AMERICAN INDIAN
GHOST STORIES
OF THE WEST

Antonio R. Garcez

Praise for the Author's Best-Selling Books

Death is not
a period but
a comma in
the story
of life.

Arizona Ghost Stories

"Gives a hauntingly accurate overview of the many reports of haunted sites all over the state. It not only lists the places from north to south, but also quotes the interviews of eyewitnesses, giving a remarkable feeling of being there with them as they encounter the unknown. Such sites as the Copper Queen Hotel in Bisbee to the Jerome Inn come to life in Mr. Garcez's investigations. His chapter on the reports of ghosts at Tombstone is perhaps one of the best accounts I have seen on this subject."

— *Richard Senate, "Hollywood's Ghosts"*

"Arizona could not have asked for a better chronicler of its supernatural landscape than Antonio R. Garcez. From Arivaca to Yuma, Arizona's most haunted places are all here! These stories will send shivers up your spine, and rightly so—they all really took place! If you have ever wanted to experience something paranormal, let this book be your guide."

— *Dennis William Hauck, "Haunted Places—The National Directory"*

Ghost Stories of California's Gold Rush Country and Yosemite National Park

"If you're a lover of the supernatural, get cozy in an easy chair and prepare yourself for the inevitable. Eyewitness accounts told in a straightforward manner!"

— *Tim Palmieri, Western Outlaw-Lawman History Association*

"As a subject where many of the books written simply regurgitate previously produced material, author Antonio R. Garcez does an excellent job of locating and interviewing primary resources to provide fresh stories of ghost folklore. Each chapter contains a brief introduction that supplies some of the background of the town and sites in question, followed by transcriptions of the witnesses' stories. Garcez's style is simple and easy to follow; the stories he has found are quickly engrossing. The fact that he put the time into his field research is impressive. Garcez can always be relied on to provide fresh stories of the supernatural and this book is no exception. He does his field research to find first-hand accounts from the people who witnessed them. When so many other writers concentrate more on information other paranormal researchers produce, Garcez deserves a great deal of credit."

— *Adrienne Foster, Book Reviewer-Epinions.com*

©2017 by ANTONIO R. GARCEZ
2nd edition—2017

ISBN 0-9740988-4-1
1st edition—2010

ISBN 0-9740988-4-1
New Mexico, USA

Some of the places that appear in these stories may have changed ownership or names since the printing of this book. Also some of the individuals who appear in this book, since its printing, might have moved on, either within this world or into the next. Their stories appear here as they were directly bestowed to the author at the time they were interviewed.

All photos were taken by the author unless otherwise noted.

The author may be contacted at the following:
ghostbooks.biz

DEDICATION

To my grandparents

My father's 'Otomi' mother, my grandmother, Maria Camargo Garcez Rios, who spoke to me as a child saying, "Never forget that your umbilical cord is attached to this land, so you will always be."

My mother's 'Mescalero Apache' father, my grandfather, Juan Ramirez, who sang and played Apache songs on his harmonica to my younger brother and me.

About the Author

ANTONIO R. GARCEZ specializes in books on firsthand ghost encounters and is considered the foremost authority and author on paranormal experiences throughout the Southwest. Born in East Los Angeles, California, Garcez graduated from the University of California at Northridge and has been self-publishing his popular ghost books since 1989, while living in New Mexico.

He enjoys researching people's supernatural experiences and conducting interviews as opportunities present themselves.

TABLE OF CONTENTS

Acknowledgments

My deepest appreciation to Hank Estrada, my partner who continues to dream with me.

Thanks to:
Arizona Department of Commerce—Arivaca Community Profile

Holbrook Chamber of Commerce/Historical Society of Navajo County (original documents held at Arizona State Archives, Department of Library Archives and Public Records)-Invitations to hanging of George Smiley and deposition of T.J. McSweeny

Taos Chamber of Commerce—City of Taos and Taos Pueblo History of the Salinas Pueblo Missions National Monument- National Park Service—History of the Salinas Pueblo

Ellen Bigrope, Curator, Mescalero Cultural Center, The Mescalero Apache Tribe-History of the Mescalero Apache

Betty L. Cornelius, Museum Director-Colorado River Indian Tribes— History of the Colorado Indians

The Colorado River Indian Tribes, Former Internees of Poston, Veterans and Friends of the Fiftieth Year Observance of the Evacuation and Internment—Historic Content and Memorial Tribute, Poston, Arizona

Author's Note

Some of the names associated with the storytellers mentioned in this book have been changed. This was done for the sole purpose of not identifying those individuals because of their cultural beliefs or their personal requests to disguise their identities. Thus, any name used in the book that might be associated with anyone known to the reader is simply coincidental.

INTRODUCTION

his book of ghost stories is a revision of my previous work, "American Indian Ghost Stories of the Southwest." With this latest expanded project, I've reached a broader selection of American Indian experiences with spirits. I've included not simply the two states of Arizona and New Mexico, but added California and Colorado. As with my original book, the stories contained within these pages are not traditional stories. They are real and told to me in an interview format. Almost all of the individuals I interviewed for this book are American Indians who have had first-hand encounters with ghosts. These individuals have seen, and in some cases have been spoken to, and even physically touched by spirit(s). A few of these individuals are not American Indian, but have an American Indian connection to their stories. I believe the inclusion of Hispanic, Anglo, African American and Japanese residents imparts a certain interesting quality.

My interviews required a considerable amount of editing. As anyone knows who has conducted interviews by transcribing from tape to the written page, the process is not as simple as it might first appear. Careful attention must be paid in order to keep the right "feeling" of the interview. Staying true to the emphasis presented by the interviewee, keeping the subject matter in context, and attempting to represent in words facial expressions and hand gestures can be challenging, but is not impossible. I also attempted to keep the narrative flow and the patois of the interviewee as close to genuine as possible, arranging sentences in an orderly manner for the story to proceed smoothly and be understood clearly. While this editing was necessary, it does not detract from the story's principal subject matter. The stories speak for themselves. Undoubtedly, some of them will arouse curiosity, speculation, fear, and even cause a few of you to probe further into the subject of the paranormal. I am content to leave you with more questions than answers. In future books I intend to survey other regions and sub-topics of the United States, compiling a collection of similar stories. I never have an idea where all this research of eyewitness accounts will lead. Frankly, like you, I am just along for the ride, and thus far it has been a ride of extraordinary wonder and unexpected amazement. Ghost stories engage me.

I am aware that it is simplistic to overemphasize the negative aspects of ghosts as evil or scary. However, focusing on these points alone promotes neither a positive nor hopeful view of our own end result. The best definitions of the existence of ghosts must be viewed through our own personal traditions of cultural and spiritual beliefs. This being said, I know that ghosts and spirits do exist and are manifest among us.

Lastly, to all the individuals whom I interviewed for this book, I sincerely thank and wish you all beauty of strength, beauty of patience, beauty of sacrifice, and the internal beauty that ultimately manifests with wisdom and humor.

— Antonio R. Garcez —

ARIZONA

"There was no climate or soil . . . equal to that of Arizona . . . It is my land, my home, my father's land . . . I want to spend my last days there, and to be buried among those mountains."

—Geronimo

 iven Arizona's particular wealth of land, Native culture, people, and unique history, I present to you a collection of its American Indian ghost stories. You'll find within the following pages—the murmuring voices; darting shadows; misty faces twisted in silent screams; empty, staring eyes of the wronged; angry footsteps of the lost; and the vaporous bodies of women with dark, empty- eyed sockets. They are all here.

Now relax, find a comfortable chair, fix yourself a strong pot of campfire coffee and prepare yourself for a long and bumpy ride into the realm of Arizona's American Indian ghost stories.

Enjoy!

—Antonio

YAQUI (YOEME)

Culturally, the Yaqui or Yoeme Nation is descended from the ancient Uto-Azteca, or Mexica people of Old Mexico. In the year 1533, the Spanish made contact with the Yaqui, and ultimately Christianity was introduced, which profoundly altered the Yaqui way of life. Interestingly, the Yaqui embraced Catholicism and the new Spanish system of government, but always kept an independent stance in this union. The Yaqui religious life of today is a result of this merger of ceremonies and cultural beliefs. San Ignacio Fiesta, Easter and Christmas are the most important ceremonies of the year for the modern Yaqui. The Yaqui have a history of being fiercely independent, and resisted Spanish colonialism until 1610, when a treaty was signed between the two. Originally they occupied eight villages in the state of Sonora, Mexico. Due to Mexican political changes, they migrated north to Arizona.

The U.S. Bureau of Indian Affairs did not recognize the Yaqui Nation as an 'historic tribe' until 1994. Their battle for such recognition was long and difficult. Considered political refugees because of their migration from Mexico, they were denied the services afforded to other American Indian Nations, and thus not recognized as an independent nation and reservation. Presently the population numbers just over 9,000. In Arizona, the Pascua Yaqui Indian Reservation was annexed into the city of Tucson in 1952. The tribal land, 222 acres, was established in 1964 by an Act of Congress and is surrounded by a desert landscape of scenic vistas, drives and trails. The San Ignacio Fiesta is observed at Old Pascua, a village located in Tucson that marks the annual fulfillment of the village's obligation to its patron saint, St. Ignatius of Loyola. The Yaqui also currently operate the successful Casino of the Sun. There is another group of Yaqui that resides close to Tempe and Phoenix in the town of Guadalupe. It is from this town that the following story was obtained.

BENJAMIN RED OWL'S (YAQUI) STORY

During our interview, I sat across from Benjamin in a humble and thankfully, very air conditioned neighborhood Mexican restaurant, located in Phoenix. Surprisingly, Benjamin's right arm was in a sling due to having been in a car accident just a few days prior. Benjamin was happy to know that I had contacted him for his personal story and stated: "It's great, it's all great. I've been wanting to tell my story for a long time, and you're just the guy I'm hoping will get it out there for others to know about." I assured him that I would do my best.

Thus, before you I present the first story I've chosen which will set the tone for all the others. I know you'll enjoy Benjamin's personal story for its emotionally inspired content and at times frightening character.

— Antonio

"My one and only experience with a ghost took place in the summer of 1991 when I was twenty-six years old. Up to that point, I can't remember ever having had any type of a paranormal experience. Of course there have been times when I've overheard friends and family discuss such things as ghosts and haunted areas, but I've never given the subject much attention. All this changed for me during one summer night in Montana. I had completed four years of graduate work in Art History at the University of Colorado, and with a master's degree under my arm, I made plans to give myself a break from all my hours of study. I thought that rewarding myself with a trip to Canada would be a nice change. Also, I knew that once I entered the job market, it would be a long time before I would have the opportunity to travel for quite some time. In fact, I already had two job offers waiting for me once I returned home. Honestly, I was in no hurry to return to an office, so I was very eager to begin my trip.

My reason for driving all the way up to Canada was to visit Jerry, a Cree Indian friend, whom I met while attending school. Jerry lived in the province of Alberta, and was a real joker of a guy. Among us Indian students, Jerry was known for his wacky sense of humor. I couldn't wait to get on the road. I packed my small Toyota with all the necessary camping gear—tent and snacks—then got on the interstate heading north to Wyoming, Montana, and my ultimate destination, Canada. Along the way, I spent nights in public campgrounds, which were located in state and national parks. Before leaving the northern-most portion of the state of Wyoming, I spent six days in the town of Sheridan. Another friend from college, Tom, lived there. Tom is a Lakota Indian who graduated two years before me with a degree in Marketing Management. Tom told me about his friend, Joseph, who lived in the town of Billings, north of the Crow Indian Reservation. Tom gave Joseph a call and arranged for me to spend a couple of nights at Joseph's house. Joseph was known as a maker of award winning horse saddles. Tom and I said our good-byes, and off I left to continue my journey north.

I took my time, stopping frequently to take pictures and to observe the beautiful prairie landscape. Because of my many sightseeing stops, I arrived at the Crow Reservation late in the evening. I turned off the highway and found a rest stop where I made camp for the night. In the morning I packed up my things and drove to the nearest restaurant, got breakfast, then drove to the Little Bighorn Battlefield Monument to have a look. Given its history, and I being Native American, the battlefield was an unsettling place to visit. The monument's visitor center was filled with historical paraphernalia. Being a history buff, I spent a good two hours reading the informational texts, and taking in all descriptions of the artifacts on display. Reading about the major battle that was fought and jointly won by the Sioux and Cheyenne against the invading General Custer was fascinating. I felt proud to be

Native American, and at the same time, saddened knowing the present social state that most Indians are locked into. After a few hours, I got in my car and drove on the two-lane road, which meandered through the battlefield itself. At one point, I decided to park and go for a hike over the rolling hills and small valleys of the battle site. As I said earlier, I had an uneasy feeling about the place. Standing on the actual ground where the battle was fought many years ago gave me an eerie feeling. I didn't at all feel frightened, just uneasy. After spending several hours hiking about the area, evening was approaching and it began to get dark. I decided to head back to my car, where I had a quick dinner of warm coke, an apple and cookies. Billings was about an hour or two away, so I got back on the highway, anticipating that I'd have a bed at Joseph's house. This plan, as it turned out, was not to be.

After just a few miles on the highway, I noticed that my car was strangely jerking. I knew something was going to give out. Sure enough, just after getting on the interstate, my car altogether stopped. I got out and pushed it to the side of the road. Having been told by a mechanic back in Denver that the car's fuel line filter needed to be changed, I suspected this was the cause of the problem. I had the foresight to buy a new filter before I left on my trip. Because it was already too dark to get under the hood and replace it, I decided to tackle the problem the next morning. After all, it was not a very long, difficult job to change out the old filter for the new one—maybe a total of 30 minutes, max. Not far up ahead, I noticed a flat area with tall trees. I decided to push my small car over to this area. I parked the car away from the highway traffic. It seemed like a safe camping site for the night.

All the hiking earlier in the day had tired me out. I couldn't wait to get into my sleeping bag and fall asleep. I opened the car's trunk, took out the sleeping bag, and lay it on the ground, with the car creating a buffer between the highway and me. I soon fell asleep. Sometime during the night, I was awakened by the touch of someone stroking my neck. Because the stroking feeling was not at all sudden or discomforting, at first I was not frightened. Then the thought hit me that someone—a stranger was touching me! I opened my eyes and, still lying in my sleeping bag, I turned around. I gazed in the direction, which I imagined a person would be standing. At first I saw nothing in the darkness. Then I saw some movement to my left. My heart was beating hard and I was getting anxious. I turned to look to my left and I saw the image of a small Indian woman. She startled me, and I think I let out a little yell of surprise. I immediately knew this person was a spirit, because her image was vapor-like. She was the same luminous color as the moon, and I could see the trees right through her. I got scared and thought I was going to have a heart attack. I couldn't move. My body was trembling. I don't know why I couldn't find the strength to get up and run. It was as if my body was locked with fear. The ghost stood about five feet away from me with a very sad look on her face. She was dressed in a yellow-colored dirty dress, and wore several necklaces made of big beads. She just stood there in front of me staring. I tried to speak, but my voice was weak and my throat was dry. One thing I do remember clearly was the strong scent of wet grass. It was a very earthy scent that I can remember to this day. It's difficult to explain, but I was able to smell and to "feel" the odor of mud, water and grass of a long time ago. It's weird, I know, but that's how I can explain it.

Soon, and with much effort, I managed to get out a real yell. She then began to fade away, beginning at her feet and ending at her head. I yelled again, and soon it was all over. She was gone. Sweat was dripping down my face. My ghost encounter took place in what appeared to be all of about five minutes. I got out of the sleeping bag and jumped into the front seat of my car. I locked all the doors, turned on the radio, and after some nervously exhausting minutes passed, I managed to fall asleep.

In the early morning I was awakened when a large noisy semi-truck passed by on the highway. Inside the car, as I moved around, I felt something at the back of my neck. I reached my hand up to scratch, and was surprised when I felt a hardened substance which had attached itself to my hair. I pulled some of this off and looked at my hand. It was hardened mud! I pulled more of this hardened mud off of my neck and head, and then I carefully opened the car door, got out and shook the remainder of the dirt from me. I didn't know what to think. Did I have a bad dream during the night, and rolled about on the ground? Or, did the apparition of the ghost woman rub this mud on me? I didn't care to think anymore about the mud. Frankly, I was eager to repair my car and get the heck out of there!

Now that there was plenty of morning sunlight, I replaced the fuel filter in my car, and after several false starts, got my car going again and hit the highway. Driving north on my way to Billings gave me a few hours to think about what I had experienced the night before. I couldn't believe that I had seen a real ghost just a few hours before. I had lots of questions, with no answers. But the most disturbing question of all was why did she cover my neck with mud? Was she trying to heal me of an injury? I soon arrived at Joseph's house. Joseph was not home, so I asked his whereabouts at a neighbor's house. After introducing myself to the older woman, she informed me that her neighbor, Joseph Dances Straight, was dead. Apparently, two months prior, while visiting his sister in South Dakota, Joseph and two friends went hunting for deer. One of the shotguns accidentally went off, and the blast hit Joseph at the base of his skull, killing him instantly. I was caught off guard by this information. The neighbor was not willing to give me any more information. I could tell that she and Joseph were close friends. I left her house filled with a personal mental numbness. Eventually, I arrived at my friend Jerry's house in Canada. I told him about what I had experienced during my short trip, describing the short ghost woman, and ultimately finding out about Joseph's death. Jerry got seriously quiet, and then told me that an Indian spirit messenger in the form of a woman had visited me. Also, because earlier in the day I had immersed myself in a powerful area—The Little Bighorn Battleground—I had "opened myself up" to this spiritual visitor. He went on to say that the messenger had rubbed "medicine" on my neck, which symbolized the manner of death which had taken Joseph.

After spending two weeks with Jerry, I returned to my home in Arizona. Never will I forget about my experience with the ghost in Montana. There are lots of things that us Indians need to be aware of. I know that modern society is a very powerful force, but we need to respect and honor our traditions from long ago. These are also very important, and necessary for our people."

COLORADO RIVER INDIANS
THE CHEMEHUEVI (NU WU)

The Chemehuevi name is derived from a Mohave word that relates to fish. However, the Chemehuevi prefer to distinguish themselves as 'Nu Wu' or 'people,' using their own language when referring to each other.

The Nu Wu are closely related to the Southern Paiute of southern Nevada. Historically, they were nomadic people who were hunters and gatherers. Linguistically, their dialect is very similar to the Ute (Kaquiisi) and the Paiute.

Originally, the Nu Wu lived in the area between southern Nevada and Yuma, Arizona, in small family groups. Ancient human habitation is very evident from the numerous petroglyphs (rock carvings), and ancient trails and pictographs (picture writings) that have been discovered in the area. The Colorado River Indian Reservation, created by an act of Congress in 1865, was originally created for just the Nu Wu and Mohave, and was located on their ancestral homeland. But in 1945, the U.S. Government relocated members of the Hopi and Navajo from their traditional lands onto this reservation.

The reservation consists of 278,000 acres of land in the states of Arizona and California. The Colorado River runs directly through the reservation. The almost perfect weather year-round and the rich fertile river-bottom land make farming one of the major industries on the reservation. It is unique in the sense that it is occupied by four distinct tribal groups—Mohave, Nu Wu, Hopi and Navajo, each group with its own separate culture and traditions. As of today, the four tribes that make up the Colorado River Indian Tribes respectively continue to promote and maintain their individual and unique traditional ways, and when necessary, come together and function as one political unit.

Within the reservation is the town of Parker, and next to this is found the Colorado Indian Tribes Museum. The museum displays artifacts, cultural items and artwork of the four nations of Nu Wu, Mohave, Hopi and Navajo. Fame is given to the Nu Wu's highly developed skill of beadwork and basket weaving. Nu Wu baskets are among the finest in the Southwest, and are exquisitely woven using willow, devil's claw and juncus. Sadly, these baskets are becoming more and more difficult to obtain, due to there being fewer weavers who practice the art.

MEMORIAL TRIBUTE

"To all men and women who honorably served in the United States Armed Forces in defense of the nation and its people, particularly to those Americans of Japanese ancestry, who, during World War II, fought so valiantly for their country while their parents and families were being interned in the Poston War Relocation Center without due process of law. And to those brave young men who gave their lives in service to their country."

During World War II, the United States was in conflict with Japan. The federal government built several Japanese internment camps on reservations throughout the southwest, purportedly for national security reasons. The Colorado River Tribes area was designated as one of these sites. This historic development brought changes to the reservation. As roads were constructed, land was cleared and innovative agricultural experiments were tested. The results of these experiments successfully raised the economy of the area.

Beginning in May and ending in August 1942, 17,876 Japanese evacuees from the Pacific Coast states and Arizona arrived at the reservation. Most of the evacuees were from California. The extreme, relentless desert sun scorched the earth, and the frequent winds whipped the sands into blinding dust storms. In winter, chilling winds easily penetrated the walls and wide floor cracks of the flimsily built tarpaper barracks. Adding to the hardships of internment, infrequent but torrential rains would quickly turn the parched dirt walkways and roads into slippery, treacherous and muddy quagmires. Amidst the trauma of forced evacuation and the indignities of internment, Japanese children were the first to adapt to the routine of camp life. They found numerous playmates, but they lacked toys and other playthings. Creative parents, relatives and friends relied on their imaginations to make playthings from scrap lumber, rocks, tree branches, shells and other available materials for the children.

BETTY CORNELIUS' (CHEMEHUEVI) STORY

My interview with both Betty and Franklin took place one early afternoon within the reservation's museum. The weather outside was definitely in the upper 90's, so I was thankful to be in an air-conditioned building. We all sat at a table and because we were alone in the museum, it was obvious that Betty and Franklin felt very free to openly discuss their experiences without having to look over their shoulders. Given the historical nature of their reservation, this story in particular was a uniquely informative experience for me.

— Antonio

"I'm Nu Wu and I've lived at the reservation most of my life, except for a period of twenty- five years when I got married and lived in Los Angeles, California. Currently I'm the Director of the Colorado Indian Museum and I've held this position for eight years. Before I tell you about the ghostly activity in the area, I need to give a quick historical background of the area, which involved the internment of Japanese-Americans at the beginning of World War II. Soon after the bombing of Pearl Harbor, an executive order enacted by then-president Franklin Delano Roosevelt stated that, beginning in the city of San Francisco and extending to El Paso, Texas, all Japanese-Americans would be placed in several internment camps located throughout the Southwest. Our reservation was chosen to be one of these sites.

A major task begun by the U.S. government at the time of the Japanese relocation was to house thousands of people, and to construct needed shelter. Lumber to construct these houses and barracks was needed in large quantities. Unfortunately, due to our hot desert climate, such large lumber-producing trees did not grow in the area. The necessary lumber was brought to the reservation by train. It so happened that both the lumber and Japanese were brought to the relocation camp by train. The Japanese were put into boxcars and taken to our reservation. There were in total between eighteen to twenty thousand Japanese who were relocated to three camps in this area, which were named Camp One, Camp Two and Camp Three. The U.S. government made the Japanese build their own community structures from the lumber that was delivered by these same trains. They built single-family homes and long barracks that were designed to house about ten families. The uniqueness of their architecture was unmistakable. These houses were built in a distinct 'pagoda' style. The roofline swung out and curved slightly upward, away from the outside walls, and there was a distinct space between where the roof and the ceiling came together. The Japanese grew vegetables in community gardens, built small ponds, built a movie theatre, and as much as we could tell, they kept up their own cultural traditions. Many babies were born in these camps and many elderly Japanese died at the camps. I heard that some of the dead were taken back to the towns where they were removed from, or shipped back to Japan. I personally am aware that several Japanese bodies were buried in the Parker cemetery, just a few miles north of here.

The relocation camps existed for approximately four years, from 1942 to 1946. When the Japanese were eventually relocated back to the larger society, the houses and barracks, which they had built, were given to the Colorado Indian Community. The barracks were cut into equal sections of about fifteen to twenty feet wide, by equal lengths long, and distributed to Indian families. A few of these old Japanese houses are still standing on the reservation. Some of these houses, which we Indians were given, were haunted. Spirits of those Japanese who lived and died within the walls of the houses they built with their own hands refused to move on. I know of one Indian family that moved into one of those Japanese houses, and they had strange things happen. The doors of the house would open and close on their own. A chair would move away from the table as if pushed by an invisible pair of hands. As if someone was about to seat him or herself down for a meal, the chair would move away from the table, then it would move back against the table! Also, lights would go on and off at all hours. Other times, many times, Indian families talked about seeing the shadowy, ghostly outline of a person who walked in their houses, traveling from one room to the next. At times these ghosts would walk through a room, approach the front door and then pass through it and go outside.

Other incidents reported are the sound of ghostly footsteps on the wooden floors of these old houses at all hours of the day and night. Families would even hear the sound of rattling dishes in their kitchens, as if the ghosts were going through the daily task of washing dishes after a meal. Some families reported hearing very young babies crying. I know that the people were concerned about these ghosts, but for whatever reason, eventually they got accustomed to their 'visitors.' They knew why the ghosts were occupying their houses, and about the Japanese sad history, so Indian families knew the ghosts would not hurt them. They just decided to live with them. Some families 'smudged' their homes with sage smoke and offered prayers to the spirits. Not too long ago, a group of traditional Japanese people visited our reservation and performed religious ceremonies. It was sad to see because they would break down and cry and hug each other. There is so much sorrow and sadness associated with the relocation. The Japanese built a stone monument on our reservation to mark that part of their history.

Being a Nu Wu, I've been very accustomed to seeing things that non-Indians would regard as supernatural. I know that these things do exist so I have been raised to be very respectful and just to let them be. I can sense the presence of shadows and light, or auras that animals have. It's something that comes natural to me. Many of our Native American people still practice our beautiful spirituality. I also know that there are 'spiritual power sites' in the hills and mountains located in the reservation and in the surrounding area. There is a lot of very powerful energy here. I know that our medicine people know about these sacred areas and spiritual sites, but we don't talk about these places to anyone. That's just the way it is."

FRANKLIN MCCABE III'S (NAVAJO) STORY

"I'm a Navajo and originally from Provo, Utah. I'm currently employed at the reservation as the Recreation Director of our gymnasium, Irataba Hall. I've lived at this reservation for twenty-two years, since I was three years old. My first experience with a ghost took place when I was approximately five years old. I recall that I was lying on my bed in my room, day-dreaming about something. Suddenly, I heard something moving about the room. I turned my head in the direction of where there was a rocking chair. Then I saw the strangest thing—the chair was rocking back and forth all on its own! There was no wind coming into the room from my window and, at the time, I was alone in the house. It just kept rocking and rocking. Then it stopped. I did tell my parents about this, but perhaps because I was a child, they must have thought it would be best to say nothing. But sometime later, when she thought I was old enough to know and after we had moved out of the house, my mother told me that a woman used to live in our house prior to us, and the woman's bedroom, where she had died, was my bedroom. Of course when I heard this, I was startled by the news, and reflected on all the time I had spent in that room by myself. As I said before, the rocking chair was my first experience with something ghostly. But as recently as two years ago, I had a more direct and scary encounter. An ongoing haunting, which is kind of common knowledge on the reservation, takes place at the gymnasium which I manage. Our gymnasium has quite an interesting history. Prior to 1965, there was a hospital located on the grounds, utilizing a portion of the gymnasium. I understand that the Japanese who were held in the nearby internment camps during the war were sent to this hospital. I don't think people would disagree with me about the fact that perhaps the hauntings at the gym have something to do with this history. A lot of people on the reservation have heard the stories about the gymnasium being haunted, and some can even give their own stories about seeing apparitions or ghosts there.

Beginning at the start of my employment at the gymnasium, others and I have many times felt the presence of heaviness, or a sense of negativity, there. My experience at the gymnasium began one evening as I arrived to finish some work I had started earlier in the day. Two friends and I arrived at around 5 p.m. Having the only keys, I unlocked

the front entrance door, and we all made our way into the kitchen. We were planning a barbecue the following day, so we were there to check on the supply of food for the event. We were alone in the building, just the three of us. As we went about our business, we were startled by the sound of a very high-pitched woman's scream coming from the basketball court. The scream was so eerie that it sent chills up all our spines. We looked at each other and immediately high-tailed it out of the gymnasium to the parking lot where we had parked our car. I guess reason must have stepped in and made me think that perhaps a woman in trouble caused the scream. We talked among ourselves and decided to cautiously return to the gym and search for an injured woman. As we re-entered the building we kept our ears and eyes ready for any suspicious noise or movement. We searched the whole gymnasium, looking in lockers and under the bleachers. All the doors were locked and the bathrooms and halls were empty. We found no evidence of anyone being inside.

Not long after this, there was another haunting incident that occurred one evening, during a youth sleep-over at the gymnasium. The kids brought their sleeping bags and everyone gathered on the stage area of the basketball court. The plan that night was to sleep on the stage floor. Once all the kids were inside the gym, I closed and locked all the doors, making sure there were no drugs or alcohol that might be sneaked into the facility. As the evening progressed, I was having a conversation with a student, while everyone was talking and having his or her own lively social interactions. I was standing, facing the student, having a clear and direct view of the two doors that open to the hallway out from the basketball court. Then something unusual caught my eye. I noticed a white ghostly figure, which was standing at one of the doors! It also must have noticed me looking in its direction, because it moved away into the hall. Startled, I kept still. Then it quickly reappeared at the next door! I can explain the image as being a big white blur-like vapor. Apparently, I was not the only one at the time who witnessed the apparition, because when I mentioned what I had just seen to those gathered next to me, a few students excitedly admitted they also saw the exact same ghostly figure. This apparition left us un-nerved to the extent that we all agreed to gather together in the middle of the basketball court and sleep close to each other in a big circle. Our sense of safety in numbers soon came to a sudden end. As we were about to call it a night, every single storage door that is located below the stage where we had been gathered just a few minutes before swung open. Seeing this, everyone got quite scared. I had to explain to everyone that there was nothing to be afraid of, and with some effort, eventually emotions settled down.

Another paranormal experience took place at the gymnasium during, of all times, a 1998 Halloween event. Once again, several persons were there to serve as witnesses. At the time, the gymnasium was decorated with Halloween paper decorations, and everyone was in the mood for a good time. The event was entitled, 'The Haunted Gym.' It wasn't long before our festive attitude ended. Hours before the evening's festivities were to begin I, along with my assistants, made sure that there wasn't anyone in the gym aside from us and a couple of helpers. We were all gathered in the basketball court discussing something or other, when the sound of footsteps began. We immediately got quiet, and the sound of someone moving paper started up. We knew that the ghosts were walking about once again. Knowing the stories of the gymnasium being haunted, we decided to exit the gym, and wasted no time in running out the door! Once outside, a few of us with a bit more bravery decided to re-enter the gym and investigate. My younger 15-year-old brother accompanied me with four other helpers, as we did a security walk-through. Once more we heard the footsteps start up, only this time they were just about six feet away from us! What a scare! We stood looking at each other with big, wide eyes. We soon joined the others waiting for us outside. There have also been instances when objects at the gymnasium were moved by invisible hands. I also know of staff witnessing basketballs bouncing about the gym without having been touched. The former director of the gym is one person who tells of watching a basketball, at rest on the floor, start to slowly move, and then begin to bounce on its own across the floor! I was alone at the gym one night and witnessed a ball, which came rolling toward me, then passed behind me. There was no way that this ball could have been pushed. I was alone at the gymnasium. The floor is level and the ball was stationary. We have begun a series of upgrades at the gym, such as applying new paint and other such renovations, attempting to make the facility a more inviting and friendly place for the public to visit. I know there are many who do not want to enter the building, but hopefully things will change. My goal is to have medicine men bless and rededicate the gym to the community by July 1, 2000.

Another ghostly experience took place just three years ago at my house. One night, while getting over an illness, I was lying in bed and happened to look out my bedroom door at the hallway. Suddenly, I felt a very heavy presence in the room. At the same time, I also heard the sound of a loud hum. I'm not sure what this sound was, but it was followed by another strange thing. The atmosphere in my bedroom felt to me as if it was becoming thick. This was followed by a strong mass of weight that began to push me down against the bed. The force was so strong and heavy against my chest that it made my breathing stop. I began to panic. Then I saw a figure appear slowly at my doorway. It moved its arms back and forth, and then it paused and looked in my direction. The ghost had the outline of a man, and it was very dark, like a shadow. With all my might, I tried to break away from the hold that this force had taken over me. With much effort, I extended one arm and tried to yell, but I could not make a sound. The dark shadow just stood at the door and stared at me. Then it moved away with a bouncing, walking motion. At the same time, the heavy weight lifted off me and I began to breathe normally.

About six months after this incident, our dogs barking outside my bedroom awakened me. I got out of bed and walked to the window to have a look. In our backyard we have a motion sensitive security light on a pole. The security light turned on as I got to the window. As I pulled up the shade and peered outside to have a look, there in the window staring back at me was the same dark, shadowy figure that I had seen before in my doorway! It was just a few inches from my own face, on the other side of the window! I was terrified! I automatically let go of the shade cord, and it quickly unrolled and hit the windowsill with a bang! I got into bed and shook with fright. I kept repeating to myself, 'Oh God, oh God.' Eventually I fell asleep.

In 1996, my mother, my brother and I had another ghost experience at about 10 p.m. That night we heard someone pound hard on our window, while an excited male voice in distress yelled out, 'Natani, Natani!' Natani is my brother's name, so we quickly ran to the window and then outside. We saw no one. The dogs didn't even bark. We grabbed our guns and looked everywhere and found nothing. We all assumed that it was a spirit voice attempting to contact us for some unknown reason. Many times in our kitchen we've experienced our microwave oven, lights, and refrigerator go on and off. This only happened in the kitchen. Now this might sound as if we had problems with our electrical wiring, but I know that this was not the case. My parents decided to have our local Mormon elders pay us a visit and conduct a prayer service to get rid of the negative presences. Prior to the service, the elders instructed my family to keep our eyes closed and not to speak, and to keep our minds clear. We all sat in a circle in the living room and as the service began, a low moaning sound started up in the kitchen, like a dog howling at the moon. As the service continued, the moaning sound became louder and louder. At one point, with my eyes still closed, I felt as if the whole house was rocking me back and forth, and I felt a powerful gust of wind that was moving in and out of the space between me and the others. Then I felt something begin to brush me on my left, and then whatever it was, started to move over to my right side. This 'thing' brushed up and down against my arms. I kept my eyes closed tightly. Then the moaning sound became clear to me as it got louder and louder. It was the word 'No.' Imagine, if you can, the word 'no' being stretched out in a loud, long, 'Noooooooo!' That's how it sounded. Then suddenly the noise was gone. About a minute passed and although we were instructed not to open our eyes, or say a word, I slowly opened my eyes. I decided to break the tension and silence by saying, 'Did you guys hear that?' As soon as I finished saying these words, everyone opened up and began to say, 'Yeah, I heard it, did you, yeah, etc.' Then the elders got up, said a quick good-bye and were out the door! We got a 'kick' out of their reaction. As of this day, that was the last incident of any ghostly activity that I have experienced."

MARICOPA AK-CHIN

The Maricopa Nation's history is one of constant battles with neighboring tribes. Their numbers were small and they claimed their homeland as being along the lower Gila and Colorado Rivers. In 1825, a major event took place when their friendly neighbors, the Pima, welcomed the Maricopa into their villages. This union obviously benefited the Maricopa, as now aggressive attackers had a much larger, united force to confront. In the year 1864, settlements of Mormons from the northern state of Utah had begun in the area, but not unnoticed by the watchful eyes of the Apaches. The Apaches loathed the intrusion of their land by these alien strangers and attacked the settlements with gusto. The Mormons obtained the help of both the Pima and Maricopa who acted as scouts and security. This focal area was in Lehi, which today the Maricopa retain as part of the reservation. Known for its beauty and creative use of shape, collectors now seek Maricopa red clay, geometrical pottery. Like the Pima, they have prospered in modern society.

ALBERT JOAQUIN MANUEL SR.'S (MARICOPA) STORY

After arriving at the reservation at mid-afternoon, I located the Manuel house among several others in the far west area of their housing development. Walking up to Albert and his wife who were sitting at their front porch, we chatted about several unrelated things, such as the weather, their children and health issues. When it came time to speak about ghosts, Mrs. Manuel spoke, "I think we should go inside where it's safer." Immediately, Albert's demeanor took on a more solemn tone and once inside, he spoke of his experiences with a reverence and sincerity of which you'll now discover for yourself.

— Antonio

"I'm Maricopa and I've lived in this area all my life. I'm fifty-eight years old. As a kid, I would see many things in my dreams, visions and lots of strange things. I worked as a farm worker some years ago, in the small town of Standfield, just a few miles away. I remember the times, when I was working some nights, several fellow workers would talk among themselves about seeing what we called, 'El Cu-cui,' or the boogieman, in the fields. The workers would speak about seeing ghost lights and other strange things. There were nights when they would get so scared that they would leave work and go home. But I wasn't scared, and everyone knew this. So my boss would send me to where this ghost was seen to finish the job on the farm. I never actually saw El Cu-cui, but I did hear it. Back in 1958 when a lot of us Indians were in the fields picking cotton, there were some guys who died out in the fields. They were young Indians who committed suicide. I never found out why. I guess they were depressed or something. Not long after their deaths, we would all hear and experience very scary things. At the time, all the farm workers slept together in a common room, and at night when the lights were turned off, strange noises would start-up and our beds would start to shake. I remember even being touched all over my body while lying in bed. My face would be touched and invisible hands would hold my arms tightly. I knew this was caused by the deaths of the guys who died in the fields. It was their spirits. I remember also smelling a cologne or perfume in the room.

That same year, there was one Indian man who was killed one night, after leaving a bar. While at the bar he got into a fight with another guy. After the fight, he left the bar and walked home. As he was walking along the road, the guy he had the fight with came looking for him in his car. When the driver spotted him walking on the side of the road, he drove his car over him and killed him. The hit-and-run took place right next to a big tree, not far from here. The next day some Indians dug a quick hole and buried the man's body. The hole must not have been very deep because the coyotes soon smelled the body, and dug some of it up. I remember walking by the shallow grave and seeing the dead man's leg and foot bones sticking out of the dirt. I didn't see his head, just the leg bones. A few days later, whenever local residents would walk by the shallow grave, they would make sure to carry some rocks with them. They dropped these rocks on top of the grave to prevent the coyotes from digging up more of the body. Eventually someone removed the body, and took it to our cemetery for reburial.

I also recall, about ten years ago, when a deadly cabin fire took the life of a baby. It must have been a very hot fire because there was nothing left of the cabin but ashes. It was located next to a big field that I used to work in. Well, one night not long after that fire, as I was irrigating the field, I clearly heard the cries of the baby that died in that fire. The cries lasted for about seven minutes. I wasn't scared, but soon after I heard the baby crying, a pack of coyotes surrounded me. I decided to get away from the coyotes. As I began to leave the field, one coyote that must have been the leader, came forward and followed me as I walked away. At the time I was carrying a gun, so I raised the gun, showing it to the coyote. When it saw the gun, it back away.

As a child, I grew up knowing the stories of 'messengers' that take the form of owls. These owls roost high in the trees. They hoot to get the attention of a person passing by. I was told that this sign is a message to the person, to let them know that something is soon going to happen to them. A death will take place, of a cousin or someone close to the person. Whenever I see these owls, I chase them away. I throw rocks at them until they fly off.

There were also times when I would see figures of people walking down the road and I would hear people talking behind trees. Even though I could see that there was no one behind the trees, I could hear their voices speaking to one another. All of this never scared me. Recently in our kitchen we have experienced strange things. In the evening, as soon as my wife and I go to bed, noises will start. We'd hear footsteps walking slowly in the living room and then in the kitchen. The ghosts would turn the water faucets on and off, and we'd hear the salt shakers being moved about the table. It's a real loud noise that the ghost makes. These ghosts seem to always be around. I guess they want to do what they did while they were alive. But like I said, I'm not scared."

WHITE MOUNTAIN APACHE
(NDE, INDEH OR TINNEH)

The White Mountain Apache have the notable history of being the direct descendants of the original Apache Tribes who settled the area many centuries ago. The ancestral homeland of the White Mountain Apache Nation is located in the east central region of Arizona. The Apache are now a nation comprised of several independent bands throughout the Southwest.

The reservation encompasses 1.6 million acres. It was established by Executive Order on November 9, 1891. Strongly traditional in culture and spirituality, the nation currently has over 12,000 members. Historically, they were hunters and raiders who did some farming, but in many cases carried out raids on neighboring agricultural-based villages for food that they were unable to obtain by hunting. The Apache consider the mountains that surround their lands to be sacred and the source of their spirituality. The Spaniards, Anglos and Mexicans were unsuccessful in their numerous attempts to subdue these true guerrilla warriors. As with almost everything ever written about the Apache, it is important for the reader to question the source of the written word, due in large part to a negatively skewed view regarding the Apache being linked to a vast amount of atrocities. In fact, this cautious approach should be taken when reading most anything printed about Native people—period.

Today a wide range of accommodations that include dining, shopping and gaming at the Hon-Dah Casino are available on the reservation.

CATHERINE TWO BEARS' (APACHE) STORY

Catherine and I sat under a traditional ramada or patio that she herself constructed of pine poles and branches in her backyard. It so happened that at one particular point in our conversation, where she mentioned encountering an owl, a large yellow butterfly came fluttering about her head and landed on her wrist. Without flinching, she looked at me and said, "Antonio, I can see the spirits are with us.

This expression is a message being given to us of their presence. I honor them."
After a few seconds of silence, we continued with the interview as the butterfly
fluttered away. I'll leave this image with you to interpret, but personally I am
convinced that Catherine and I were both honored with a simple and spiritual
expression that day.

— *Antonio*

"In 1992, I was attending the University of Arizona in Phoenix. I was
in my senior year and majoring in biology. During the summer of that
same year, five seniors (including myself), four graduate students and
a professor were conducting fieldwork at Theodore Roosevelt Lake.
The lake is located in the Tonto National Forest, about a two-hour
drive northeast of Phoenix. Our two-month study and research focused
on native amphibians of the lake, specifically bullfrogs. Throughout the
years, this particular species of frog had begun to change the ecology
of Arizona's lake and streams. Although the bullfrogs had increased in
population, other smaller native populations of frogs were showing the
beginning signs of extinction. Bullfrogs have a voracious appetite and
will consume anything smaller than them, including snakes, other frogs,
lizards and mice. Our focus of study was to specifically record data,
and to ultimately discover a link to the bullfrog population explosion.
Although I enjoyed the research fieldwork, it was wet, muddy, and smelly
and I had to wade in waist-deep cold water. In order to catch the frogs, I
had to dress in watertight rubber overalls. Also part of my uniform was a
net laundry bag, which I tied to my belt, a pith helmet with a flashlight
strapped on top, and of course a fish net attached to a six-foot pole. My
colleagues and I would get in the water at about eight in the evening
and begin our 'hunt,' which would last until around ten or so at night.
We initiated a process of surprise by which we would catch these fast
and alert bullfrogs by slowly wading towards a floating mass of leaves
or plants. Using the light strapped to my helmet, I would scan the area
until I spotted the bright telltale sign of a bullfrog's reflecting eyes. Once
spotted, I would make my way towards the frog, careful not to make any
ripples and, using my fishing net, quickly catch it and place it inside the
net bag tied to my belt. This system, although primitive, would bring

in about ten to twenty frogs a night per student. Each pair of students had a section of lake in which to capture the frogs. After finishing our work for the night, we would drive back to the lab and place the frogs in a large stock-water tank for study the next day. Our evening captures took place three nights a week. Due to the many frogs in the area, we had enough specimens and paperwork to keep us very busy.

So what does capturing bullfrogs have to do with ghosts? Well, one evening during a night of bullfrog catching, something very, very strange happened to me. Another girl and I went off for the evening to do the night's frog gathering. We went into the water at about eight in the evening. The frogs were making their croaking sounds as usual, and we got right to work. But at about nine o'clock, I began to feel sick. My stomach was turning. I figured it was something I had eaten earlier at dinner. I decided to end the evening's hunt and get back to my warm bed. I informed my partner that I would be taking the truck, and for her to catch a return ride to the lab with the others. 'No problem,' she said. So off I drove. The road was dark. I had to drive slowly due to javelinas (wild desert pigs) and other small desert animals that were out and about. It was summer, so to get fresh air, I had both the windows in the truck lowered. Suddenly, I felt something come in through the passenger side window! Something hit the right side of my body and gave me a terrible scare! I quickly put on the brakes and nervously turned on the interior truck light. That's when I saw it—a small owl! Apparently the owl had flown across my path on the road, and mistakenly entered the truck through the open window. Well, there it was, on the floor of the truck flapping its wings with its beak wide open. I can look back now and say, that confused bird gave me a good scare! I opened my driver's side door and scrambled outside. I walked over to the passenger side door and opened it, to allow the owl a way out. But when I opened the door, the owl was gone! Where had it gone? I carefully looked under and behind the truck seat, but there was no owl. If it had exited the truck on its own, I would have heard it, or even seen it because the dome light was still on inside the truck. This was definitely a strange thing that had just occurred. The owl in my truck simply disappeared! Knowing something about animal behavior, I knew that this was not usual. Also, being an Apache gave me a cultural knowledge about such things. Traditional Apache people do not consider owls to be positive animals to be associated with. I knew this owl was not a good omen. Owls to Apaches are messengers of bad news, and even death. My parents have told me that some medicine people who do evil use the owl's spirit in their witchcraft.

I quickly got back into the truck, rolled up both windows and drove at a fast speed to the cabin. I admit that at the time, I was scared being all by myself. When I entered the cabin, I went straight to the bathroom and showered. I still had the stomach-ache, but now I was more concerned about my recent owl incident. After making sure that all the doors in the cabin were locked, and the outside light was on, I got into bed and waited for the return of the others. After about twenty minutes, no one had returned, and I began to get worried. I got out of bed and looked out the window, and saw nothing but darkness. I thought it best to try and sleep, even though my stomach was a ball of nerves. As soon as I got back into bed, I heard the sound of footsteps in the front room. I knew there was no way someone could have entered the cabin without opening the locked door and making a sound. Something bad was definitely going on, and I was scared! As I gazed from my bed at the open doorway that led into the bedroom, the footsteps stopped. Then there was silence for a few seconds. Soon I heard the voice of what sounded like a small child speaking in my Apache language, 'Can I go see mama. I want to see mama. Can I go see mama?' I couldn't stop trembling. The words were very clear, and because they were spoken in Apache, that made them even more terrifying to me. I had had enough of this, so I jumped out of the bed and, in the darkness, scrambled for the light switch on the wall. Nervously, I tripped over my own shoes, fell to the floor hitting my left shoulder, and smashed my big toe against the dresser. I was in pain. I figured my toe was broken. I managed to crawl across the floor, then find the wall with the light switch, turn it on, and crawl to the bathroom.

No sooner had I entered the bathroom, when I heard the sound of my fellow students' trucks returning to the lab. I was an emotional mess. I decided it would be best not to tell anyone about what had happened to me. After all, what could they say or offer me? One thing that I did need was to get some medical help for my toe. It was already swelling up when my roommate came in the door. I told her that I had fallen, and that was all. I was driven that night to the student university clinic in Phoenix, where an x-ray was taken. I was given the good news that the toe was not broken, but I eventually lost the nail. Still it hurt quite a lot and it was very bruised. Unable to do any more night wading for frogs in cold lake water, my research ended. I spent the remainder of the summer at home. Once I arrived home, I told my parents all about the experience with the owl, and the child's ghostly voice. They told me to pray and to never again be out alone in that area. My parents could not offer an explanation regarding the owl that came into my truck, or the ghostly voice of the child. All I was told was that sometimes these 'things' are forces that foretell a future event. As of this date, I have not had anything happen to me that I can connect to that summer night in 1992. But that does not mean I won't. I'm hoping not to ever experience anything like that again. I'm not the type of person that goes looking for ghosts and things. Ghosts scare me."

SAN CARLOS APACHE (T'IIS-EBAH-NNEE)

The San Carlos Apache Indian Reservation is located east of Phoenix in southeastern Arizona and was established by Executive Order on November 9, 1871. The total landmass of the reservation is just under 1,900,00 acres. The reservation was reduced in size a total of five times for the benefit of copper and silver miners, and land-anxious Mormons whose demand for water surrounding the Gila Valley reduced it further. It is the seventh largest U.S. reservation, with over 7,100 people. Within the reservation borders are forested alpine meadows and wooded mountains, as well as desert plains. Anthropologists speculate that the Apache Nation entered this region around 1450. The San Carlos Apache call themselves 't'iis-ebah-nnee' or 'grey cottonwood people' and their language is closely related to the Di-neh' (Navajo). The San Carlos Apache now consider themselves to be a unified people, even though their history shows they were originally several separate bands of the same Native nation.

After his surrender in 1873, the great Apache chief Cochise, along with his followers, were forcibly taken by the U.S. military to San Carlos. Soon after, the famous medicine man Geronimo and his followers fled the oppression of the San Carlos Reservation. Presently, the reservation fights the continuous battle of chronic unemployment among its people, with the hope of developing industry and tourism. Encouragingly, tourism is taking hold as a source of income and employment. The tribe is directly promoting its lakes and forests, focusing on campers and sportspeople. The cattle-ranching industry and the mining of peridot, a semi-precious green stone found within the reservation, is also a source of employment. The largest nearby town of Globe provides needed medical and shopping facilities.

HENRY TALL HORSE'S (APACHE) STORY

As I turned off the main highway unto the roughly paved road that led to the center of the reservation, I was surprised by the starkness of the area. Given the extreme hot weather, there were no visible people anywhere to be seen outdoors. Slowly maneuvering my car through the dirt roads, I passed a few humble homes, and the carcass of a dead calf laying aside the road. It struck me that the poverty of the area should be a wake-up call to the governmental department that oversees this reservation and its honorable people. This being said, I eventually met with Henry whereas he provided me with a very personal interesting story which I know you'll appreciate.

— Antonio

"My mother died when I was two years old, and since that time, I've lived in San Carlos with my father. My experience was with two spirits. Everyone seems to think that ghosts only appear during the night, but in my case, I saw them during the day. These spirits didn't harm me, but I still got pretty scared. My experience was a strange and powerful one that I know will stay with me for a long time.

One spring morning, when I was nineteen years old, a close friend and I decided to walk over to the nearby San Carlos River and fish for catfish. Before heading out, we found two metal beer can openers. We used two stones to pound them flat, and made them into spear points. We sharpened the metal points, grinding them against a large flat boulder. Then we wrapped each of these points with wire to the ends of long thin, but strong, poles. It was a primitive but effective tool in spearing fish. My friend and I went fishing like this many times before, so we were eager to catch a lot of fish. It was about 10 a.m. when we got to the river. We followed the riverbed until we found a spot with a few trees to shade us from the sun, and a pool of water that we hoped had some fish. We each sat on the sand at opposite sides of the pool. Because the pool of water was a short distance from the main river, the water was still. In this still water, it was easy to spot the movement of swimming fish. We fished for a few hours, and caught five fish. We decided to head home and fry the fish for lunch. Most Apache I know don't like to eat fish because of our traditional beliefs, but that is changing. My friend and I enjoy eating fish. After our catfish lunch, my friend went home to his house and I took a nap.

Around 6 p.m. I decided to walk back to the river, only this time I just wanted to walk and not fish. I followed the path back to the pool of water where my friend and I had been earlier. As I got closer, in the distance I heard a very strange sound. The sound was a humming or

buzzing noise that I couldn't identify. I decided to investigate by following the sounds up the riverbed ahead of me. The sun was starting to go down in the west, but there was still plenty of light. As I got closer, the noise seemed to change to something like the flapping wings of a large flock of birds. I decided to slow my pace in order not to surprise whatever might be making the noise. I walked as carefully as I could through the trees and spiny weeds. I had a feeling that animals might be nearby, so when I thought I was close enough, I stopped and got behind a large tree branch to hide myself. Flies were buzzing around my head, but I didn't want to make any noise by swatting them. I got down on my stomach and lay flat on the sand, so I wouldn't be seen. In the distance, not far from me, I could see two large, dark shadow-like figures. They were about 70 yards away from me and I was unable to make out what they were. At first I thought they were two large dogs. They were about the same size as German shepherds. I strained my eyes to see the figures. Suddenly they changed into a shape that took on a human form! They were definitely not dogs, and I knew they were definitely not human either! As I said before, there was plenty of sunlight, so darkness was not a problem. Also, I noticed that something like a cloth, or maybe possibly animal skins, hung loose over their bodies. I couldn't tell what this stuff was. The figures had arms and legs, hands and feet, and their faces were covered with this cloth-like stuff. This covering made it impossible to a make out their faces. I saw them bent over on their hands and feet, walking just like a four-legged animal.

While I was watching all this take place, coming from the direction of the figures was the flapping wing noise that I had heard earlier. There were no birds anywhere and no wind blowing either! But I could hear the noise of what sounded to me like a tremendous flock of birds' wings flapping! These mysterious figures stood up, bowed down, turned around, and slowly moved away from each other. Several times they got down on all fours, and for many minutes, turned in complete circles. It seemed like they were dancing. Something inside told me that these 'things' were not normal, but in fact 'spirits.' I was scared. I tried my best to keep very still, but I was shaking all over. After a few minutes, the spirits changed their steps and began to move from side to side. I know this might sound crazy, but the figures changed from animal to human to animal and back again. I couldn't believe what I was seeing! Suddenly, they did something that scared me even more — they stood upright on their feet, and leaped towards each other. I'm telling you, this really surprised me. I didn't expect them to do this, or to be so fast. I felt that if I moved, even a finger, they would discover me. Who knows what they would have done to me? Because they were moving all around the riverbed so much, I was afraid they would eventually spot me. I decided to keep lying flat on my stomach, hoping to camouflage, to blend into the background as much as possible. If they spotted me, I was ready to run for it. I kept quiet and watched them repeat their strange dance over and over again. A few times one of them would jump about ten feet into the air. It was terrifying and, at the same time, fascinating to watch.

I stayed hidden behind the branch for a few more minutes, until I felt a bug sting my leg. I felt it crawl into my pant leg and sting me on the ankle. It must have been a wasp because it hurt like heck! I didn't want to make a sudden move, but knew I needed to get rid of it. I slowly sat up and stretched my arm over to scratch my leg. Through it all, I didn't take my focus off the spirits. Luckily, they didn't notice me. But when I turned my head, I hit it against a branch that was a few inches above me. The sound of the moving branch gave me away! I saw the spirits freeze and immediately they turned their heads in my direction! I saw them crouch down and instantly disappear into thin air! That was all I needed. I stood up and ran for my life, breaking branches as I ran through the bushes. Several times I lost my balance and fell to the ground. Each time I got up and ran back down the river retracing my steps, stumbling many more times before arriving at the road, which led back home. It's difficult for me to describe how scared I was. I was shaking all over and a bit bloodied.

When I got home, my father saw me covered in sweat and dirt and asked me where I had been. I excitedly told him the story of what I had seen. He looked at me with a strange gaze that I had never seen before and shook his head saying, 'Those were not things you should have been watching. You should not have been sneaking up on those spirits. They need to be left alone when they dance. You must not ever sneak up on spirits again.' He also told me, 'The spirits come down from the mountains from time to time. They have been doing this since Apaches first came to this area. The spirits live in the mountains and canyons. They follow the water because there is power in water. The river is like a big vein and water is the blood of life for spiritual beings. You need to go back there to where you saw the spirits, and leave them an offering.' I told my father that I would do as he said, but as of this day, I have not gone back to that spot. I don't want to see any more spirits. Knowing that the spirits did not wish to cause me any harm has changed my view of spiritual things, but I'm still not wanting to meet any more of them. I was raised with the stories of spirits that lived in the nearby mountains around our reservation, and was told of witches and ghosts that took many animal forms. Years ago it took my own personal experience with the dark, dancing spirits to prove to me that these were not just stories. I know these spirits are real because I have seen them."

HUALAPAI

In times past, beginning around 600, the Hualapai were a tribe who were primarily hunter-gatherers. But where water was available, the Hualapai cultivated gardens of corn, squash and beans. Today there are just fewer than 2,000 Hualapai who live at the tribal headquarters in Peach Springs, Arizona, and 50 miles east of Kingman on historic Route 66. The total reservation encompasses 108 miles of the Colorado River and a segment of the Grand Canyon. The topography of the reservation varies from rolling grassland and shear, rugged canyons to pine forest. Elevations range from 1,500 feet at the Colorado River's banks to over 7,300 feet at Aubrey Cliffs. The Hualapai Nation has managed to maintain their culture, language and well-deserved pride. The future looks positive for the Hualapai, especially since they currently have one of the highest numbers of students who are enrolled in college of any reservation in the state.

ROBERT RED SKY'S (HUALAPAI) STORY

This following story is an eye opening one that I assure you will leave you with much food for thought. Anyone who has ever gone hunting in the wilderness might have at least one or more stories of encountering 'something' strange or unexplainable. The following story given to me by Robert might just linger in your thoughts for a long time to come. I've visited with Robert twice since our initial meeting. He's introduced me to other areas of his reservation where many unexplained paranormal 'power spots' exist. Because of my own strong spiritual beliefs, I have never visited these areas without him. At this point I caution anyone who might go exploring unto reservation lands for the purpose of simply 'experiencing' ghosts. You have been warned.

— Antonio

"One winter in the month of January, when I was seventeen, my brother and father, along with my father's two good buddies, went on a deer-hunting trip in the Hualapai valley. This was a hunting trip that none of us will ever forget. Even now a strange feeling comes over me when I think back to what we all witnessed years ago, on what started out to be just an ordinary outing. That winter day I experienced an example of the power of spirits that comes forth from the land the Hualapais call home.

Two weeks before, my father had spoken to three Indian fellas in town. These guys mentioned to him about the big deer bucks they had seen browsing and running within a deep canyon. To offer further proof, they asked my father to walk with them out to the road where their pick-up truck was parked. The men proudly pulled off a large plastic tarp, which was covering the bucks they had killed. He told me those guys had some of the most beautiful bucks he had ever seen. He asked the three guys for detailed directions regarding the location of their successful hunting. As they gave him directions, he wrote down every road, turn and curve. In our Indian way, we don't hold back information about such hunting areas. It's traditionally right that we share such information among our people, and it's something that goes back a long way with the Hualapai.

My father arrived home and told my brother and me about the deer. Soon we had planned a hunting trip. My father was convinced he too could shoot a deer or two just like those guys in town had. He got on the phone and invited two good friends of his. The date was set. We knew the weather would be cold so we packed a good supply of food and warm clothes. My father enjoys eating hot chile so my mom made him about two dozen beef burritos with some very hot red chile, all rolled up in foil. These he planned to heat up on the campfire. We loaded the pick-up with three days' supply of food and water, the burritos and our hunting gear, and then off we drove to meet up with my father's two friends.

We soon came to the main turn-off from the highway.

We started out in the early morning, and although it was a very cold winter morning, there was no snow on the ground. The weather was perfect. We soon came to the main turn-off from the highway. It was a dirt road, which was not too rough for the first five miles but then got very rough as we made another turn onto another road. The sun was already up in the east as we started our way up over a hill. We stopped at the top of the hill and took a short coffee break. As we stood standing around the two trucks in the empty landscape drinking our hot coffee, we suddenly heard a strange sound come from the west. It was like the sound of a hundred hoof beats, the sound of many horses going at a full gallop. It came from nowhere; it just sort of started up and lasted for a few seconds, then it ended. We expected to see a herd of horses come up onto the hill, but there was nothing visible, not even a dust cloud. None of us could explain what it was. We nervously joked about it being a flying jet, but the sky was, as far as we could see, clear of any aircraft. Not saying another word, we finished our coffee, got back into the trucks and continued on our way.

The time now was eight-thirty in the morning and I could tell that the trucks were not going to be able to continue any further on the very rocky road we were driving on. We decided to stop and make camp in the middle of a distant, small grove of juniper trees. The wind was still and the air was cold and crisp as we opened our tents and arranged them around a rock fire ring that my brother formed. After making camp we decided to eat some food, and then head out with our rifles towards the hills in the direction we were told the deer would be. We followed an old coyote trail that went down the eastern side of a ridge. We were careful not to talk loudly, or make loud sounds with our footsteps. Deer are very alert and can be easily spooked. We noticed that the area was littered with deer droppings. A good sign!

We followed an old coyote trail that went down the eastern side of a ridge.

The area was sparsely spotted with medium to tall junipers, and in the distant narrow valleys were a few groves of cottonwoods and oaks. My father knew that deer like to browse in these areas, so we were constantly trying to pick out any movement in the distance. Suddenly, just as before, the weird sound of hoof beats started up again. We all stood still and waited. Then, just as before, the sound came toward us and soon disappeared.

This time we were not so quick to dismiss the sound as being a jet plane. We softly spoke among ourselves, but said nothing about it being an omen of bad medicine. We knew it would not be a good thing to talk about it any further, because to do so would bring us a bad hunt. We again picked up the hike and continued towards the valley below. The time was now one in the afternoon, three hours since we left our campsite. As we entered the valley and the grove of tall trees, we were startled as a porcupine came out from behind an old stump and gave us all a fright. It was difficult to keep from laughing loudly. We all felt a sense of relief at our little brother's sudden appearance. As we exited the other side of the grove of trees, my father, who was now walking ahead of us, spotted some deer on the side of the hill. He stopped his walk and lowered his left hand, exposing the palm, which was a signal for us all to immediately stop. We stood still and viewed the deer, quietly scanning the large herd before us.

There were ten does and three really beautiful bucks. What a sight! This was what we had all dreamed of. We spoke in soft voices, communicating to each other how best to get a shot at the bucks. Then, without warning, something scared the deer. They must have seen something big or dangerous because they bolted and went running. They couldn't possibly have seen or caught our scent among the trees. We automatically got down on our bellies and watched as the deer darted just a few yards away from us. We froze like statues, trying to camouflage into the surrounding brush and trees. Just as it appeared that the deer were going to reach us, they darted in another direction and disappeared behind a small ridge.

We were speechless, and wondered about the sudden change in the deer. We thought there must have been a hungry mountain lion or something very scary that had attempted to attack them. We rose to our feet and looked toward the area where the deer had been grazing and did not see anything unusual at all, neither a mountain lion nor even a bird. Nothing. Things were now becoming too strange for us to dismiss all these experiences. Something other than coincidence was at work here. My father spoke first and said, 'I think we should perhaps offer a prayer for guidance and ask for protection from whatever is tracking us in these hills.' My father's two older friends agreed and in our Native language we all bowed our heads and prayed.

After praying, we decided to continue tracking the deer and headed in the direction of their escape. It didn't take long before we found ourselves in another canyon walking between tall stone walls. A small stream of water bubbled out from a large sandy area, which formed a shallow pool of water. All around the outer edges of this pool were green, mossy plants and deer tracks. We knew we had found a deer water hole. The only problem was that we were a long hike away from our supplies and shelter. We knew that it would be better to head back to camp and start out earlier the next morning. We climbed up and over a large pile of boulders, then hiked along the canyon wall for a short distance, then headed up and out of the canyon. We made it over the boulders with no trouble, but when we began to hike along the canyon wall, my brother called to my father to look at something on the walls. There were ancient petroglyphs, stone pictures that were carved on the canyon walls centuries ago by prehistoric Native people.

These carvings were not the usual ones, which we were accustomed to seeing on other walls in other canyons. These were not pictures of sun, bird, stars and lightning symbols. These were pictures of people without heads, or with the heads and arms of animals. There were pictures of owls and figures with opened mouths. My father and his friends spoke out loud, 'These pictures tell that this canyon area is full of supernatural forces. The pictures of headless people mean that bad witches and animal spirits were working together to make bad medicine

here many years ago.' We all agreed that to get out of this canyon as soon as possible would be the best thing to do.

We hurried our hike and soon reached the top of the canyon. We reached our camp just after dark. We got dinner going on the fire and after eating our fill, drank a few cups of coffee. Not once did we mention the weird sounds, the deers' reaction or the petroglyphs we had experienced that day. It is best not to talk about such things. To do so, we believe, would call to us the dark forces. We decided at around eight that evening to call it a day and get into our sleeping bags. After placing more wood on the fire, we all stretched out, close to the fire ring. We were very tired from all the hiking of the day, and were eager to get enough rest for the next day's activities. Very soon after zipping up into our bags, we fell into a deep sleep. I must have been the last one to nod off because I remember hearing everyone's snoring before falling asleep.

The next thing I remember is being suddenly awakened by a loud snapping sound coming from one of the burning logs in the fire. I opened my eyes and stared at the black, moonless sky above. I remember thinking to myself, what a beautiful sky it was, as I viewed all the stars filling the dark spaces from one vast direction to the other. Then I turned to face some movement, which caught my attention in the brush a short distance from our camp. I saw what looked like a naked person crouching down on his legs staring at me! I thought that I must have been imagining this because of how tired I was. I closed my eyes and rubbed them with my cold fingers. I again turned my attention to the figure in the distance and sure enough, it was still there, just staring at me. I began to get scared, thinking it might be someone who was going to rob us. I knew that my rifle was just a few feet away from me, but I would need to react quickly in order to do any good.

As I observed this person, I realized that he was the size of a child. I watched as he made a quick motion and stood straight up. That did it for me. I threw off the sleeping bag and yelled for everyone to get up as I went for the rifle. I yelled, 'Hey, there's a guy over here.' Everyone reacted quickly by jumping out of their sleeping bags. I told them about the person I had seen in the bushes. My father listened to me and then said, 'I had been seeing that guy for some time before you woke us. There are other spirits with him as well. I've been seeing two more of them moving from juniper bush to juniper bush.' This got my brother a bit scared. He spoke. 'Well, what are we going to do? Will they hurt us, do they want us to leave this place?' My father's friend responded, 'I think we should pack up and leave this place. These are not good spirits. We saw the pictures on the rocks. Those are not good pictures. Those are pictures of witches and people who work with bad spirits. I really think we should leave this place tonight.' We threw more wood on the fire and we got it burning brightly. We decided to take my father's friend's advice and leave the canyon that night.

As we packed up our gear, I again noticed the shadows of people, or spirits, running from bush to bush. I let the rest of the men know what I had just seen. My father decided to sing a prayer and the rest of us joined in. My father's friend then ended the prayer by announcing, in the direction of the spirits, that the Creator was watching over our well-being and that they should leave us alone. Suddenly, we heard the low sound of laughter and hoof beats leave our camp. This is when I knew our power of prayer helped us chase away whatever was watching us.

We all got in our trucks and drove home that night. We did not speak again about our experience until the next morning. During breakfast we told our mother about our experience. She said that during the day and night we were gone, an owl had been making hooting sounds in the tree in our front yard. This was very unusual and she knew that this was an omen that something bad was happening to us. She herself began to pray for us to return safely home. Aside from this experience I have had a couple more that have taken place, but I don't think I'd like to talk anymore about this."

TOHONO O'ODHAM

The Tohono O'odham, or 'Papagos,' as they were named prior to 1980, presently exist on a reservation, which extends over a hundred miles following the Arizona and Mexican border. This reservation is also the second largest in the U.S. It begins north in the Casa Grande area, east in the Aguirre Valley, west in the Sand Tank/Sauceda Mountains, and then ends south in Old Mexico, where a small population of Tohono O'odham presently reside in the state of Sonora. They still practice much of the traditional ceremonies and beliefs that were alive prior to contact with Spanish missionaries in the late 17th century. The people chose to renounce the negative name 'Papagos' which means 'bean eaters,' for the more appropriate and suitable name that they have always called themselves, Tohono O'odham. The Tohono O'odham are a true

desert-farming people. In years past, they used a 'dry farming' technology (like the Hopi to the north), which utilized the infrequent thunderstorms and rains that flooded the washes and valleys. They planted traditional seed crops in these areas and simply waited as the earth's wet season provided the needed moisture for germination. Presently, these farming practices are no longer in use by the people and instead, they utilize water provided by modern wells.

An Italian Jesuit missionary named Father Eusebio Francisco Kino made contact with the Tohono O'odham in the year 1687. This meeting changed the culture of the Tohono O'odham forever. New crops and domesticated animals were introduced, as was a new political system and religion, Catholicism. Today, church structures remain as evidence

of this legacy. The Tohono O'odham provided the prime labor and artists who built all these beautiful buildings. The joint knowledge of the Tohono O'odham and Europeans regarding construction and design is admirable and will for all time be deserving of notable recognition.

DAVID WAR STAFF'S (YAQUI) STORY

David's story is unnerving given its location and time of night. I tend to wonder how anyone might have reacted in a more rational manner if found to be in a same situation as he. During my research, I rarely come across stories compelling such attention as his. Fortunately for David and his cousin, they were aided by two strangers who just happened to be in the area. Let's simply hope we all can be so lucky as they were.

— Antonio

"It was February in the year 1991 when I had my experience with a ghost. I was seventeen years old at the time. One Saturday evening in Phoenix my high school was having a basketball game, and after the game my cousin Ralph and I left the school gymnasium at around 10 p.m.

My cousin is from Tohono O'dham and I was going to spend the weekend with my aunt's family. Like myself, my aunt is Yaqui. She married a Tohono O'dham man some years ago and had two kids. One is my cousin Ralph. We got on Interstate 10 and then switched on to south Highway 15 for the drive to the town of Sells on the Tohono O'dham Reservation. About 40 minutes into our drive we were deep in the desert. Because my car needed new tires, I had to drive just below the speed limit. The threads were just about completely worn out. I guess I had the type of car that we Indians call an 'Indian Car.' It was a pretty beat-up looking car, but it got me where I wanted to go. Anyway, there we were driving in the middle of the desert with the CD player going, and the darkness all around. Suddenly, a large javelina crossed the road, and I hit that wild pig with a big-old 'bang!' I didn't have time to even think about stepping on the brakes because all at once there was just the road before us, and the next there was this javelina. I knew we had some big trouble with the car because the radiator began to hiss and steam began pouring out. I immediately drove to the side of the road, and stopped the car to check on the damage. Sure enough, that big pig had hit the front grill head-on, and a piece of metal had punctured my car's radiator.

Directly behind the car in the darkness we could hear the pig loudly squealing. It was a weird experience to be alone at night in the desert and to hear the loud dying sounds of an animal just a few yards away. It kept up the terrible squealing sound for a long, long time. I had a flashlight, but I sure wasn't going to go check on its injuries without a gun. I know that javelinas can turn on you, giving a nasty bite when cornered or injured. My cousin said, 'You know, with a busted radiator, we're not going to be able to go any further tonight.' 'Yeah,' I answered. 'We're going to have to spend a cold night in the car, or else start walking and hope someone picks us up.' We decided to stay with the car, open up the hood and hopefully, if anyone driving by saw us, they might give us a lift. After about a half hour, the javelina stopped screaming. As we sat in the front seat, we waited and waited for a passing car. A few passed by, but none stopped. I looked at my watch. The time was 12:10 a.m. Aside from being cold, we were both sleepy. We decided to turn off the car's radio in order to conserve the battery. We also decided to go outside and sit on the car's trunk, to keep from falling asleep. We kept each other up with jokes and talking about the basketball game. After a while we ran out of jokes and things to say. We each started to yawn every few minutes. I looked at my watch. The time was 1:40 a.m. 'Damn,' I thought. 'When are we going to get home?'

A few more minutes passed then I heard the sound of something in the bushes. I turned to look at Ralph. I could tell by his reaction that he also heard the sound. We kept still and alert. The sound was of someone slowly walking and breaking twigs and brush with each step. The sounds were coming from the direction where the javelina was lying on the road. The moon was bright enough to make out forms in the darkness, but we were not able to see anything. Then from out of the bushes, about twenty feet away, we saw a barefoot man! I turned on my flashlight and focused the weak yellow light on him as I yelled, 'Hey, what's up?' The man stopped and turned to face us. Because of the weak batteries in my flashlight and the man's distance from us, it was not easy to make out his features. I thought he was a desert tramp. There are a few of those old guys living out there. Ralph yelled out, 'Watch out. We hit a javelina and it's somewhere out where you're walking!' Again there was no reply from the man. Then it occurred to both of us, what's this guy doing in the desert at this hour? This was not normal. Things were becoming kind of weird. We got a little scared. We both yelled out, 'Hey, you, can't you hear us, get away from there.' The man stopped, turned in our direction and looked at us. We were definitely 'on the edge' at that point. I thought if this guy has a gun, in which direction would we run? I spoke to Ralph, 'This guy is some kind of weirdo. We better be careful.'

Then the man took a few more steps toward the highway, and we both got a real good look at him. He was dressed in very little clothing.

On his thin waist he wore a tight-fitting dark colored cloth that draped down over one knee. Around his neck were several long necklaces with large white beads or shells. He wore his hair short with bangs above his glaring eyes. One obviously strange thing was his hair. It was either greasy or wet, because when I focused the light from my flashlight on it, it shone. He was about five feet tall and very thin. He was an older man, because his face showed the signs of age. Ralph and I yelled to him, 'Hey, you!' Again he did not respond. He didn't even look at us, but continued to walk across the highway and into the brush on the other side, where he disappeared. I use the word 'walk,' but he was floating about five inches over the asphalt! I could see his bare feet making the slow movement of walking.

As he re-entered the brush, unlike before, we didn't hear any of the twigs breaking under his footsteps. Ralph and I looked at each other and jumped off the trunk, ran inside the car and quickly locked the doors! We knew this was no tramp. It had to be a ghost! You had to be there to feel the energy to know that this was a real ghost. What else could it have been? We spent the night, scared and hoping for a car to stop, or for the morning to quickly arrive. We were scared! We kept thinking that the ghost was going to appear to us again, only this time at the car's windows! Our imaginations kept us from sleeping. We tried to think about other things, but it was difficult not to keep focusing on the ghost. We kept the car's inside dome light on, and the radio tuned loudly to a rock station. Eventually, because we were so tired, we finally did fall asleep.

As the hours passed by, sometime before dawn, we were wakened by a passing truck with two guys who were headed for Sells. They sure did give us a good scare when they knocked on the car's window, but soon we were introducing ourselves, and they offered to take us home. The guys told us they were artists driving from California. They were on a photography trip, taking pictures of the desert and Indians for an art project. We tied one end of a rope to the back of their truck and the other end to the front of our car, and they towed us home. We never mentioned our experience with the ghost the night before. But when we did get home that morning, we told my aunt and her family everything. Everyone agreed that what we had experienced was the ghost of an ancient Indian from the spirit world. Since my encounter with that ghost, I've decided, if at all possible, never to drive at night through the desert again."

HOPI
(HOPITUH)

The Hopi Reservation lies within the larger Navajo Reservation in the northeast quadrant of Arizona. The nearest town of Tuba City is located to the west while the largest city of Flagstaff is located to the southwest. The Hopi area itself is quite isolated by many miles of desert and canyons. Highway 264 provides the major access to and from the reservation. When mentioning the Hopi or Hopituh Nation, it is difficult not to focus on such essential elements as farming and gardening. Existing and thriving in a desert environment is testament to the adaptive ability of these unique and deeply spiritual people. Hopi can trace their physical ancestral birth to their homeland as being approximately 1200 and earlier. Archaeologically, garden terraces at Third Mesa or Bacavi prove this. Farming methods used in times past are still in use to this day. Examples are the ingenious use of gardens located on mesa walls, which are irrigated terraces that are water-fed by the villages located above. Another method is 'dry farming.' This technique involves the planting of seed within arroyos (washes) and valleys located on the lower plateaus where seasonal rain produces the moisture necessary for their germination and growth.

The Hopi cosmology is composed of four worlds, or 'ways of life.' At the present time, the Hopi believe that they are in the fourth way. As they moved from the third way to the fourth way, they and other people were offered corn by the creator, or Ma'saw. Aside from the Hopi, all the other people eagerly and boldly took the largest of the corn that was offered. The Hopi in turn were left with the shortest and smallest blue corn. The Hopi immediately knew that this was symbolic of their life to come, as it too would be short and difficult. Thus, their response was to manifest the virtues of cooperation, humility and respect among themselves and others. They also knew that the earth was a wonderful and giving, living spirit and its health would depend on the Hopi people as its caretakers. Today the Hopi live in three separate and autonomous mesas or villages, and within each village are sub-communities. First Mesa includes Waalpi (Walpi), Hanoki (Hano or Tewa), and Sitsomovi (Sichomovi). Second Mesa includes Songoopavi (Shongopavi), Musungnuvi (Mishongnovi) and Supawlavi (Shipaulovi). Third Mesa includes Hoatvela (Hotevilla), Paaqavi (Bacavi), Munqapi (Moencopi), Kiqotsmovi (Kykotsmovi), and Orayvi (Oraibi).

DONALD FIRST CRY'S (HOPI) STORY

Oh boy, what a story you're about to read. As you might imagine, conducting the research for all my writing has always placed me in a needed situation to travel about the Southwest. And because of this traveling I have had to spend

many nights in hotels and out-of-the-way motels. Some of these establishments definitely have appealing qualities while others have me praying for the rescuing morning light to make my escape. Donald's story might prompt you to consider other 'issues' when picking a hotel room—'extra' questions you might need to ask the front desk. His and his wife's encounter with the spiritual world in their hotel room might just also change your own future thoughts regarding a vacation.
— *Antonio*

"My girlfriend Becky and I are both Hopi. I've spent most of my life on the reservation, except when I left to work for eight years in San Diego, California. My older brother and I were offered well-paying jobs as roofers in new home construction. Becky has worked at the reservation school cafeteria for just a couple of months, and we plan to get married next year. My experience with a ghost took place two years ago. Up to that time I had never had any kind of spooky stuff happen to me. I know that a lot of ghostly things do take place in the hills and mesas that surround our tribal lands, but I never really paid much attention to the stories. Anyway, two years ago Becky and I spent a summer weekend in the gambling town of Laughlin, Nevada. We never thought this short get-away was going to be anything but a fun time. We've driven together to Laughlin many times before without ever having encountered a ghost. So this first weird experience shook us up for a long time afterwards.

Whenever we've driven to Laughlin, our normal routine is to arrive at a hotel, check into a room, then hit the 'one arm bandits' downstairs. We've both done this since we were in our early twenties. Sometimes we win big, and sometimes we lose, but we have a good time nonetheless. This time, we arrived at the hotel on a Friday evening at around 7 p.m. We checked into a room on the 14th floor with a view of the Colorado River below. We emptied our suitcases of clothes, which we hung on hangers in the closet. Then we decided to watch a little television before heading to the lobby downstairs for a bite to eat. As at other times, we both knew we would spend most of the night gambling, so we were in no hurry.

As we were lying on the bed watching a comedy show, I felt an uneasy feeling strangely come over me, a feeling of depression that I had never experienced before. I thought that maybe I was getting the flu or had gotten food poisoning from lunch. I also felt a sort of a weird 'thickness' come over me. I know it sounds strange, but I felt something like a cold mud had covered me. I couldn't make sense of why I was suddenly feeling so bad. At one point, I looked away from the television and focused my eyes on the open window. Without being conscious of it, I began to think crazy thoughts of darkness covering me like a cloud. I began to shake like a leaf. My heart was throbbing and I was filled with a sense of dying. Becky must have noticed something was up, because I felt her hand touch my shoulder and say, 'Donald, Donald, what's the matter?' I answered, 'Nothing. I'm just not feeling too good. Maybe I'm getting a cold or the flu.' I told Becky that I needed to close my eyes and rest, but she looked at me funny and said, 'You're drenched in perspiration. Donald, just look at you.' I told her that I would be alright, but I needed to relax for a few minutes. Becky sat back on the bed, but kept an eye on me.

I turned my attention back to the television, and soon I began to feel better. Then that feeling of disaster, a sort of panic came slowly over me once again, and I automatically began to glance out the window as before. I thought I was having an anxiety attack, because my hands began to shake and a feeling of fear began to take control of me. A friend of mine once had an anxiety attack when we were at a restaurant, so I am aware of the symptoms. I yelled to Becky, 'Look at me; something is happening to me!' Becky came to my side and said, 'Donald, what is it? What's going on?' After a few seconds, I decided to get up off the bed and walk to the bathroom and splash water on my face. Becky followed, and looking at me through my reflection in the mirror said, 'Donald, should we take you to a doctor? You might be having a heart attack.' I answered, 'No, no. Let's just go get something to eat.' As quickly as this thing came over me, it left. I soon regained my composure and told Becky that I was feeling much better. Whatever it was that had come over me was now gone. We decided to leave the room, go down to the lobby and get some dinner.

I began to feel much better and even got lucky when I won $800.00

playing the $1.00 slots! At about 2 a.m. we decided to call it a night, and took the elevator to our room on the 14th floor. Getting ready for bed, I brushed my teeth, then closed the drapes and got into bed. We both quickly fell asleep, but my sleep did not last for long. I was awakened a few hours later when Becky grabbed my arm and shook me hard. 'Donald, Donald, wake up, wake up, there is some guy in the room!' Becky said that she had awakened with the strong feeling of someone's eyes staring at her. When she opened her own eyes she saw the figure of a young man standing next to the bathroom door. Out of fear she grabbed my arm and woke me from my sleep. I watched as Becky pointed to look by the bathroom. At first I didn't see anyone and then I heard a loud 'thud!' It sounded like someone had fallen to the floor. I leaped out of bed and cautiously turned on the lights. As I looked around the room, I noticed there was nothing out of place. As much as I could tell, we were alone in the room. I carefully walked to the closed bathroom door, reached for the knob, and opened it. I reached inside and felt for the light switch, then turned it on. There was no trace of anyone. Although we could easily explain away the figure of the guy Becky had seen as being a bad dream, we could not explain the falling thud sound we had both heard. Throughout the night, we would hear the thud sound again and again. Being too tired to stay up any longer and discuss it further, we returned to bed and fell asleep. The next morning Becky told me she was unable to sleep and was awake most of the night.

After breakfast we walked to the parking lot, got into our car and drove to the local mall to do some shopping. We entered a dress shop where Becky began a conversation with a fellow customer, a woman who happened to work in the same hotel where we were staying. She introduced herself to us and said she was a prep-cook there. The woman was a Paiute Indian from California and she and Becky hit it off right away. I excused myself, and decided to wait outside the store on a bench, while Becky finished her conversation. When Becky caught up with me, she told me that the woman had given her some strange information about the hotel where we were staying. Apparently, three days before, there was a guy who had unintentionally killed himself on the 14th floor of the hotel. He was a drug addict who mixed a batch of heroin in the bathroom of his hotel room and died of an overdose. While doing her job, the maid found the body the next morning. The Paiute woman had informed Becky of this after Becky mentioned that we were staying on the 14th floor. Although the woman was unaware of the dead man's room number, she told Becky it was a room that had a window that faced the river below. The cook also had Becky promise that she would not tell anyone at the hotel about what she had said, for fear that she would lose her job.

Well, this new information sure did give us a new perspective. Becky became very nervous and told me she did not want to worry or scare me, but that the figure she had seen in our room the night before appeared to her once again that night. She told me that she did not get much sleep because the ghost made a sound that caused her to look in the direction of the bathroom. Once again, she spotted the ghost standing against the wall, in a leaning position. His eyes were dark black, and opened wide, and even though his mouth moved to make words, no sound came out. Then the ghost suddenly disappeared. Becky said she closed her eyes and convinced herself that what she had seen was something her imagination had made up, but she spent the night drifting in and out of sleep. With this new information, Becky and I returned to our hotel and demanded a room change. Since that

weekend, we've not had another experience with the supernatural. And I have not had another anxiety attack or anything like one."

VILLAGE OF ARIVACA

Arivaca, in southern Pima County about 11 miles north of Arizona's border with Mexico and mapped by Father Eusebio Kino in 1695, is in an area which contains some of the oldest mines in the United States. Arivaca, which is unincorporated, is about 56 miles southwest of Tucson. The post office was established in 1878. The locale may have been a Tohono O'odham Indian village before Natives revolted in 1751 against the Spanish, who were attracted by precious metals and excellent grazing land. The Spaniards used forced local Indian labor to work these mines under the direction of Tumacacori Mission padres.

In 1833, the Mexican government approved a petition by brothers Tomas and Ignacio Ortiz to raise cattle and horses on 8,677 acres of land that formed the Arivac Ranch. (The original Indian word, OLa AribacO, means 'small springs'.) Although boundaries for the ranch were never certain, the rights were bought by the Sonora Exploring and Mining Company in the year 1856. This company operated mines near Arivaca and Tubac. Also located on the ranch were reduction works for the Heintzelman Mine.

Charles Poston, the father of Arizona, acquired the property in 1870 and later asked the U.S. government to confirm his right to 26,508 acres. The U.S. Surveyor General recommended confirmation of 8,680 acres, but the U.S. Congress failed to heed this recommendation. Poston's rights were obtained by the Arivaca Land and Cattle Company, which asked the U.S. Court of Private Land Claims to approve the land claim. The court refused, saying it was impossible to identify the land that was intended to be granted. The decision was upheld by the U.S. Supreme Court on March 24, 1902, and the land became part of the public domain.

Today Arivaca is primarily a retirement and residential area.

FRANCIS TORRES' (HISPANIC) STORY

I interviewed Francis at her home. Arivaca is a small village town tucked within a quaint desert valley. Within this quiet town lies Francis' two-bedroom home. Viewing it from the street, the house would not give any indication as to the frightening manifestations that transpired just a few years ago within its walls.

Francis preferred that I not describe the outside of her house because she said that by doing so, some neighbors might identify her and start to gossip. Given her concern, I have chosen to also not use her real name. This interview was conducted in Francis' kitchen. During the interview we kept hearing a few 'thuds' coming from the walls. After the third thud, Francis excused herself, rose from her chair, walked to a back room and shortly thereafter returned to the kitchen holding a picture of St. Benedict and a lit candle. Francis said, "I'm not taking any chances. Whatever is here knows we're talking about it. This should take care of them." Francis then placed the picture and candle on the table and the interview continued without any further interruption.

— Antonio

"My story about El Coyote took place just a couple of years ago. I have made sure not to tell many people about what happened in the house because, being a small town, the gossip gets around really quickly. I used to rent and live in the house next to the one I now live in. I also knew the old woman who was the owner of the property. When I moved into the house next door, she and I began to talk and we became very friendly with each other. Some mornings we would have coffee in my kitchen. She sure was a talker. She told me about her son who lived in Tucson, and I got to meet him a few times before she died. I recall that the first time I visited her, she showed me around the inside of her home. I noticed that one of her bedrooms had a door with nails hammered into the doorframe. Hanging on one of the nails was a small metal crucifix. I asked her about this, because it was very strange to have a door nailed shut the way it was. Her explanation was that she had nailed the door because of El Coyote. I asked her, 'Who was El Coyote?' She said he was a bad spirit that needed to be kept locked up. I immediately thought that living by herself for so long made this old woman go crazy. I asked her why the spirit had the name of El Coyote.

She said she had given it that name because, although she had never really seen the spirit's face, its body looked like a wild dog. I thought to myself that this poor woman needed to get out of the house more often and mingle with people because she was most definitely not a rational thinking person.

I didn't think much more about the 'friend' that she kept locked up in the bedroom. I never heard any loud noises coming from her home and, after all, she was really sweet.

One day while she was at the post office, I walked to the rear of her house and looked inside the bedroom window where she kept El Coyote. I didn't know what I would expect to see. As I looked inside, I saw a room that was without furniture. It didn't even have any rugs. Poor old woman, she must have invented this ghost as her own personal friend. I began to feel sorry for her because I myself have never married and I know that it sometimes does get a bit lonely. There wasn't anything unusual about the room, so I never mentioned it to her again. Well, two days later, I paid her a visit to show her a large holiday greeting card that had arrived at my house. I knocked on her front door and when she did not answer, I walked to the rear door, which was left unlocked and walked inside. I immediately smelled gas. I took a few slow steps into the house and kept calling her name. There was no answer. I got concerned and quickly walked through the house. When I entered her bedroom, I found her lifeless body in bed. I called the police and they discovered the cause of her death was due to a flexible copper hose leading from the wall to her gas heater that had developed a small hole. The day before her death, she had spent the holiday in Tucson with her son and his family. I know she had died happy because, after returning home, all she did was talk to me about how nice her visit to her son's house had been.

After the funeral, her son told me that he was going to sell his mother's house. I asked him if he would sell it to me, and he agreed. I also asked him if he knew anything about the closed door that was nailed shut, and about El Coyote. He said that his mother only mentioned El Coyote a few times, but that he thought it was an imaginary friend his mother made up. After buying the house, I had two friends who lived in the town of Nogales come to Arivaca and help me with repairs. I was overjoyed to finally own a house of my own. I began to remove old wallpaper and paint from every inside wall. Of course, the first thing I did was to remove the nails on the bedroom door where 'El Coyote' was kept locked away. During the repair work, I never noticed any strange noise, or saw any ghost. Except for the cold temperature that hovered in that rear bedroom, there was nothing strange at all.

Finally, after a few weeks, the house repairs were completed. After moving all my belongings into the house, I soon began to notice that the rear bedroom was strangely very much colder than the rest of the house. At first, I was not much bothered by it, but it did make me wonder. At times, when I would enter the room, it was so cold that I got goose bumps on my arms. At other times, it was like stepping outside into a cool night. I thought about what the old woman had told me, but realized that perhaps my imagination was working overtime. As the weeks passed, things began to get much worse. Day and night I began to see strange shadows in the house. I don't mean shadows shaped like a person—they were more like a large blanket that covered the wall! One afternoon, I was washing dishes and I heard a strange voice. Because I was in the kitchen, I had the television volume in the living room turned up high, so that I could listen to the show. I thought that perhaps the voice was coming from the television. I stopped washing the dishes because I had a very strong feeling that someone was in the kitchen with me. I turned around to look behind me. I saw this huge black shadow—it covered the whole wall! It moved slowly, and then quickly darted across the room and into the hallway. It couldn't have been the shadow of a passing car because the kitchen is located in the rear of the house. And it couldn't have been a passing plane, because I would have heard it flying so low. No, I knew this was something that had to do with the spiritual world.

Even though I was a bit shaken, I walked into the hallway and looked in the bathroom, closets, and the bedrooms. As soon as I entered the last bedroom, the familiar cold feeling came over me. My instincts told me I had to get out of there, fast! I closed the door behind me and left it closed until the following week, when a handyman paid me a visit. I had ordered a pair of new closet doors that were delivered by a Nogales contractor who carried them off his truck and into the bedroom. Everything was going fine. I was in the living room watching television as the loud noise of his electric drill started up. I remember walking to the bedroom and asking the contractor if he wanted some coffee. He said no and I left him alone to finish the installation. Just a few minutes later I suddenly heard him yell, and as I began to get off my chair, he came flying down the hallway and out the front door! I thought he had hurt himself, so I raced out the door to meet him at his truck that was parked in the street. He was pale. He told me that 'something' had taken hold of his arm. When he turned around he saw a very large man with angry eyes, grabbing hold of his upper left arm. It took all the strength he had to free himself from the ghost's strong grip. The contractor did not know anything about the bedroom, or about the woman who owned the house before I did. His experience left him shaken and I was very concerned about spending any more nights or days in the house with that 'thing' walking around. I volunteered to go back into the house and return with his tools. I softly prayed to myself as I walked into the bedroom, and I guess God helped me, because I didn't see El Coyote.

After the contractor drove away, I walked back to the bedroom and placed a crucifix on the door and closed it shut, just as the woman before me had done. I decided to tell my cousin, who lives in the town just south of Arivaca, about what had happened. She asked, 'If there is an angry spirit in the bedroom, it must be protecting something. Why wouldn't it want people in the bed- room?' That weekend my cousin, her husband, Pablo, and a friend came to my house to investigate. We entered the bedroom and searched the closet and tapped on the walls. As we walked about the room, we all took turns walking over one particular spot on the floor that was colder than the rest of the room. 'That's it, it's here!' my cousin said. 'Whatever this ghost is protecting, it is under this area of the floor.' Pablo went outside and located a small door that led to a crawl space under the house. He returned to tell us to get flashlights. The two men opened the door and they both entered the crawl space, as my cousin and I watched. Soon we heard Pablo yell to us to come outside. The men had found something. As we all gathered in the yard, they showed us a small Indian pottery bowl and some old stone beads. No money, no bones—just a bowl and beads. We placed the bowl into a cardboard box with crumbled-up newspaper, as packing material.

I didn't want these things in my house and I decided to take them to the nearby San Javier del Bac Mission at the Pima Reservation. After driving up the mission's driveway, I waited in my parked car for a moment, just to think things over. I wasn't sure if giving these Indian things to a priest would be the best thing to do. Instead, I decided to take a short drive to the reservation office and speak with someone. I met an office worker and explained to her that I needed to know if there was a person who could help me. After telling her my story, she gave me directions to the house of a woman who heals people on the reservation. As I was parking the car on the dirt street, the woman and her son were driving up to the house. I introduced myself and quickly told her about what I had in the cardboard box. She seemed uneasy, but said she would take care of it. My meeting with her only took about 15 minutes. I know that I must have appeared very nervous, because I remember speaking to her very quickly. I opened the car's trunk, took out the cardboard box with the pot and left it on her porch.

As I drove away, I began to feel very comfortable and relaxed. Somehow I knew that I had done the right thing. A feeling of relief came over me. Since that night I have not had another experience with El Coyote in my house. Today, I use the bedroom as a workshop for ceramic figurines that I paint. I paint several different figurines of people, animals and flowers, but if you look closely you'll notice I don't have one single painted pot. I guess you can tell why I stay away from keeping pots in that bedroom!"

NAVAJO
(DIN-NEH')

The name by which the Navajo are known is not so much the name of a people as the name of a place. The neighboring Pueblo people referred to the area of the Southwest that the Din-neh' occupied as Navajo. The

Spanish later arrived referred to the Din-neh' as Apaches de Navajo. This label was in time shortened to simply Navajo. Given all this excess phraseology, the Navajo have always referred to themselves as Din-neh', which means 'the people,' and their homeland as Dinetah'. Current usage of either two nouns is acceptable. However, it is best to use the name that the Din-neh' have chosen for centuries.

Today the Din-neh' are the largest Indian nation in the United States. Presently they account for fifteen percent of the Native American population as reported in the 1990 U.S. census. Their tribal numbers are in excess of 250,000 members. Occupying a vast area of the Southwest, spreading across parts of Arizona, New Mexico, Colorado and Utah, Din-neh' land encompasses an area larger than the states of Connecticut, Rhode Island, Massachusetts, and New Jersey combined. Chinle, near the geographic center of the Navajo Indian Reservation in northeastern Arizona, is at the entrance to Canyon de Chelly National Monument. Chinle became a center for population growth and trade after 1868 when the United States signed a treaty with the Navajos. The first trading post was established in 1882, the first mission in 1904, and the first government school in 1910. Today the community, at an altitude of 5,082 feet, has been designated one of the major 'growth centers' on the Navajo Reservation by the tribal government. It is an important trade, administrative, and educational center within the Chinle Chapter (a local government unit) and is headquarters for the Chinle Agency, one of five Bureau of Indian Affairs administrative jurisdictions on the reservation.

JOSIE YELLOW GOURD'S (NAVAJO) STORY

I interviewed Josie on the Navajo Reservation not far from the town of Chinle, which is located in the northeast quadrant of the state. Josie is a 41-year-old widow and mother of twin daughters, aged 16. Our interview took place inside their mobile home, which is situated on deep red, rusty-colored desert land with wispy juniper trees growing in contorted shapes. Overhead is the endless vastness of the turquoise blue sky.

Within such beauty, this location would be complete if not for the reality of poverty that lingered all around. As with some Native Americans, Josie daily endures such inconveniences as living without modern plumbing, electricity or heating. The interview was conducted in Josie's kitchen. On the table were various small plastic tubes and glass jars containing a rainbow of assorted tiny, brightly colored glass beads. Josie and her daughters sew these beads onto leather and make hatbands, necklaces, earrings and bracelets. Once completed, they take these articles to local stores in town and either sell them or exchange them for personal items. Josie spoke in a calm, even tone when relating her personal experience with a witch and ghosts. Her daughters were in the adjoining living room and silently listened as their mother told me her story.

— Antonio

"My 70-year-old grandfather enjoys living in the traditional manner of us Navajos in a Navajo roundhouse or 'hogan,' which is right next to our mobile home. He also prefers to speak only our Native language. After my grandmother's death, he lived alone in his hogan for over twenty years. Both he and grandmother lived together in a previous hogan, but after she died, grandfather burned their original hogan, as is our tradition to do when the owner dies. A new hogan was built for grandfather a short time later, and this is where he now lives. About eight years ago, in the month of November, grandfather—who otherwise was in good health—began to suffer from headaches and body aches, which eventually caused him to be bedridden. When grandfather's condition worsened, he began to refuse food. After discussing his situation with my older brother, we both decided that it would be best to take him to a doctor in Window Rock. Grandfather was hesitant, but soon realized the logic in our decision to seek medical help. After being admitted into the clinic, he was taken through the long process of many blood tests and   x-rays. My brother and I spent three days in Window Rock at a friend's house while grandfather was being cared for. When the results of the tests eventually came back from the lab, to our surprise and relief, they indicated that he only had a rise in blood sugar, which could be treated with drugs. Aside from this, his other tests were normal. Both my brother and I were still not totally convinced that all was well with him. We had seen the turn for the worse that our otherwise active and mentally alert grandfather had taken. His state of constant pain and fatigue was very unusual for him. The doctor prescribed pain medicine to help him sleep.

After filling the prescriptions we returned home. On the drive home, grandfather stated that he wanted to seek the help of a local medicine man in Chinle. Grandfather wanted to have a 'Sing'. Among us Navajos, we have a curing ceremony, which we call a Sing. The 'Sing' ceremony involves the participation of an elder medicine man or woman, special songs are sung, incense is burned, and a drum and other ritual items are used. It is a lengthy ceremony and highly respected among traditional Navajos. My brother and I assured my grandfather that we would honor his wishes and contact a medicine man back home. Arrangements were made with an elderly medicine man, and a date for the Sing was set.

Four nights before the ceremony, a strange thing happened to me. It had been snowing heavily during the day, and that evening, the moon was bright and full. At around 11 p.m. the barking of our dog, which we keep chained to our porch, awakened me. Usually she barks at skunks that live under the mobile home, or in response to the yelping of coyotes that sometimes come around our property. This time her barking sounded different to me. It made me get out of my warm bed and walk to the window. As I parted the curtains on the front door, I saw the image of a woman I did not recognize walking about my grandfather's hogan. I reached for my jacket and boots, and walked outside. My dog was growling and barking. In the moonlit night, I followed this strange woman as she made her way to the rear of the hogan. When I yelled at her, 'What do you want?' she did not respond. I decided to confront this strange woman. With my dog still barking loudly, I quickly made my way to the hogan as my footsteps crunched noisily into the foot-deep snow. About twenty feet away from the woman, I saw that she was wrapped in a dark shawl from head to toe. Her face was hidden from my sight. Something inside me made me stop in my tracks. As soon as I stopped, the woman suddenly turned away from me. What happened next made my mouth open wide. The dark woman took off like a flash! She did not run, but seemed to float over the snow-covered ground without leaving a trace of footsteps! My dog barked and barked. I turned in the direction of the trailer and ran back. I missed a step and remember taking a hard fall. Once I reached the trailer I rushed inside and locked the door! Both my daughters told me that they had witnessed

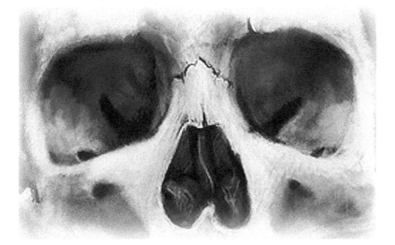

the whole affair from the safety of the mobile home window. I was out of breath and shaking. I knew that I had seen something evil outside. My girls were also shaken, and that night we all slept together.

The next day I wasted no time in telling my experience to my brother. After hearing my story, he knew that what had taken place that night had to be witchcraft. A ghost or witch had for some reason visited our property. My brother said, 'Who knows how long these evil visits have been going on without us being aware of them?' We all decided that it would be best not to tell our grandfather for fear that such information would upset him, and we didn't want to risk him becoming even more ill. We also knew that this new information needed to be related to our medicine man. My brother drove me to the medicine man's home, and we informed him of what I had seen. He was not surprised by my story. He said, 'Oh, I know who this is.' Then he explained to us that there was a Navajo medicine woman who lived not far from his house who wanted to gain a reputation in the Indian community as being a powerful spiritual person. After I heard the medicine man's description of who this woman was, I could recall her from a visit she made to my grandfather's hogan several weeks before grandfather became ill. I remember grandfather telling me that this woman had visited him because she wanted him to be her boyfriend. When grandfather refused, she got very angry with him and yelled obscenities. She left our property in a rage! The medicine man further explained, 'It is difficult to gain power without earning it in the correct manner. This woman has decided to seek the help of certain animal spirits instead of asking the Creator for direction, and doing what is right.' He also said, 'You need to know that this woman wants to hurt your grandfather. Your grandfather refused to do what she demanded, so now she has taken revenge. She chose to make him ill, but she will not stop until he is dead.' My brother and I could not understand why this medicine woman would want to be so evil as to hurt our grandfather.

Our concern now was for our grandfather to be healed. The medicine man said that he would be ready to confront this woman's witchcraft during grandfather's Sing. The night of the ceremony came and we all gathered inside my grandfather's hogan. We used kerosene lamps for light and a fire was started in the wood stove. Soon the medicine man arrived and the ceremony began. Grandfather was seated on top of a blanket, which was placed on the dirt floor. In front of him the medicine man placed the items which would be used for the cleansing: a bowl of water, a leather bag of corn pollen, a basket with a beautiful eagle feather, and various other items. The medicine man began to drum and sing his songs, calling the positive forces of Mother Earth and the four directions. He sang towards the heavens and asked the Creator for vision, help, and power in defeating all evil. His singing continued for about an hour or so. He reached for the basket, which held the eagle feather and grabbed hold of the feather's stem. Saying a prayer, he passed the feather over grandfather's head and body. Then the medicine man returned the feather to the basket and closed his eyes. All our eyes were focused on the medicine man's face as it began to slowly change. His eyes closed tightly and his mouth began to display a severe expression of pain. His clenched teeth were very noticeable in the warm orange glow of the lanterns. I held onto my brother's arm so strongly that I knew I must have left bruise marks. I was scared from watching what was taking place before us. This small elderly old man seated on the ground before us was changing into something spiritual. A force had taken over him, and what we were seeing was scaring me. Grandfather was so weak with illness that I had to brace his body with one hand so he wouldn't fall over. As grandfather closed his eyes and prayed to himself, he was unaware of the transformation which was taking place with the medicine man. With a quick motion, the medicine man turned over on all fours, and with the gestures of a determined dog or wolf, began to crawl around, sniffing the air and pawing at the ground. Then he crawled his way to a corner of the hogan, and began to dig vigorously with his bare hands at the dirt floor. His breathing became loud and filled with energy. He dug and dug with the force of a man much younger and stronger than he. I took a quick glance at my brother. His

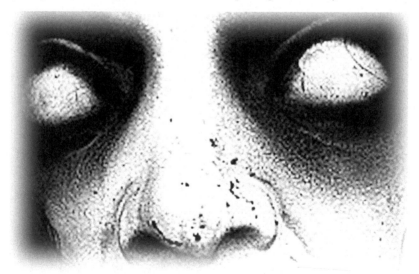

face showed that he was also in awe at what was taking place before us. I turned my eyes to the medicine man who had now dug a hole about a foot deep. Then he stopped his digging and seemed to recover from his trance. In a dazed voice, the medicine man asked my brother to bring a lamp over to him, which he quickly did. Then the medicine man reached into the hole he had just dug, and to all our amazement, pulled out a soil-covered sweater, which belonged to my grandfather! The medicine man said, 'Here is what the witch used for her evil medicine against your grandfather, but now I will use it against her. She used this sweater as her only way to witch him. She will no longer be able to have control over him!' After saying this, he sang a song while placing the eagle feather and corn pollen over the head and shoulders of my grandfather. My grandfather took a deep breath and fell to one side. My brother was ready to catch him as he fell. Grandfather said he was tired and wanted to sleep. We left him there in his hogan covered in warm wool blankets. The ceremony was over.

We followed the medicine man outside the hogan as he carried the sweater and placed it on the ground. He asked for a lamp, and emptied the kerosene from it over the sweater. He lit a match and tossed it on the sweater. The fire slowly began to burn and consume the sweater. Then, in the distance, we heard a piercing loud scream, a howl. We turned in the direction of the sound and spotted a ball of light, which rose up high into the sky, then bounced away and disappeared into the desert! The medicine man informed us that what we had just heard and seen was the witch. He said, 'She will never be able to recover her strength. I found her power and she will be eaten up by her own evil.' After that night, grandfather returned to his old self. I am convinced of the powers which some bad people can use to harm others. So much jealously and evil exists in the world. However, it is good to know that in the end, the power of the Creator always wins. I have seen it."

TOWN OF HOLBROOK

Holbrook is on the banks of the Little Colorado River in northeastern Arizona's Navajo County high plateau country. In 1881, railroad tracks were laid in northeastern Arizona, passing through an area known as

Horsehead Crossing. The following year a railroad station was built at Horsehead Crossing and the community's name was changed to Holbrook in honor of Henry Randolph Holbrook, first chief engineer of the Atlantic and Pacific Railroad. Holbrook, at an elevation of 5,080 feet, became the county seat of Navajo County in 1895 and was incorporated in 1917. Holbrook is an important trade center for

northeastern Arizona. Its location on historic Route 66 and on Interstate 40 at the junction of four major highways, between the Apache Sitgreaves National Forest to the south and the Navajo and Hopi Indian Reservations to the north, makes tourism important to the local economy.

THE NAVAJO COUNTY COURTHOUSE

This historic courthouse is located at the northeast corner of Arizona Street and Navajo Boulevard. Currently it houses the Chamber of Commerce offices and the Historical Society Museum. In 1976, a new governmental center was established south of the city. All county offices

were then moved from the courthouse to this new location. In 1981 the County Board of Supervisors requested that the Navajo County Historical Society open a museum in the old building. Local residents graciously donated furniture, keepsakes and other wonderful items along with written family histories to include in the displays, which are presently on view in the museum. Aside from the many notorious trials that were held in the courtroom, only one hanging took place in the courtyard on January 8, 1900, at 2 p.m. The name of the executed was George Smiley who was hanged for the murder of T. J. McSweeney.

The following are reproduced invitations to the hanging of George Smiley, for murder, which occurred at Holbrook, issued by F. J. Wattron, Sheriff of Navajo County.

This first invitation, the news of which was sent out by the Associated Press, brought a letter of condemnation from then President William McKinley to Governor Nathan Oakes Murphy, of the Territory of Arizona. Governor Murphy severely rebuked Sheriff Wattron, and issued a stay of execution, whereupon the Sheriff sent out the second sarcastic invitation. The following is the deposition of T. J. McSweeney after being shot, filed on October 4, 1899. McSweeney died shortly thereafter.

Holbrook, Arizona, Dec. 1st 1899

Mr. T. B. Berryhill

You are hereby cordially invited to attend the hanging of one

George Smiley, Murderer.

His soul will be swung into eternity on Dec. 8, 1899 at 2 o'clock, p. m., sharp.

Latest improved methods in the art of scientific strangulation will be employed and everything possible will be done to make the proceedings cheerful and the execution a success.

F. J. WATTRON.
Sheriff of Navajo County.

Question: What is your name?
Answer: T. J. McSweeney.

Question: Where do you reside?
Answer: Have been residing at Dennison.

Question: You are employed as section foreman of the Santa Fe Pacific Railroad Company at Dennison?
Answer: Yes, sir, at Dennison.

Question: What is the man's name who did the shooting?
Answer: George Smiley.

Question: What do you think caused him to commit this act? What were his reasons?

Answer: He claimed I ought to give him a time check when he quit. I had to go to El Paso to have my wife's eyes treated and I asked Mr. Crowley to send a man down there and this fellow worked one day for Garrity and then quit and then, of course, Garrity was the man to give him his time check. I had no more to do with it.

Question: He worked for Mr. Garrity after you had taken leave?

Answer: Yes, sir.

Question: Go ahead and tell me just what he said?

Answer: He just walked right up to me and either said, "Give me my time check," or "I want my time check," but before I had a chance to reply, came right up and struck me.

Question: What did he strike you with?

Answer: I do not know; something hard.

Question: Where did he hit you?

Answer: In the mouth and face, just one blow.

Question: What did you do then?

Answer: I started to run and he shot me in the back and I kept running.

The invitation reads:

Revised Statutes of Arizona, Penal Code, Title X., Section 1849, Page 207, makes it obligatory on Sheriff to issue invitations to executions, form (unfortunately) not prescribed.

Holbrook, Arizona, Jan. 5th, 1900.

Mr. _A. B. Wetherill_

With feelings of profound sorrow and regret, I hereby invite you to attend and witness the private, decent and humane execution of a human being; name, George Smiley; crime, murder.

The said George Smiley will be _executed_ on January 8, 1900, at 2 o'clock p. m.

You are expected to deport yourself in a respectful manner, and any "flippant" or "unseemly" language or conduct on your part will not be allowed. Conduct, on anyone's part, bordering on ribaldry and tending to mar the solemnity of the occasion will not be tolerated.

F. J. WATTRON,
Sheriff of Navajo County.

I would suggest that a committee, consisting of Governor Murphy, Editors Dunbar, Randolph and Hull, wait on our next legislature and have a form of invitation to executions embodied in our Laws.

MARITA R. KEAMS' (NAVAJO) STORY

I interviewed Marita at the courthouse, where she was employed as receptionist and information clerk for the museum and Chamber of Commerce. Marita is a Navajo woman who has had numerous encounters with ghosts at the courthouse. She believes that perhaps one of the spirits that follows her around the property is the ghost of the executed man, Smiley. "I know he's around here all the time.

I can feel him looking at me," she says. What follows is a detailed account of something that cannot be contained behind glass cases and roped-off rooms. When the lights are turned off at the Navajo County Courthouse and all daily business has ended, another type of activity chooses to begin to stir, an activity of curiously weird noises, voices, and more. Marita can tell you what she has experienced,  *but of course the true challenge is to experience these eerie events for yourself. The museum's hours are 8 a.m. to 5 p.m.*

— Antonio

"I've been working at the courthouse for three years, and before that I was working at the Petrified Forest National Park gift shop. I have had numerous experiences with the ghosts in the building, and I also know of others who have experienced strange things first-hand. My experiences gave me the impression that I was not welcome in the building. I guess I was being tested. Being a Navajo, we are taught that if you keep any possessions of the deceased— a shirt, furniture or whatever—the spirit of the dead person will attach itself to the item and you might have some trouble on your hands. In the museum there are lots of items of the past, which are displayed in the showcases, such as old Indian grinding stones, arrows and clothing, as well as lots of non-Indian items. The museum director has informed me that some of the items that have been securely locked behind glass cases have been strangely found outside of these cases, and placed in other locations by 'someone.' Our museum's kitchen display seems to attract most of the activity. Utensils and other items are re-arranged to fit an unseen person's own whim for order. A museum employee named Jane refuses to open any of the display cases unless someone is with her. She keeps her own experiences to herself.

Interestingly enough, our own museum director is hesitant to be alone in the building. All our employees have experienced our names being called out from the second floor. In my case, I heard a friendly female voice, but others have heard both male and female voices calling them when they are alone in the courthouse. Another employee who was the former city tourism director had quite an experience of his own to tell. His experience happened while he and his family were driving past the courthouse late one night. He noticed that the lights were on in the second floor, when they should have been turned off. He drove his car to the rear of the building and informed his wife and teenage son that he would return after finding out who might be in the courthouse at such a late hour. He opened the back door and just as he was about to enter, his wife called out to him from the car that there was a woman on the stairs on the second floor landing. This strange woman was looking out the window at them. He returned to the car and sure enough, there was a woman whom he did not recognize

staring down at all of them. He, his wife, and son entered the building and searched for the strange woman. Although they did a thorough search, they never found her. Just a few months after I began working here, a group of kids carried a Ouija board up to the third floor on a Halloween night and apparently made contact with the ghost of the building. The ghost identified himself as George. George is the name of the man who was actually hanged right outside the courthouse in 1900.

I was alone one evening in the courthouse when I heard a loud banging metal sound coming from the second floor. As loud as it was, I was not about to go upstairs by myself and investigate. I just remained where I was, hearing the sound. The next day, I asked a co-worker about it and he said, 'Oh, the ghosts make that happen now and then.' I decided not to inquire any further. Just a few months after my first experience, I was once more in the building after locking up for the day. It was dark and I was on the second floor, standing next to a window. Suddenly, I began to hear the sound of someone walking down the staircase from the third floor approaching the second floor where I was. The doors were locked and I wasn't sure who this stranger might be. The thought crossed my mind that I could be in danger. As I kept quiet and listened for the footsteps, I noticed that they stopped.

Trying to be as quiet as possible, I listened for any sound. There was no further noise coming from the stairs. I convinced myself that perhaps my mind was playing tricks on me. After all, I had heard others speak about the courthouse being haunted. Maybe this was just my crazy imagination. Suddenly, the footsteps started up once more! I carefully made my way to the open door and peered out onto the staircase. I saw no one. I realized that I must have been experiencing something ghostly. I sure didn't want to stay in the building any longer. I quickly walked down the stairs, grabbed my purse and keys and shot out the front door!

There is another event I have experienced several times during the winter — doors opening and closing on their own. Once I even witnessed the doorknob of the front door of the courthouse turn, and the door open and close. We have double doors that are located directly behind the front desk, which lead out to the rear of the building. I once heard these doors swing open. I walked to the doors to investigate, and I found that the doors were locked, just as I had left them.

Besides my own experiences, public visitors to the courthouse have, at numerous times, approached the front desk to tell of experiencing cold chills, or a feeling that a ghost is following them. Like these visitors, I have also experienced these same feelings. It feels like a blanket of very cold air is passing right through me. I know this sounds strange but I'm also not the only one who has experienced this. Visitors have told me that this feeling is strongest in the room where an old chuck wagon is displayed, exactly the room where I have always felt the same thing happen to me.

Another strange unexplained thing that continues to happen in the courthouse are the faucets in the men's room that are turned on by an invisible hand. At the end of the day, I thoroughly check every corner of the courthouse, making sure that everything is as it is supposed to be. There have been several instances when I've returned after checking the men's room and found the faucets are running. I don't know who could have done this since I have been the only 'living' person in the building. I have a suspicion that it is the ghost of George. I remember another day when I was seated at the front desk and the greeting card rack began to turn on its own, and then abruptly stop. I thought that there might be a small child behind it who was having fun spinning the rack. I rose from my chair and walked over to have a closer look. There was no one near it! There was also a time when, for several nights after leaving the building, I would feel the presence of someone following me to the parking lot and into my car. I felt the usual cold chills, and this presence would not leave me. I would even take frequent glances at my rear-view mirror hoping to spot something in the back seat.

At other times I'll feel the invisible hand of someone playing with my hair. I have felt my body being touched so many times that I chose not to discuss this with anyone anymore. They might even think I'm crazy. There are times when I'll be so annoyed with George's behavior that I'll yell out, 'George, please stop doing this!' I won't experience any more activity for several days afterward, so I know he is paying attention to what I say. Once we had a court ordered defendant sent to us as a volunteer to do work at the museum. As a part of his sentence, he was ordered by the traffic court to do community work. Our employees' first impression of this volunteer was not a very positive one. This guy had heard some of the stories about our ghosts, and when he arrived for work, he began to make fun of George, and openly state that he was not afraid of ghosts. We didn't trust this worker and didn't want to leave him alone in the building unsupervised. In the museum we have a donation box and a few small, valuable items in the gift shop that would not be very difficult to steal. Well, one day I asked him to bring me some brochures from the rear of the building, where the old jail cells are located. Today we use these original cells as storage areas for office supplies. A few seconds after I heard him scream, he exited the building. But before doing so, he came running to me saying that the bars and metal were making loud noises and the ghosts were trying to get him. I just smiled and giggled when he told me this, then he shot out! I knew that our George was keeping an eye on this guy."

CALIFORNIA

CALIFORNIA REPUBLIC

t has been estimated that during the gold rush era, California Native Americans numbered around 300,000. By the 1900 census, only 15,000 remained. Driven off, unable to sustain themselves on their homelands, hunted as 'wild animals,' and decimated by foreign diseases, nearly 95 percent of California's Native American population was exterminated. The gold rush and the ensuing invasion of white settlers into their homelands, was for these historically peaceful, and unique Native Americans, nothing more than a policy of utter genocide. Originally inhabited by various Native people such as the Miwok, Chukchansi, Yokuts, Paiute, Mono, and many others, northern California's Native people today remain rich in culture and Native art.

Within this section, once again, are personal interviews with a range of Native individuals. So, without further adieu, I present to you the ghosts of the California Gold Rush area, and Yosemite National Park.

COLUMBIA STATE HISTORIC PARK

Columbia is a rich gold town, which has become a living history museum. Columbia State Historic Park started life in 1859 as a commercial hub for the area's miners. Today, Columbia State Historic Park is an educational sightseeing attraction for people from all over the world. It is also a vital, living community for those who live in and around it.

The original buildings with their iron doors from the 1840's have been restored to house businesses in keeping with the historic theme of the park. Approximately 96 percent of the buildings are original. In 1860 a fire destroyed several of the buildings; they were replaced within the year.

The town was accepted as a state park in 1945 at the urging of area residents who wanted to preserve the mother lode's most intact gold rush town.

The history of Columbia is rich in gold. According to most reports, the first miners arrived there in 1850. Dr. Thaddeus Hildreth, his brother George, and a handful of other miners found gold while camped near today's main parking lot. Another version said a group of Mexicans panned for gold at the same spot in relative secrecy for four or five months prior to the Hildreth party happening upon them. Within a month, about 6,000 miners lived in a tent and shantytown called Hildreth's Diggings. The name was changed to American Camp, then to Columbia, all in 1850. By the end of 1852, the new town had more than 150 stores, saloons, and other businesses, a Sunday school, Masonic Lodge and a branch of the Sons of Temperance.

In addition to being a state park, Columbia has been the setting for many movies, television shows and commercials.

PARK RANGER LOGAN TEJON'S (TULE RIVER) STORY

Ranger Logan Tejon and I sat across from each other at his home located in the little gold rush town of Nevada City. Today, Logan prefers to wear his hair in traditional style, long and divided into two large braids. Unknowingly I scheduled his interview in good time, because a few weeks later, he sold his house, then made the permanent move south to Mexico—a retirement he had planned to do for several years. I imagine that today you'll find Logan swaying in a hammock somewhere on Mexico's Pacific shore. Given all this, I found his personal story to be truly intriguing and fascinating. I'm positive that you'll agree with me.

— Antonio

"My story took place over 16 years ago. At the time I was employed with the California State Park Service. I'm a Native American from the Tule River Indian Reservation just west of the town of Porterville. My mother, who worked for the tribal office, informed me of a job announcement that the tribe had received through the mail. The job was for a park ranger at the historic village of Columbia. I fit all the required criteria for the position and after submitting my application, I was hired a few months later.

After I located a small house in the nearby town, I soon started my new job at the park. My position was Historic Interpreter. Like everyone else who was employed at Columbia State Park, our positions did not just limit us to function within our professional title. We were required to understand other obligations at the park. This usually meant that we 'crossed over' to other job descriptions when necessary. For example, I might be asked to lead a tour during the day, then do security watch the following night, etc. On a few occasions I would substitute in other areas of the park when an employee called in sick, or missed a day or two.

My ghost experience at the park took place one early evening as I was taking a group of tourists on an interpretive walk. I had no idea that within a span of a few hours, my outlook on the paranormal would begin to change as it did on that tour.

Towards the end of the tour, one member of the group who was about thirty-something asked me, 'Excuse me, but do you know if the park is haunted?' I responded, in as much of a professional manner as I could, 'Well, that's a common question. Due to the antique look of the buildings, and the town's exceptional rich history, I can see how some people might associate it with ghosts.' I also informed the woman that

I personally had never had any type of encounter with a ghost at the park. However, by her negative facial reaction, I could tell she was not convinced in the least by my answers.

When I informed the group that the tour would be ending in just a few minutes, the same woman and her boyfriend both came forward and asked me if I could spare a few minutes alone with them, so they could describe a ghost experience they recently had at that park. I told them that would not be a problem. And at the end of the tour, we three sat at a bench under a tree where they proceeded to tell me their story:

'Last night at about 9pm my boyfriend and I were walking through the park when we both spotted the ghost of a small man standing next to one of the doorways. He was dressed in dark clothing, and as we walked past him, he simply stared at us, not giving us a wave of his hand, or any courteous gesture.'

Caught off guard by her story, I asked her, what made her think this man was a ghost? She said, 'As we walked past him, we noticed that his face was very pale and had distinct dark outlines. This gave us a creepy, scary feeling.' The boyfriend continued by saying that he said, 'Let's stop across the street and watch what he does.' She said, 'We acted as if we were tired from walking, and sat down on one of the public benches. We were only about fifty feet away from the man, so even though it was dark, we easily had a clear view of him.' The boyfriend then said, 'The man might be a tourist acting out a fantasy of playing a ghost and scaring people, or he might even be employed with the park service.'

The woman continued the story by telling me they both watched the man for about five minutes until she had had enough, and told her boyfriend the ghost was scaring her. The ghost man was still as could be, staring straight ahead, and this was freaking her out. My boyfriend saw how this was affecting me and spoke to the man, 'Hey, what's up!' At that, the ghost man slowly turned away from us, and seemed to float towards the doorway of the building directly behind where he had been standing. As he reached the door he disappeared in the darkness! We both immediately were amazed and puzzled. My initial fear left me and I convinced my boyfriend that we should walk over to the door and investigate. We cautiously walked over to the building and looked through the door's window. It was dark, except for the dim light of a small adjacent room. We turned the doorknob, but it was locked. As I said, we followed this man immediately after he disappeared from us. He didn't even have enough time to place a key into the door, open it, and enter in the few seconds we observed him. And for God's sakes, he floated across the ground!

I attempted to explain to the couple that as far as I was aware, the park service did not employ actors to play the role of ghosts, especially after closing hours. They were not convinced, and urged me to ask the superintendent about their experience. I assured the woman that I would try and find out who was behind this. They both were so concerned with what they saw, that she gave me her home phone number and address so I could give them the outcome of my investigation.

The next day, I asked several employees and no one knew anything about any employees or actors dressing up and portraying ghosts. I filed a report with the supervisor, and left it up to her to do the remainder of the follow-up investigation.

Some months after this incident, a film crew had scheduled to shoot some footage in Columbia. The old west setting of Columbia attracts several film crews throughout the year to the park. Not only does Hollywood love the movie-shooting location of Columbia, but film companies from other areas of the world also seek out its uniqueness. Columbia's old buildings must give off a very historic and authentic aura of the old west, because we get film crews into the park many times throughout the year. This time, the film company that was scheduled to come into the park had traveled from London.

The crew arrived without incident, and began setting up their trailers and positioning their lights. I was employed to provide the necessary security for the set, and was also hired by the film crew to give the film staff a tour around the park and nearby town. I guided them to the local restaurants, historic sites, etc.

One staff crew member, searching for the best locations to film, was in charge of operating a mobile camera unit. I accompanied him as he set up his camera and actors at different locations throughout the park. His shots were taken in buildings, under porches, on top of buildings, and generally throughout the park. At the end of the day he and I met to discuss the shooting schedule for the following day, the purpose being to shoot around, and not to disrupt the flow of visiting tourists.

I remained with him as he entered a movie trailer filled with the company's editing equipment. He took a quick review of what he had filmed that day. He seemed strangely baffled by what had been recorded on the film. He rewound the video and appeared just as perplexed. He asked me to take a look at the video screen. We both spotted a strange person who appeared in one of the shots, that was not part of the acting crew. He asked me if I knew who this individual was, or if he was employed with the park service. He re-ran the video for me, and sure enough there appeared a small man dressed in a dark hat and clothing, standing by one of the old buildings. The video caught this strange man as he stood by the building, turned and walked towards a very old large tree. He again turned to his left, then 'disappeared' by a doorway. He didn't just walk into the doorway and enter the building; he 'disappeared' under the doorway. I had no idea who this person was, but I immediately recalled the story the couple on my tour had described to me about the ghost they had seen, just two months prior.

I got a chill, and asked the cameraman if this man had appeared in other shots. He said this was the only one, and then said, 'Logan, if I didn't film this myself, I would have thought this guy was staged. But I think we've captured a ghost on film.' I was surprised. I could only respond with a nervous, 'Wow!'

Once word got around about the ghost on the video, other park staff eagerly asked to view it. One female employee related to me in confidence that she had never seen the ghostly man, but she had her own experience with voices in that same building! She said she had not told anyone about her story, because she hoped the memory of it would leave her in time. But after viewing the film, she decided to describe to me what happened to her one afternoon:

'At about 6:30 one evening, I entered the store to check on a light bulb I noticed had been left on. When I walked to the rear of the store, I immediately felt the presence of someone in the room with me. This was strange because I knew I was alone, and I didn't hear footsteps, or the door open behind me. There was enough sunlight entering from the windows, so I was not at all in a darkened room. As you know, Logan, the room is also not very large, so I could obviously tell if I were alone or not. The strange feeling that someone was standing right next to me was very strong. I turned around and faced the front windows. I said, 'Anyone here?' Suddenly I clearly heard a male voice state the words, 'Woman don't belong here. Woman don't belong here!' I froze in place and said, 'Who's there? Who's there?' I kept still. Without warning, I felt a pressure of a 'cold hand' being placed at the area between my shoulder blades! That was enough. I shot out of that room like a bullet! I've not told anyone about this experience before. But since that day, every time I pass that store, I turn away not wanting to see what might be glaring back at me from the inside the window.'

As for myself, I've not had any further contact with the cameraman, or his crew from London. And aside from these incidents, I've not heard of any other ghostly activities that have taken place at Columbia. There must be others who have had something strange happen to them at the park. Given the large amount of tourists who visit Columbia each year, I wouldn't be surprised if there exist photographs with images of ghosts that just happened to have been captured on film. As I said earlier, I haven't worked at Columbia for over 16 years. A lot can happen in 16 years. The ghost man must have appeared to someone within this time."

CITY OF SACRAMENTO

Framed by the Sacramento River on the west, Interstate 5 on the east, the Capitol Mall on the south, and the "I" Street Bridge on the north, Sacramento, California's capital city since 1854, is both rich with history, and is visually captivating.

The Native Americans who inhabited the Sacramento area were of the Miwok, Maidu, and Shonommey Nations. For thousands of years, these people lived by hunting deer and gathering acorns, which provided the bulk of their diets. The land was bountiful, and consuming only what they needed to survive, these resourceful men and women utilized all that was available to them.

Acorns, being a substantial part of their diets, were gathered, ground into flour, and leached of its tannic acid by using repeated applications of water. This mush was cooked in woven, watertight baskets using heated stones that were placed into the moist acorn mush. The stones were continuously stirred and eventually the mush was cooked and made edible.

In the early 1800's, Gabriel Moraga, a Spanish explorer, gave the name Sacramento, meaning Holy Sacrament, to the surrounding land and river. In the year 1848, the discovery of gold in Coloma changed the area, and the Native lifestyle forever.

Sacramento became a center of urban activity. Large mercantile buildings, as well as homes and pioneer supply warehouses, were established. The Sacramento River served well in the economic success of the town's development, as it was utilized as a route of commerce and transportation. As the railroad developed, the town became even more of a focus of commerce. In the early 1850's, devastating fires and floods took their toll on the citizens. Even cholera made a deadly visit to the

Sacramento Valley. Eventually, after four years, things began to get back to normal, and Sacramento grew in stature and western prominence. Today, California's capital reigns supreme over an extraordinary state of magnificence.

SUTTER'S FORT STATE PARK

Eight-year old Patty Reed carried this doll across the plains to California. During the bitter months snowbound in the Sierra Nevada Mountains, Patty had "Dolly" to confide in and to comfort her. She later donated the doll to Sutter's Fort, the original destination of the Donner Party.

Sutter's Fort began its history as a small settlement, founded by John Sutter, a German-born Swiss entrepreneur, in 1839. This one time small, lowly gathering of settlers would come to mark a supremely important position in California's history, and the great migration to the west.

John Sutter acquired the land grant for his settlement from the Mexican government and called it New Helvetia, meaning New Switzerland. However, the settlement generally became known, and was soon accepted as Sutter's Fort. Self-sufficiency was paramount to the fort's survival.

The fort, primarily constructed with Native Americans doing the bulk of the labor, soon became widely known as a way-station and trade center for pioneers. Another aspect of the fort's role in history was when it sent several rescue parties to locate the doomed Donner Party that was trapped in the Sierra Nevada's during the severe winter of 1846-47.

Perhaps the most famous of its roles was in 1848, when John Sutter sent a work party to Coloma to construct a lumber mill. During the building of the mill, construction foreman James Marshall spotted the glint of yellow gold among some stones. Efforts were made to keep the news of this discovery quiet, but to no avail. Soon word spread, and the rest of this worldwide rush of fortune-seekers is now the basis of California's history.

With much excitement and the quick departure of Sutter's workers away from the fort in search of wealth, the fort was soon left deserted. John Sutter was left without a work force, and by the 1880's, the fort's only original building, the Central Building, remained. Sutter's Fort was reconstructed in 1891, based on an 1847 map. Sutter's Fort and the California State Indian Museum are both located in an easily reached location in downtown Sacramento.

Shavehead, chief of the Hat Creek, Atsugewi people. The Atsugewi's homeland was in the area now known as Lassen National Park.

CALIFORNIA STATE INDIAN MUSEUM

The museum is housed on the same two-block city location as Sutter's Fort. In the museum's collections is sheltered one of the finest collections of California Indian basketry. From cooking or boiling, to flawlessly beautiful and delicately decorated feather baskets, all regions of the state's Native American population are represented.

Other important displayed items are musical instruments and ceremonial dance regalia. There are exhibits that also highlight tools, hunting and gathering implements, and contemporary art. The spirituality of California's Native peoples is a dominant theme throughout the displays. Outside demonstrations include the Gathering of Honored Elders (held in May), the Art Show and Acorn Day (both held in Autumn), and the Arts and Crafts Holiday Fair (held Fridays and Saturdays after the Thanksgiving holiday).

LINDA BLUE'S (MIWOK/MAIDU) STORY

This interview originally began outside the actual museum, but as the dark clouds were beginning to form a thunderhead above, Linda suggested we move inside so as to not get rained on. Entering the building, I noticed we were the only visible ones in the facility. Because of the approaching weather I was confident that the interview would proceed uninterrupted. Within the course of Linda's narrative there would be unexpected grating or rasping noises being made at the far end of the museum. Linda held a short pause, then mentioned to me, "That's where the very old artifacts and baskets are displayed. I know 'they' are listening to us right now. They're always about the place, watching, and I believe, taking care that we treat their property in a respectful manner."

— Antonio

"I'm Miwok/Maidu from the Wilton Rancheria on the Consumnes River, located about 38 miles southeast of Sacramento. This year marks my third season that I've been working at the State Indian Museum. My official title is 'on-call' Park Aid employee. I help out with the usual museum interpretation duties, such as describing to visitors the various rare California baskets, and other items of historical importance that are displayed.

Before beginning my employment at the museum, I was told by fellow Indians about the history of adjacent Sutter's Fort being built upon an Indian burial mound. I have knowledge of several burial sites that have been disturbed about the fort area.

Our museum is housed in a building just a short walk behind the fort. And working at the Indian Museum has not been a "spiritual" problem for me. Anthropologists have also discovered Native American artifacts on the grounds surrounding the museum and fort. I know from working on archeological sites on my own reservation, that our ancestral spirits do care about their belongings. Fortunately, the state is now sensitive to our beliefs, because Native American employees are given the option of being re-assigned to other sites if they wish.

It's also well known that some Native Americans refuse to work at Sutter's Fort because of sudden and unusual illnesses that are reported by them soon after entering the area. Because of this, today I can't name one Indian that I know who works at the fort. Employees have mentioned to me that they have seen dark figures walking in the museum and on the museum grounds. Of course, I, myself, was hesitant at first to work so close to such a sacred site. But, because I sincerely respect my ancestors, I know I'll be alright. A very disturbing trend is when non-Natives dig up Native Indian burial sites, and disrespectfully take the offerings and jewelry that the dead person was lovingly buried with. For instance, it was a common burial rite for Indian people to bury strings of hand-made shell beads with their dead. We call these burial beads, 'Cry Beads.' I've seen these funeral beads being displayed and sold at swap meets, auctions, etc. Non-Indians can't seem to relate, as we do, to the spiritual significance that these funeral items have to our culture. So they literally remove our burial offerings, then restring and sell them. For us Natives, it's very sad to witness. My own spiritual experiences at the museum are not uncommon from others who have spent any length of time there. For example, when I'm alone standing at the front desk, soon after closing the doors for the day, I'll sometimes hear the soft sound of older Indian women begin a chanting song. Their songs are most evident in the rear of the building, where the older baskets are displayed behind glass.

There will be times when I'll

We call these burial beads, "Cry Beads."

quietly walk to the rear of the museum, then pause for a few moments at the basket display. Soon I'll hear the spirit women singing in their Native language. I don't recognize the words, but they're definitely Indian songs. The songs are not loud, but are more of a soothing, soft chanting. The chanting will continue without pause. As I walk, returning to the front desk, I'll still hear these women's sweet voices chanting away behind me. My explanation is that the chanting is due directly to the museum displays. Because the baskets being displayed have been collected from all over California, the singing spirit women could be from any one of the many Indian Nations that existed in the state. Deep within my soul, I can 'feel' these spirit women's connection and attachment to their baskets. I know they're overseeing that their work is being cared for, that it's being honored in the right way. It's almost as if they want their baskets to return home to their own people. Employees have also mentioned to me that they have seen dark figures, or shadows walking among the museum displays, and also on the museum grounds.

Other strange, but common occurrences are the various artifacts that move on their own, within the museum. These particular Indian displayed items are moved off shelves, as if the spirits are annoyed. Several times I've witnessed spoons, beads, and small baskets that I know have been securely attached to a pedestal, 'tossed off' the pedestal and on to the bottom of the case.

Other things that have frightened employees, both Native and Anglo, have been the shaking of padlocks that hang on the cases. We've all seen this take place. We've stood by and watched as the locks that are mounted on the display cases move as if some invisible hands were pulling to forcibly open them. Our collective response has been, 'We've got to get out of here. Something is not right!' As recently as three weeks ago, some employees came to me and reported that the padlocks on the cases were once again moving. So I tell them, 'Don't worry. It's a common experience here. You better get used to it, 'cause it's not going away.'

Not long ago, we had a group of about 100 gypsies visit the museum grounds. One gypsy woman came into the museum and engaged me in conversation about one of their family members who was being hospitalized in a local hospital. Immediately I felt a strange feeling come over me. I felt that something was not right. This woman had a strong spiritual presence about her, and it was affecting me in a negative manner. As she spoke, I felt her energy, or power, pushing against me. I actually felt her energy forcing me away from her. This was very strange because it came over me without any warning. I moved several steps back away from her, when something unseen, and very powerful, struck me from the side. Just then, another gypsy woman came to join her friend. Without them moving or saying a word, I was physically pushed from side to side by these women's power.

Somehow I escaped this spiritual 'tug of war,' and walked over to a fellow ranger who was standing nearby. I asked the ranger to take over because I wasn't feeling well. I knew these women were trying to tap into my spirit, and take my Indian power from me. Their power was very strong and hard to break away from. It was a terrible and strange moment for me, an experience that I've never before had.

I'd hope the spirits who are attached to the baskets in our museum understand that we honor them and their art. I hope they do. Our people are very strong people. I enjoy being surrounded by my culture. We know how to identify and protect ourselves from bad spiritual things. We pray and use sage to 'smoke' our homes, and to honor our families. The 'Chaw'se,' or 'Big Time' gathering at Indian Grinding Rock State Park in the Sierra Nevada foothills is also a special spiritual time for us. This gathering is attended by many Indian families from all areas of the state, and is primarily focused on unity and thanksgiving ceremonies."

YOSEMITE NATIONAL PARK

A special tribute to Julia Florence Parker

Julia Florence Parker (born 1929) is one of the preeminent Native American basket makers in California. Julia is a Coast Miwok-Kashaya Pomo basket weaver, prolific artist, teacher, and storyteller. Since 1960, Parker, a long-time resident of Yosemite Valley, has worked as a cultural specialist at the Yosemite Museum and interpreted the cultural history of Yosemite Valley tribes to park visitors.

I personally had the honor of visiting with Julia and her daughter

Lucy, over the many years beginning when I was 18 years old and visited the park. Our friendship began when she offered me and my dog the opportunity to spend the night in one of the traditional wooden bark shelters outside in the Indian village compound behind the museum.

In the morning, I woke up to the sound of wooden sticks beating against a log accompanied by singing voices of men and women practicing and preparing for a pow wow later that day. The smell of fresh brewed coffee,

frying spuds, and bacon were also deliciously evident through the village that morning. Throughout the years I have made regular visits to Yosemite, where I have observed Julia busy demonstrating her artistic woven creations to the observing public. Her grace and hospitality will always remain within my spirit.

YOSEMITE VALLEY

Often called "the incomparable Valley," Yosemite Valley may be the world's best-known example of a glacier-carved canyon. The dramatic scale of its leaping waterfalls, rounded domes, massive monoliths, and towering cliffs, has inspired painters, poets, photographers, and millions of visitors.

The park embraces a great tract of scenic wild lands set aside in 1890 to preserve a portion of the Sierra Nevada that stretches along California's eastern flank. Ranging from 2,000 feet above sea level to more than 13,000 feet, the park encompasses alpine wilderness, groves of giant sequoia trees, and the Yosemite Valley.

The valley's sheer walls and flat floor evolved as alpine glaciers lumbered through the canyon of the Merced River. The ice carved through weaker sections of granite, plucking and scouring rock but leaving intact harder portions, such as El Capitan and Cathedral Rocks. Glaciers greatly enlarged the canyon that the Merced River had carved through successive uplifts of the Sierra. When the last glacier melted, its terminal moraine, left at its farthest advance into the valley, dammed up the melting water to form ancient Lake Yosemite in the newly carved U-shaped valley. Eventually sediment filled in the lake, forming today's flat valley floor.

Today Yosemite Valley is a mosaic of open meadows sprinkled with wildflowers and flowering shrubs, oak woodlands, and mixed-conifer forests of ponderosa pine, incense cedar, and Douglas fir. Wildlife—from monarch butterflies to mule deer and black bear—flourishes in these diverse communities. Waterfalls around the valley's perimeter reach their maximum flow in May and June. Most prominent are the Yosemite, Bridalveil, Vernal, Nevada, and Ililouette Falls. However, some have little or no water from mid- August through the early fall. Meadows, riverbanks, and oak woodlands are sensitive and have been severely damaged by long-term human use.

Indian people have lived in the Yosemite region for as long as 8,000 years. By the mid-nineteenth century, when Native residents had their first contact with non-Indian people, they were primarily of Southern Miwok ancestry. However, trade with the Mono Paiutes from the east side of the Sierra for pinon pine nuts, obsidian, and other materials from the Mono Basin resulted in many unions between the two nations.

A life-like statue of Chris Brown "Chief Lemee" Southern Miwok 1900-1956, welcomes visitors to the museum.

Chris Brown (1900-1956) was a Miwok man born in Yosemite Valley. Known as "Chief Lemme," he performed Miwok dances for visitors to Yosemite from the 1920's until 1953. The dance regalia he is shown wearing is a mixture of Southern and Northern Miwok style. He also made and used a Paiute or Plains-style drum, which he decorated with designs of his own creation.

Demonstrations of Native American culture have long been popular with visitors to Yosemite. The Indian Village, located behind the museum, was built in the late 1920's, and is open year-round. Although daily demonstrations of Miwok dances are no longer presented, demonstrations of Miwok and Paiute culture take place there during the summer. The Native people of Yosemite developed a complex culture rich in tradition, religion, songs, and political affiliations. Making use of the varied local ecosystems, they used plant and animal resources to the best of their abilities.

Actual photograph of Chief Lemee wearing a shoulder cape of great horned owl feathers, clamshell disc beads, and a bone whistle around his neck.

KIMBERLY H. CUNNINGHAM SUMMERFIELD'S
(TSA'LAGI/MIWOK) STORY

Kimberly and I met one day within the Yosemite Indian Museum where the interview was conducted. Seated on a bench in a semi-darkened room and surrounded by artifacts and priceless works of Native art, Kimberly first described her passion for her culture and followed it up with a most intriguing list of spiritual experiences that both she and visitors alike have reported. Today Kimberly is most proud of her skills as a paid park storyteller, retelling visitors the stories 'given' to her by elders of the community. However notably, ghost stories are the exception in this regard.

— Antonio

"My foster parents are from the Toulomne Rancheria. My birth family is from Yukia, California. I am by birth, Tsa'lagi or 'Cherokee,' but my foster parents, in the knowledge and ways of the Yosemite Miwok, raised me. I began working at the park at the age of 15, as an Indian Cultural Demonstrator. Today my title is Park Ranger/ Interpreter, and I'm also a member of the park's Indian cultural staff.

The Indian museum is housed in a park building that was dedicated in 1926, and is constructed of local stone granite. At one corner of the building is an Indian burial whose location is kept secret from the public. We don't give out information as to the location of the burial; we respectfully keep that information to ourselves.

I know of many spiritual experiences at the park. Yosemite is filled with spirits. And as Native people, we believe in the existence of both human and animal spirits. They dwell within the valley mountains, streams and waterfalls. They can be seen and heard moving about, and at times even singing. We believe this. Personally, I'm always experiencing spirits at the park. Right here in the museum are many spirits who regularly pay their visits.

Just last week, my two co-workers and I were in the process of closing the museum for the day. We turned off the lights and turned on the alarm system. Finally, standing at the exit, before locking the doors, we took one last glance at the interior and left. The next morning I came to work at 7:30, and as soon as I stepped inside the museum, I 'felt' that things weren't right. It was a feeling that just came to me. I felt something was out of balance. People say that when a spirit is present, the room will get cold. Maybe that does happen, but I've only experienced the room changing to a very warm temperature, when something of a spiritual nature is about to take place.

Suddenly, the lights that are located in the middle of the museum, specifically spot-lighting the collection of ceremonial regalia, began to flicker. They'd dim, then slowly get bright, and flicker. It appeared as if someone were playing, or sending out a 'light code.' I explained to my co-worker, 'I don't know what's going on, but I'm not going in there!' No one has ever fully explained to me why the lights that focus only on the ceremonial displays behave the way they sometimes do. All I can say about this is that I know there are spirits in the museum. I've seen them as they walk by, and approach the area where I am standing.

"The faces were casts from living persons who have since died and visitors have reported to me that they've actually seen the eyes, or mouths move!"

108

Shadows of people will move about the museum. I've gotten so used to seeing them that I even talk to them. I know that they're always around. Artifacts that are kept under glass, in display cases, occasionally get moved around. I imagine that the creators of these beautiful baskets and such are still emotionally attached to them. It's understandable because of the love, and care, the creative energy those people put into their work.

We have one park ranger, a non-Indian, who we confided to about the spirits in the museum. He made no qualms about his disbelief in the supernatural. But one evening, as he was closing the museum for the day, something abruptly changed his mind. He said that as he was doing a walk-through of the museum, not only did he hear voices, but also he actually saw the spirits! Since that evening, he's not been the same.

Again, I believe that the artifacts we have in the museum were very personal to the people who skillfully and lovingly made them. I've never gotten the feeling that the spirits are angry, they just are checking up on things. The museum does not display anything that is disrespectful to Indian people. The park staff places much importance about not displaying burial jewelry or offerings.

I need to tell you about the mannequins in the museum. The diorama-displayed mannequins are actually molded from Indian's faces, cast from no-longer-living people's faces. There have also been times when I've heard loud shrieks being yelled out by visitors who swear that they've seen the mannequin's heads turn to look at them! I've even had visitors become so scared by the mannequins that they will quickly leave the museum without speaking a word. But I know what took place. Visitors have reported to me that they've seen the eyes, or mouth move on these mannequins.

My aunts always cautioned me as a child, never to look or stare at a spirit straight on, because that can cause the spirit harm. I was told that if spirits chose to appear to us, it's because they have a lesson or news to give. I was also taught never to be disrespectful or to speak rudely when referring to spirits. This is something I also teach to my own children. The dead must be respected."

RANGER ROBERT L. FRY'S (ANGLO) STORY

Robert and I met for our interview within the museum. Robert was busy completing an instructional, Native string project, which he himself fashioned for the museum's display. A friendly fellow, I found Robert to be a very knowledgeable and likable guy. His personal character has befriended him to numerous folks and without exception, Native people. Because of this, his interaction with staff, notably Indians of the park, have provided him with much to retell in this interview.

— Antonio

"My position at the park is Ranger Naturalist/Interpreter. I'm by profession an ethno-biologist with a focus in the Native American use of plants. I've made bows, arrows, including nets, string and other plant fiber crafts. Some of my work is displayed in the museum. This year marks my 42nd year at the park, 13 years as a full-time employee. I came to Yosemite in 1960. Before being employed at the park, I was a high school science teacher. Native people who I've spoken to privately have described seeing and hearing very unusual things. Without a doubt in their minds, they sincerely believe that spiritual beings do exist at the park.

A common belief the Indians hold dear is that their dead ancestors return to earth, and to Yosemite, in the physical form of a bear. Because a bear's feet have a heel with five toes facing front, a bear's footprint resembles a human's. When a Miwok happens to encounter a bear, they are taught to look directly at its eyes, and speak to it normally, just as they would speak to another person. The Miwok never killed bears because they believed them to be sacred or spiritually pure.

A Miwok female friend once described to me that not long after the well-known chief Lamee died in 1955, a bear began to visit not only her house, but the other Indian women's homes in the area. The bear would wonder around the houses and scratch at their windows. During his life the chief, although never married, was very fond of provoking laughter, and good-natured pranks on the women. My friend believed that the chief visited her, and other women, in the form of this bear. She said even though they honored his visits, they still remained all a bit unnerved.

I'm also aware that culturally, the Miwok have a great reverence, and sometimes fear, of waterfalls. To the Miwok, all waterfalls held great power, and if not honored correctly could prove to be dangerous.

Children were never allowed to play or act disrespectfully when in the area of a waterfall. Pohono or Bridalveil Falls is a waterfall which is considered to be very 'haunted' by the Miwok. I personally think it is a very spooky place. The Miwok name for the falls, 'Pohono' translates to 'bad puffing wind.' Pohono is, in my opinion, one of the most beautiful waterfalls in the park. It's 620 feet high and unlike the other falls in the park, it never ceases to have water spilling over its rim. A common ritual when passing Pohono is to lower one's voice, or cease to speak, until quite a distance away. Indians believe that spirits dwell at the base of the Pohono, and these spirits should not be disturbed.

The famous collector, Ripley, once labeled Pohono, 'The waterfall that flows uphill.' He coined this phrase because, at times, usually in the month of September, there is a peculiar wind that hits the face of the waterfall with such force, that if the flow of water is low enough, it will push the water back, and cause it to stop flowing for a few seconds. Soon after, a huge amount of this restricted water will spill over the side in a gush. Personally, I had an unusual experience with Pohono, which took place at 2 a.m. At the time, I was headed to a favorite fishing spot. The weather was calm, but as soon as I entered the area of the falls, I noticed that strangely, the trees were whipping wildly back and forth. Knowing what I did about the spiritual identity of the falls, I felt the strong urge to get out of my car, which I did, and said, 'Oh, Pohono, I honor you.' Feeling personally convinced I did the right thing, I soon drove away.

Dave Jarel, the head of the park's heli-attack crew, described another strange thing associated with Pohono to me in 1973.

There had been a very heavy winter, which dropped a lot of snow in the park. Badger Pass Ski Area, which is located about five miles back from the fall's rim, is used by many skiers to reach Dewie Point. There were two skiers, a doctor and his son, who decided to also use this route. They got lost in a snowstorm and the son decided to turn back, but the father chose to continue. The father became lost and somehow ended up at the water's edge of Bridaveil Falls. Obviously there was no way down. Unable to locate him, his body was not discovered until the early spring thaw.

Dave said that as he was making a pass over the falls in his helicopter, he noticed a red patch of cloth at the rim. He swung the helicopter around for a closer look and recognized it to be the lost skier. As the ground crew approached the body, they noticed he was frozen in a sitting position on a rock, with his chin in his hand blankly staring at the valley below. His skis were eventually located wedged among the boulders down below at the fall's base. He had apparently taken them off in frustration, and tossed them over the side. I say frustration because the road down below is opened year round, and he must have died watching the cars pass below, unaware of his grave situation up above.

One year, the skull of a young girl was found at Summit Meadow, again in the Badger Pass area. Many years after this girl was murdered in the park, the murderer was arrested in the state of Texas on another charge. I guess his conscience got the better of him, because he described in grim detail to the authorities, where and how he had committed the murder in Yosemite. I happened to be with the medical forensic examiner from Seattle who was examining the skull's teeth. We searched for bones and other evidence, but all we located was the skull. The examiner explained how animals will usually drag away most of the body's ribs, arms and legs except for the skull. Due to its round shape, the skull is difficult for animals to bite or grasp a hold of. The skull is usually the only portion of the body that is left at the murder site by animals.

I also know the story of a man who committed a gruesome suicide in 1958 by jumping off Half Dome. He was staying at the Glacier Point Hotel, which in 1969 was consumed and destroyed in a massive fire. He left a note in his room stating, among other things, that he was going to hike the nine miles to Half Dome. At the site where he jumped was found another note, which was folded in his coat pocket, stating his

"Pohono," or Bridalveil Fall.

intentions. At the base of the rock, the search party located most of his body, minus his hindquarter.

Glacier Point also had an incident of a suicide/homicide. A disgruntled man apparently pushed the woman he was with over the edge, and then he followed her by jumping to his death.

Another sad case which I'm aware of, is of an obese 350-pound man who committed suicide by jumping to his death off Taft Point. Taft Point is just west of Glacier Point. This man happened to be an employee of the park.

I know that each of us experiences paranormal events in our own personal way. And I also think the human mind is flexible enough to believe whatever it wants. I believe and 'feel' a parallel 'connection' to Native people, and to the men from ancient times that fashioned arrowheads. These people didn't have much control over nature, and when you have very little control, you become very respectful of nature's power. To the Native people of Yosemite, it was a given fact that the spiritual forces of coyote, frog, bear, lizard and all the rest had their functions. Arching everything was the great Creator who lived beyond the setting sun. Before contact with western culture, when Yosemite's Native inhabitants died, their bodies were cremated so to set the spirit free to join the Great One."

COLORADO

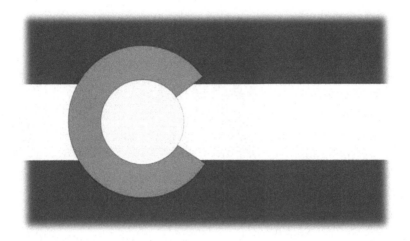

olorado is unique and quite special. With more than 20 million visitors to the state each year, there is much to see and to discover. Within its state borders are immense blue skies, mountains that appear to reach to the very earth's stratosphere, extremes in its temperature ranges, and a haven for both humans, plants and animals. Colorado welcomes visitors to relax, renew and enjoy what can only be described as heaven on earth. Early Native Americans knew this to be very true. They honored the land for thousands of years and continue to do so today, remaining so very thankful to have been the recipients of this land by birth. Personal stories presented to me by Native people were numerous and it was difficult to eliminate some while retaining others. I know that after

reading these particular stories, you will be transferred to another manner of thought. My expedition into Colorado's spiritual reality was undoubtedly an eye opening experience for me. Admittedly, I willingly learned new objectives and new insights which added to my already rich personal repository of experience and knowledge. For all this I remain grateful.

TOWN OF CORTEZ

In the southwestern area of Colorado lies the town of Cortez. Many historically fascinating sites of  the area's first ancient inhabitants—the Anasazi — are easily reached, including the entrance to world-famous Mesa Verde National Park, a World Heritage Cultural Site. At the park you'll be able to explore the landscape where these ancestral Puebloan people constructed 1,000 years ago, cliff dwellings that they carved out of the red sandstone walls of the canyons.

Cortez has numerous parks and trails. The colorfully decorated Cortez Cultural Center offers, among other things, a forum for Native cultural arts, educational programs, interpretive exhibits, outdoor dramas, and Native American dances.

The two nearby independent learning centers, Crow Canyon Archeological Center and Anasazi Heritage Center, provide the visitor with a grand display of southwest ancient cultural history. The Four Corners area, where Cortez is located, is a community that is contemporarily diverse and proud of its ancient cultural legacy.

BLANCA FULLER'S (ANGLO) STORY

Blanca described her story to me at her home. We were sitting in her living room as her partner, Rebecca, listened in. After she told me her story, Rebecca stated, "I think it would be important to tell him about the arrowheads and the pottery shards you guys had collected earlier in the day. I think that might have had something to do with the man that appeared to you."

I turned to Blanca and asked her about this. Blanca said, "Well, yeah, we found an area where there were several ancient fire pits. We knew these were fire pits because of the obvious black charcoal marks on the ground. All around there were pottery shards and arrowheads that my brothers and I gathered and placed in our pockets. I only kept one. I'll show it to you when we're done with the interview. When we walked back down from the mountain, thinking that the experience with the ghost had something to do with the artifacts in our pockets, as we hiked past the pits, we threw the artifacts in that direction."

Blanca's story will give some readers cause to leave such things as ancient artifacts alone. If you happen to be hiking in the wilderness, and come across something in the order of pottery shards, or other evidence of ancient human workmanship, it would be best to leave it where you found it. That is unless, you don't mind the possibility of having the person who made it, many centuries ago, pay a little 'friendly visit' to your home.

— Antonio

"I've lived in Cortez all my life. I've only discussed my ghost experiences with just two close friends and my immediate family. My strange experience took place within the national forest. I'll tell you what happened to me, however a few of the specific details I'll keep to myself. I have my reasons for doing this. Two of my brothers were also with me when we encountered the spirits. Of course they've told their wives, and I've informed my life-partner, Rebecca. I'm not aware of anyone else knowing our story.

When I reached the age of 18, my two older brothers decided to surprise me by giving me a memorable birthday. They wanted to take me into the mountains and hike and camp in the nearby canyons to the south of town. They both knew how much I loved the wilderness, so I was ecstatic! I had gone into the mountains before with my father, as a teenager, but since his death two years before, I had longed for another opportunity to retrace our father and daughter experience. My brothers both knew how much I would appreciate the opportunity, so when they told me what their birthday present was, I hugged each one and without hesitation said, 'When do we leave?' The following week we gathered all the necessary equipment, and set out on an early Friday morning for a full weekend of camping.

My mother drove the three of us several miles into the mountains. We entered the national forest and eventually she dropped us off at the beginning of an unpaved county road. We knew the direction we would be traveling in, and what the terrain would be like, so we were well prepared.

After walking for several hours, we came upon some landmarks that years before my father and I had made along the trail. For instance, we had gathered a few rocks and made a small pile to one side indicating that the trail we were on was the correct one. My brothers and I hiked for a few more hours until we decided to take a lunch break. The weather could not be better, blue skies and billowy white clouds. I was literally and figuratively in heaven. After lunch we continued on our way up and around a large mesa. At home we had decided to reach the top of this natural monument before nightfall, and make camp for the night. We were making good progress until my brother Eric slipped and fell. His water bottle and glasses went flying! Due to the weight of his backpack, his balance was off center, and that caused him to have a pretty hard fall. But aside from hitting his front teeth on the ground, he was not hurt, just a bit bloody, but all-in-all still intact.

We reached the summit at around 6 p.m. that evening, and located a good spot to make camp. Our mother had made us several burritos, which she had tightly wrapped in aluminum foil, so we had plenty to eat that night. We did manage to get a good fire going, and cleared away some brush and rocks in order to have a comfortable area to lay our sleeping bags.

As the night was approaching, the darkness was both beautiful and somewhat spooky. The night sky was filled with stars and we spotted several shooting stars among all the constellations that were visible. Before our fire began to die out, Eric placed a few more sticks on the glowing embers, and a rebirth of flames soon started up. I was glad to be there on that mountain, and glad to have my two brothers who I loved with me.

Soon our conversation turned to talking about my girlfriend Rebecca who I had recently started dating, and was definitely falling in love with. My brothers both knew I was attracted to women at an early age, and reminded me of the time when I chose to play cowboy with them. I wanted to be Roy Rogers and hated, simply hated being told to play the role of Dale Evans! We laughed and laughed. I loved my brothers and I remember getting a little teary-eyed by telling them so that night. I guess I even cried a little bit. Thinking back, it must have been the isolation of being in the open, and in the wilderness, which encourages honesty and the expression of human emotions. At least for me it did that night. And I'm glad for it.

Anyway, a few minutes after that conversation, something, a movement in the nearby bushes, caught all of our attention. We turned in the direction of the noise and spotted the dark form of a mountain lion! We froze and didn't take our eyes off it. I'd seen lions before, usually quite a distance away, but never one so brazen as to come just about 20 feet from me. We had no time to react, but I do remember saying, 'Stay still, let's see what it does.'

The lion took a couple of steps, then turned its head in our direction. Its yellow eyes shown brightly in the camp fire, and I was about to reach for a nearby stone to pitch at it. But when I moved my arm, it must have noticed and quickly turned and ran off into the darkness. Wow, we were all startled by this! Eric got right out of his sleeping bag, then quickly gathered a handful of rocks, and with all the force he could muster, pitched each one at the direction of the cat. My other brother and I also did the same, and even loudly rattled a few large branches of firewood for good measure. With all of us causing so much noise, I doubted that any animal within a mile would have chosen to come close to our camp after that raucous noise. When I think back, that was a pretty brazen animal. It was also pretty large; the largest mountain lion I'd ever seen.

So you might imagine how difficult it was for us to sleep that night. Any small noise, coyote howl, or owl hoot would cause one of us to sit upright and say, 'Did you hear that?' Luckily, the moon was semi-full, so that offered us the comfort of having a bit more light. Everything around us seemed to glow a silvery blue. Eventually, we did get to sleep. But several hours later, before sunrise, something woke me.

I was awakened by the sound of cracking twigs. I opened my eyes and standing directly above me, bent over, was a man! I was so scared I tried to yell to my brothers, but I just could not make a sound! I remember his hair was cut right below his ears in a straight line. And his eyes were the deepest and darkest black I'd ever seen. His features were definitely those of an Indian. Although he was standing right next to me, I don't remember if he was wearing any clothes. All I remember was seeing the portion of his body above his waist; everything else below was a foggy blur.

He stood there, more or less, just checking me out and didn't make a sound. Because I was so startled and scared, I couldn't make a move. But I did manage to get a few words out. I softly said, 'Who are you?' That was the extent of my conversation because he bent his body back, turned away from me and disappeared!

I thought to myself, 'I've just seen a ghost, an Indian ghost.' I sat up and glanced quickly over at my brothers, both of whom were in their sleeping bags with their eyes wide open! I asked them, 'Did you see that!' Jim spoke, 'Yeah, yeah, what the hell was that? We've been watching him for a few minutes before he walked over to you.' Eric spoke, 'I saw him first and woke up Eric. That was some strange shit!'

The sun was beginning to turn the dark sky a light blue and morning would soon be coming. The three of us seemed to be, on some level, in shock. We lay deep inside our sleeping bags and shared our thoughts with each other. 'Was this an Indian from long ago, or just a guy who died recently?' Jim said. I told them, 'I think it was a ghost from a thousand years ago, because look how he had that strange haircut and his eyes. I'll never forget the look of his eyes. They were so ancient.'

Soon we fell back to sleep and around an hour or two later, one by one, we woke up. After making breakfast, it took us no discussion at all to arrive at the conclusion that we were not going to spend another night on that mesa. We brushed our teeth, ate breakfast, rolled up our bags, packed everything up and began our long descent back to the main road.

Eventually, we did come across someone who was driving along the road we were walking. In fact, it was my brother Jim's friend, who was taking pictures for a photography class project. He asked us about our hike and we all looked at each other, and instinctively knew better than to share any information about our experience. We just told him how wonderful and beautiful everything was. On the ride home he didn't asked any further, specific questions, other than to simply discuss generalities.

So there you have it. That's what took place up on that mesa several years ago. It's interesting to know that all three of us witnessed the spirit. If it would have only appeared to me, or one of my brothers, there might have been some doubt, but it appeared to the three of us at once. Pretty difficult to explain away, don't you think?

As I said in the beginning, only a few people know about what took place. We decided to keep it, more or less, a secret among ourselves. Now, of course with this book, a lot more people are going to know about our experience. But I hope some of the readers are not going to go into the hills looking for ghosts. That just wouldn't be the right thing to do in my mind. I believe the ancient ones need their privacy; they want to be left alone. I hope people understand that."

TOWN OF DOLORES

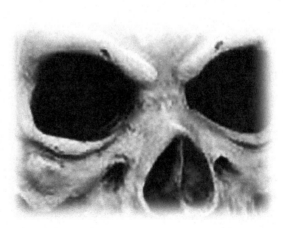

Being situated just west of Canyon of the Ancients National Monument and northeast of the Ute Mountain Tribal Park, Dolores is considered the gateway to Mesa Verde National Park. To the southeast of town are the world famous cliff dwellings at Mesa Verde National Park. Colorado's second largest body of water, the McPhee Reservoir, is located northwest of town.

It is not uncommon to experience such large animals as deer or elk as they graze in the nearby hills, or even cross the highways. Such big game attracts seasonal hunters, as well as photographers who prefer to take aim and shoot with a camera.

During the height of Dolores' history, the town was a major railroad stopover along the Rio Grande Southern route that lay between Durango and Ridgeway. Given its railroad history, the town displays an exact replica of the original train depot on Railroad Avenue. It is housed within the Rio Grande Southern Railroad Museum and Dolores Visitors' Center. In addition, a curious visit that a tourist might also enjoy while passing though Dolores would be to its well known Galloping Goose Museum.

ANASAZI HERITAGE CENTER

The Anasazi Heritage Center is an archaeological museum that displays and preserves artifacts and records from excavations on public lands in the Four Corners area, one of the richest archaeological regions in the United States. The museum is also the headquarters for Canyons of the Ancients National Monument. Their goal is to increase public awareness of archaeology and cultural resources in the Four Corners area of the Southwest.

Anasazi is the Navajo name for a farming people who lived in the Four Corners between AD 1 and AD 1300. The population size varied over time, but at its peak many thousands of Anasazi families occupied the southwest corner of Colorado. Their modern descendants, the Pueblo Indians of New Mexico and Arizona, prefer the term Ancestral Pueblo rather than 'Anasazi.' The Spanish word, 'pueblo,' refers to the traditional apartment-house style of village architecture that survives today.

The museum features permanent displays on the Ancestral Pueblo people, and on the techniques that allow modern archaeologists to reveal the past. Many exhibits are hands-on and interactive. Visitors can weave on a loom, grind cornmeal on a metate, examine tiny traces of the past through microscopes, and handle real artifacts. Changing special exhibits and events feature topics of regional history and Native American cultures.

The museum's pueblo-style building was created during the McPhee Dam and Reservoir project, which included the Dolores Archaeological Program, the largest single archaeological project in the history of the United States. Between 1978 and 1984 researchers mapped about 1,600 archaeological sites. Included were hunting camps, shrines, granaries, households and villages, along the Dolores River in the reservoir area. About 120 sites were excavated to salvage their information value. The artifacts were removed from the area that was scheduled to be flooded by the McPhee Reservoir project. Many of these artifacts are displayed in the museum; the rest are available for study and research.

The museum is 7,000 feet above sea level at the foot of the San Juan Mountains in southwest Colorado. It overlooks McPhee Reservoir and the Montezuma Valley, and is about 17 miles by road from Mesa Verde National Park. On the museum grounds are two 12th century settlements, the Dominguez and Escalante Pueblos, named after Spanish friars who explored this area in 1776 and became the first to record archaeological sites in Colorado. The pueblos were excavated and stabilized 200 years later.

MICHAEL DEVLIN'S (ANGLO) STORY

My interview with Michael took place at his home in Cortez. I had heard about his spiritual experience from another interviewee in Denver the week before. I made it a point to contact Michael and travel specifically to Cortez to schedule an interview with him. Michael's home is intricately decorated with a Native American theme in mind. On one wall are framed lithographs, and on another wall are a bobcat pelt, and earthen jars filled with feathers of various birds. The living room gave me the appearance of it being a mini museum.

Michael pointed out a specific old, small earthen jar that was topped with a clay lid. Michael stated, "This small pot contains a few human bones. I located it in southern New Mexico at a dig about 10 years ago. I believe the site was a burial." When I pressed him further regarding his purpose for removing it from the burial site, Michael answered, "I know I should have left it where it was, but there were so many pots like this one at the site, I didn't think taking one would matter much. Anyway, I plan to return it sometime."

This manner of thinking was disconcerting; and, in my view, very disrespectful and adverse to a positive focus regarding Native Americans. After my interview with Michael, I did not mince words when describing my disagreeable thoughts on his keeping such human remains in his house. Michael agreed to return the pot to its rightful resting place. In fact, three months after our interview, I received a letter that included two pictures showing Michael placing the pot in the pit where he had originally removed it.

Since our initial meeting, I have kept in contact with Michael, and I am personally assured knowing he has remained true to his word in respecting the remains of the dead that he has, and will, at times come into contact with.

— Antonio

"I've worked at the Anasazi Center for several years, and never in my life would I have believed that what I experienced within the park could have happened to such a disbeliever of spiritual things as myself. Today, I'm still able to clearly recall the memory, and the impact the experience made on me. I know that I have been changed spiritually. I now have a better understanding and respect for those individuals who report their own personal experiences with ghosts.

When I first studied at the center, I was under the tutelage of a professor of archeology from Denver. Beginning with my first graduate study semester, I was one of the students that was chosen for the archeological 'dig', and the other student's name was Bob. Both Bob and I were working on completing our master's degrees in archeology that summer. After successfully completing our respective research papers, we would graduate in the fall of that year. We were both excited to begin.

During the first week of our research, Bob and I began by mapping out a forty-by-thirty foot area of land. This area was marked out using stakes and tape. Then we transferred this information onto a grid in our notebook. Within the first week this mapped-out area began to take shape as we cleared its top surface layer of weeds, stones and debris. All the soil that we had removed from the site was sifted through a mesh screen to separate any artifacts that might have been overlooked. The work was tediously slow but very necessary.

Within the first week we advanced a little more than halfway through the process, and by the following week we had already discovered a tray full of pottery shards and one deer bone awl. The ancients used the awl as a leather hole-making tool. In addition to these we also found several examples of shell and stone beads. Without much digging, all these artifacts were recovered from the surface, which was quite impressive. We knew that given these initial discoveries, the area had to be a rich source of more significant artifacts and other examples of human history.

One day, during the first month of my work, I received some bad news. My brother, who was working for an oil company in Germany, had been terribly injured. Thankfully he was alive, but he had lost the sight in his left eye. He would also need, in the future, numerous plastic surgery operations on his face. This terrible news affected me to my core. I cried for most of the day, feeling helpless and very sad. The news was a burden that I carried throughout the day and into the night. I needed to clear my mind so at around eight that evening, I decided to drive the six miles to the isolated site, and find a large rock where I could sit and contemplate my brother's future, my brother who was now partially blind. Gazing upon the heavens I was comforted sitting there in the open desert, viewing the stars that were so bright. The night was clear and the moon was full. This time to reflect was just what I needed.

As I was about to rise up off the rock, in the near distance I spotted what I thought might me a coyote moving about 40 feet away from me. I sat back down and waited, hoping to see where it was headed, but I soon discovered that what I had thought was a coyote was instead a man! I waited to see what this guy would do next.

He moved about the ground in a sweeping motion. That's the only way I can describe his movements as being sort of a side-to-side movement. In my mind, I struggled to find out who this person was and what to make of his strange movements. There was nothing for me to do but watch.

Strangely, I was not in the least bit scared as he turned to face me. I looked him straight in his eyes and spoke, 'Yeah, I'm over here. What's going on?' He did not respond but within only a split second, he was standing right in front of me! I was totally caught off guard by this and tried to let out a scream, but I couldn't. I was frozen stiff! I looked him straight in the eye and was transfixed with fear.

He glared at me and I noticed that his skin was so pale, it gave the appearance that he had never seen a single day of sunlight. His eyes were a clouded light gray color, without showing any life in them at all. I immediately knew that this thing standing in front of me was a ghost, and I was scared! I was so uneasy that I began to breathe rapidly and hard. The next thing I remember was passing out and waking up, with my face flat on the ground! The night was still dark and I had no idea how long I must have been lying on the ground because I wore no watch. I slowly struggled to get up. Once I did, I walked to the truck and drove back to the center, where I entered my sleeping quarters. As soon as I lay on the bed, I was out cold!

When I awoke in the morning, I felt as if I were still needing more sleep, so I fell back to sleep. I didn't wake up until 11 that morning. I have no idea why, I just know that my body was totally exhausted from the night before. I was fully aware of my surroundings and did not feel as if I was drugged, and why would I have been? I felt a strong desire to get up and out into the fresh air.

Once I stepped outside, with the warm sunlight washing over me, I felt much better. I can only describe this feeling as the time I spent a week in a hospital when as a young boy, I had had my tonsils removed. After the operation I developed an infection which kept me in the hospital for a week. When I was released, my father carried me in his arms to the car. As my father walked into the sunlight, such a refreshing feeling of peace came over me, one I'll never forget. That exact same feeling came over me as I was standing in the sunlight that morning. It was a wonderful feeling of safety and peace.

I don't know why that dark and menacing spirit approached me that night in the desert, and what I could have done to prevent the fear that gripped me, from taking over me like it did. I wasn't drinking, nor was I under any medication that could have caused such a severe experience. It was nothing my imagination created. I was not even thinking of such an unusual subject as ghosts. I do believe that what approached me was a ghost and its reason for doing so remains a mystery to me to this day."

TOWN OF EADS

Eads is located in Kiowa County, which is in the southeast area of the state. The area is veined with irrigation canals and the Arkansas River. The land is also dotted with the skeletons of weathered, ruined structures of homesteads of years past, and farms and ranches. The most important aspect of this wind-whipped land is its history. The mountain branch of the Santa Fe Trail had great significance to this area's development. Historically, this area is fascinating.

Here are the world's longest fossilized dinosaur tracks and the immense Comanche National Grassland. The Comanche, Cheyenne, Arapaho, and Prairie Apache knew this land well. The Hispanic and Anglo cultures also left their own individual marks on the land. If you're an enthusiastic naturalist, historian, or appreciate the raw ecological evidence of nature's lasting impression on the land, then do not pass this landscape of history by. Once you visit this area of the United States, you'll immediately 'feel' the presence of those who have come before. This is not an easy area to walk away from unchanged.

SAND CREEK MASSACRE NATIONAL MONUMENT

"Each evening she would start telling us the story of Sand Creek ... she would always cry when she told the story, and I always wondered why she cried ... and then when I started growing older

I began to realize what she had been through, seeing all her people getting killed..."—

Nellie Bear Tusk, 2000

On November 29, 1864, Colonel John M. Chivington, a Methodist minister for 20 years, led approximately 700 U.S. volunteer soldiers to a village of about 500 Cheyenne and Arapaho people camped along the banks of Big Sandy Creek in southeastern Colorado. Although the Cheyenne and Arapaho people believed they were under the protection of the U.S. Army, Chivington's troops breached the 1861 Treaty of Fort Wise by attacking and ultimately slaughtering over 150 people, mainly women, children, and the elderly. For protection of his people and as duly authorized and directed by the United States government, Cheyenne Chief Black Kettle had raised both the U.S. flag and a white flag of truce, both of which were fully visible to the troops. Despite

Chief Little Robe, Southern Cheyenne. Little Robe's family were among those at the Sand Creek Massacre. Among the deceased was the Chief's father, also called Little Robe. One of Little Robe's children, a son named White Bird, became a noted Cheyenne into the early 1900's. Credit: Oklahoma Historical Society

the display of these flags, Chivington's men marched ahead with their personal need to complete the utter destruction of these peaceful people. The Colorado troops then desecrated the dead and plundered the camp. Later, they were greeted as heroes in the city of Denver. Dismembered corpses and body parts were paraded along the streets of Denver, with much glee and delight by the soldiers.

Photo of U.S. Army Colonel John Chivington with U.S. Army Colonel John Chivington ★

For the soldiers, losses were minimal, with about nine or ten killed, and three dozen wounded. After the attack, most of the surviving Cheyenne fled north towards the Smoky Hill, seeking refuge among relatives. During the ensuing months, Sand Creek was investigated by a Military Commission, a Joint Committee on the Conduct of War, and a Special Joint Committee investigating the condition of Indian Tribes. These committees condemned the action of Colonel Chivington and most of his officers and troops, labeling the event a massacre.

A delegation of Cheyenne, Kiowa, and Arapaho chiefs in Denver, Colorado in September 28, 1864. Black Kettle sits 2nd from the left, in the front row.

"I saw the bodies of those lying there cut all to pieces, worse mutilated than any I ever saw before; the women cut all to pieces ... With knives; scalped; their brains knocked out; children two or three months old; all ages lying there, from sucking infants up to warriors ... By whom were they mutilated? By the United States troops ..."

— *John S. Smith, Congressional Testimony of Mr. John S. Smith, 1865*

"Fingers and ears were cut off the bodies for the jewelry they carried. The body of White Antelope, lying solitarily in the creek bed, was a prime target. Besides scalping him the soldiers cut off his nose, ears, and testicles-the last for a tobacco pouch ..."

— *Stan Hoig*

"Jis to think of that dog Chivington and his dirty hounds, up thar at Sand Creek. His men shot down squaws, and blew the brains out of little innocent children. You call sich soldiers Chris- tians, do ye? And Indians savages? What der yer 'spose our Heavenly Father, who made both them and us, thinks of these

things? I tell you what, I don't like a hostile red skin any more than you do. And when they are hostile, I've fought 'em, hard as any man. But I never yet drew a bead on a squaw or papoose, and I despise the man who would."

— *Kit Carson*

Prairie Chief, a Southern Cheyenne; son of Wolf Grey / Grey Beard and Old Standing Woman. Prairie Chief's family was at the Sand Creek Massacre. Wolf Grey appears on the list of Sand Creek people which was compiled in 1865 at the treaty of the Little Arkansas, Kansas. Wolf Grey or Grey Beard was shot and killed in 1875 while being taken to prison at Fort Marion, Florida. Prairie Chief passed in October, 1917. Credit: Oklahoma Historical Society

Colorado Territorial Governor Evans, who ordered the bloody attack, and whose political career was subsequently ended because of this loathsome decision, wrote a rebuttal of sorts. Colonel Chivington, who had initially responded via deposition, addressed the people of Colorado with a synopsis of the investigation. Chivington and others defended their attack at Sand Creek, claiming bias, political agendas and even officer jealousies had distorted and misrepresented the facts. Today, the Sand Creek Massacre remains as only one of many historical reminders of the numerous sorrowful events imposed upon Native Americans within their own land.

In 1998 Senator Ben Campbell (CO-R) introduced a bill that resulted in legislation known as the Sand Creek Massacre National Historic Site Study Act. This legislation directed the National Park Service to identify the location and extent of the Sand Creek Massacre and define its suitability as a potential unit of the National Park Service. The Sand Creek Massacre Site Location Project used historical documentation, oral history, traditional tribal methods, aerial photography, archeology and geomorphology. On November 7, 2000, President Clinton signed into law the Sand Creek Massacre National Historic Site Establishment Act. The Act recognizes the national significance of the Sand Creek Massacre and authorizes its establishment as a unit of the National Park Service.

Approximately 12,500 acres in Kiowa County, Colorado were authorized for inclusion within the National Historic Site. Though debate continues regarding the specific location of internal features, most researchers agree that the core area of the site contains the location of the Indian village, the point from which the Colorado regiment first spotted the encampment, the location of the village's horse herds, the general path of company and howitzer movement and attacks, positions of the hastily-dug Cheyenne and Arapaho protective sand pits, and the military bivouac area of November 29-30. The National Park Service worked in partnership with the State of Colorado, the Cheyenne and Arapaho Tribes of Oklahoma, the Northern Cheyenne Tribe, the Northern Arapaho Tribe, landowners, Kiowa County, and other partners in the process of establishing the National Historic Site. Over the years the area of the Sand Creek Massacre has continued to be visited and commemorated. Sand Creek descendants remain active in tribal communities in Montana, Oklahoma, and Wyoming, and Council Representatives continue to work alongside the National Park Service.

"I think that by locating these places and having an actual place to go and pay homage to the people who died there, for us it's going to bring closure to a lot of tribal pain that we are presently experiencing.

— *Dr. Richard Little Bear, 2000*

Over a century since the tragic event, the Cheyenne have finally begun to realize some sense of healing by honoring the memory of the Sand Creek Massacre victims through the on-going following efforts:

• Repatriation of human remains and artifacts held in museums taken during and after the massacre.

• Researching, gathering and archiving Cheyenne oral history of the Sand Creek massacre;

• Protecting and preserving the village site of the Sand Creek massacre through federal legislation the Sand Creek Massacre National Historic Site Act of November 7, 2000;

• Assisting the State of Colorado in

A survivor of the Sand Creek Massacre, Cohoe later spent time in prison at Fort Marion, Florida. During his time at Fort Marion, Cohoe was among Indian prisoners who depicted their history and traditional cultures through the medium of ledger art. Cohoe passed away in 1924. He was survived by two sons, Coyote Walking and Black Bird (Charlie and Bruce Cohoe). **Credit: Oklahoma Historical Society**

reinterpreting the Civil War monument at the State Capitol to affirm that what occurred at Sand Creek on November 29, 1864 was a massacre of innocent men women and children and not a "battle";

• Originating the First Annual Sand Creek Spiritual Healing Run of 1999 from the Sand Creek Massacre Site in Kiowa County to the steps of the state capitol in Denver.

Clearly, the Sand Creek Massacre National Historic Site shall remain a reminder of the tragic extremes sometimes reached during times of conflict; it symbolizes the struggles of Native American tribes to maintain their way of life on ancestral lands, and represents a significant element of frontier military and Native American history. Each of these mandates, historic sources and partnerships will help insure that the site is preserved in perpetuity for future generations of Sand Creek descendants and world citizens.

OPHELIA CHANGING BEAR'S (KIOWA/ARAPAHOE) STORY

Ophelia and I met prior to the beginning of a pow-wow one early evening. By coincidence, Ophelia's son David and I are both bead workers, making traditional crafts for personal use and to trade at pow-wows. It was during our conversation that David mentioned that his mother was knowledgeable in spiritual matters. After he introduced me to his mother she became very interested and willing to share her thoughts. A few months after our meeting, Ophelia has since 'let go of her physical body and taken the spiritual road herself,' but thankfully, because of her willingness, I was able to record a bit of her personal remembrance for you.

— Antonio

"I was born in Anadarko, Oklahoma, in the year 1923. My mother was a member of the Kiowa Nation and my father was from the Arapahoe people. Both of them had much to tell about their memories of the Sand Creek Battle. I remember as a small girl, when we would visit Sand Creek, father would always make offerings of tobacco to the souls that were killed at Sand Creek. I was told to never speak about, or to mention, the name Sand Creek without first bowing my head to honor our relatives. All of them were to be prayed for and honored.

I don't have too much to say about the stories; they are mine to carry with me until I also leave this life. What I will say is that I know that Sand Creek is a very sad place. Many terrible and sad memories still linger there. I haven't visited the area for over 60 years, but once when I did visit with my parents and two older brothers, we all knew and felt that that ground was holy. A hawk followed us everywhere we walked. It flew in the air and just kept up with us, just floating way up high where we could see it.

I hope people who visit will always remember to keep it holy and not to speak in a loud voice when they visit. The trees, the ground, and the wind all can hear what people say. Mother Earth knows what's in people's hearts. So, be reverent and make offerings. It's a sad place."

RALPH COVINTON'S (ANGLO) STORY

Ralph and I met for his interview at a Santa Fe city park. Ralph just happened to be in New Mexico for a gallery showing of his brother's artwork and I, being a resident of New Mexico, it was convenient for me to meet with him in town. Seated at a bench one afternoon under the shade of cottonwood trees he described his spiritually rich encounter with one entity. Unexpected as the encounter was, Ralph was to that day still visibly moved by what happened to him just a few years before. I know this story will be one story you'll be thinking about for some time to come.

— Antonio

"Today I live in the small town of Lamar, but I was raised in Eads, and born in Chivington in 1923. The town of Chivington is what most people who happen to visit might refer to as a ghost town. Not much is left of it, just a few houses and dirt, with lots of dead trees and open ranges, with a few cattle here and there. I left Chivington in the late 1960's. The only ones left from our family are just my brother and me, that's all, just the two of us.

As you know, the town of Chivington was named after the Arapahoe and Cheyenne Indian killer, Col. John M. Chivington! I don't hide my distaste for that terrible idiot! I had a couple of friends who were Native Americans, and I personally know how honorable those people are. My wife was a Kiowa from Oklahoma. I know about the way history can change things, for the worst, depending on who's writing it all down. Native American people are, by and large, the best thing this county ever had, and I hope your readers know this.

I was around the age of 14 or 15 when I first began to have the experiences happen to me that I would call hauntings. I was visiting my grandparents at the time that also lived in Chivington, just a couple of miles away from where our family house was. My grandparents' house was a small, three-room house. No running water or electricity. When we wanted to take a bath, we had to heat the water on the wood-burning stove in the kitchen, and we would also share the bath water!

One spring evening after we had all gone to sleep, as I was lying in bed, I heard the sound of a dog barking in the distance. For some reason, this sound alarmed me. It was not unusual to hear this. The dogs in town would sometimes bark at foxes, coyotes and other dogs, but for some reason, this night was different. Apparently, no one else heard the dog because I could see in the darkness that everyone was fast asleep in his or her beds. I did finally go to sleep, but that night I had the worst nightmare I have ever experienced.

I dreamt that a woman, an Indian woman who was covered in dirt, was standing next to my bed. I woke up on my back, in a sweat, and just lay in bed staring up at the dark ceiling. My brother, Glen, who was asleep next to me, did not notice anything because he never woke up and was snoring away.

But I felt that my dream was more than a dream because of it being so real. From that night on, I would have many nightmares of that Indian woman who would approach my bedside, but when I'd wake up, she would not be there. I knew I was dreaming, but the nightmares sure did seem very real to me as a child.

At around the age of 17, my dreams began to take on a new focus. The nightmares became more constant, and the nightly visitations of the Indian woman were becoming even more frightening to me. Until the time when she actually appeared to me! One night, I was having a dream about running after our horses. It was a strange dream. I was barefoot and running as fast as the horses. As soon as I caught up to them, I suddenly woke up! I was on my left side, facing the wall. As I was lying there in bed, I began to suddenly hear the sound of footsteps coming up to my bed. A little bit scared, I didn't turn around. I just automatically froze, listening to the strange footsteps. Then I heard the steps come right up to my bed and then felt the hand of someone pulling at my hair! I acted like I was asleep—playing possum. Somehow, I eventually did fall back to sleep.

From that night on, my dreams of the Indian woman started back up once again. And as soon as she would reach my bed, I'd wake up. I'd look about the room and not see anyone. Like I said before, my nightmares were becoming more constant. I knew that if I were to tell my mother or father about them, they'd think I was going crazy, so I just kept them to myself. But one night, things did change.

After having the usual dream of the Indian woman, I woke up and I remember that as I lay there in my bed, the smell of what I could only think might be wet wood was overpowering. It was a very strong aroma of something old and damp, something resembling a dampness or moldiness.

I lay there and thinking that a skunk or some type of smelly animal had 'let go' in my bedroom, I sat up in bed and quickly visually scanned around the room. That's when I noticed that one area of the room was a lot darker than the rest. I fixed my gaze on this darkness and soon saw that it was beginning to move! The shadow became smaller and took the form of a person—the Indian woman in my dreams!

Her shadow moved slowly towards me and it began to grow larger and with more defined details. I lay silently in bed in shock! Despite the darkness I could see her fine facial features, and the pattern of her dress were becoming clearer. As she got to about five feet from my bed, something within me took over. Suddenly, instead of fear, I began to feel a deep concern and sadness for this woman. I could somehow sense that she was in pain, and something like an emotion of deep pity took hold of me.

With a dry mouth, I spoke to her, 'I don't know why you're here but I care about you and I'll try to help you.' She slowly turned her head and opened her mouth, but I didn't hear any words come out. Then I again said, 'I'll help you with whatever you need.' She kept still and then I felt my face and body grow hot, as if a thick wool blanket had been wrapped around me! As I lifted my right hand to my face, I must have fainted because the last thing I remember is waking up in the morning. I knew I did not dream of the woman, she was real; the ghost was real because something inside me told me so. I was not dreaming, I was sure of it!

The next night I decided that if I were to have another visit from this woman, I was going to make sure I did not faint. Somehow I was going to be braver and keep talking to her until she responded to me. I guess because of having had so many dreams of her in years past, she had become somehow familiar to me. Not as a friend, but as a sort of familiar being. I know this is a strange kind of relationship, but that's how I was thinking at the time.

Sure enough, about two nights later I heard a noise in my room and there she was. This time, as before, when she spoke to me her mouth moved but no sound came out. But after she closed her mouth, her words, or what I thought might be words, came after, as if in a delayed time. Something like if you were to clap your hands together, and just a few seconds later, the clapping sound is heard like an echo. This made no sense to me.

In a few minutes she had disappeared. In the morning I awoke with a sense that I could communicate with her if I kept it up, and persisted in allowing her to feel comfortable. I didn't know what else I could do, so the next night, before going to bed, I placed a small piece of a chocolate bar next to the table in my room where she would appear. I hoped she would appreciate that as my gift to her.

I didn't have to wait very long, because right after I placed the chocolate on the table and said, 'Well, I hope you like chocolate,' I felt the room grow cold, then the scent of wet earth filled the air. I looked around the room and didn't see anything unusual, but in the distance, I slowly began to hear the sound of lots of commotion going on— the sound of yelling and gunfire! I looked outside from my window and didn't see anything. The night was still and even the dogs weren't barking.

While I was wondering what that sound was, I heard the sound of something moving in my room. I struck a match and didn't see anything, and the chocolate was still where I had placed it. So I decided to get into bed. But as I got under the covers, I felt a hard object between the wall and me. I reached out of the covers and discovered a stick!

I took a long slow breath. My hands began to shake. I knew I had not put that stick in my bed and my brother, Glen, was not home at the time, because he and mother had gone to Lamar to stay with my uncle for the week. And father was returning with the two of them in two days. I was alone in the house.

I knew it had to be the Indian woman who had left it there for me. I said, 'Thank you,' out loud. Then I placed the short, thick stick on the same table where I had left the chocolate bar. That night I did not get a visit from the Indian woman, and I have not had another dream about her since then.

I've kept the stick for many years and when I married my Kiowa wife, I told her the story about my dreams and how I had come to have the stick. She told me to wrap it in a blanket, and to sprinkle sage over it, and to place it upon a small bed of cottonwood and juniper branches. And most importantly, to keep it hidden from anyone's view.

We've always kept the stick wrapped up and hidden in a box, high up on a shelf in our garage. When my wife died in 1976, I brought the box into the house and kept it in my own bedroom. It's a small stick, about 23 inches long and about five inches round. I'll always keep it with me. I've told my brother Glen not to forget to bury me with it. I want to always have that stick, which was given to me by that Indian woman when I was a young man, even when I'm dead and leave this Earth. I hope that I will meet up with my wife, and that both of us can personally thank the spirit of the Indian woman for her gift."

CITY OF FORT MORGAN

Situated in the northeast quadrant of the state, Fort Morgan is the boyhood, high school town of the famous bandleader, Glenn Miller.

As in years past, the town still retains its farm-ranch community outlook. The town also lies on the historic Overland Trail. Contained within the town sits the Fort Morgan Museum. The museum presents an overview of the area's history from the original inhabitants, the Plains and Pawnee Indians, through to the new arrivals, the farmers and ranchers who settled within the area.

North of town lies the Pawnee Buttes, of which the formations were the setting in James Michener's classical novel of Colorado, "Centennial." Traveling north of Fort Morgan, and bordering the state lines of Nebraska and Wyoming, lay the Pawnee National Grassland. This wondrous and vast landscape of rolling hills and shallow valleys is a uniquely special area of solemn silence.

BARRY LYNCH'S (ANGLO) STORY

I interviewed Barry at his home in Denver. His personal story is one of those unique tales that make me smile, and reaffirms my own personal beliefs in the lasting power of our ancestors, and their strong ties to their land. I will never discount how important it is to reaffirm, and to be mindful of this. Although I myself have not yet visited the Pawnee National Grassland, which is the focus of Barry's story, I have visited the grassland area located within the Crow Indian Reservation in Montana. My experience there was very, very 'special' and worthy of reverence. Barry's story presents a moment of time, frozen for reflection and wonder. Here's an example of spirits not manifesting on our terms, but as is often the case, they will choose to present themselves where and whenever they wish.

— Antonio

"As I was driving through Ft. Morgan about 14 years ago, I decided to stop at a small restaurant in town. I sat in a booth next to a young guy who was about five years older than myself. He spotted me as being new to the area, and asked me about my travels and where I would eventually be headed. I told him that I was just traveling through, attempting to see as much of the United States as I could within two months, before starting college in Wisconsin. I really had no set schedule except to reach Wisconsin by fall.

He asked if I had been up north to the Pawnee National Grassland. I asked him if it would be a worthwhile visit. He answered that the area was wonderful and very necessary to experience if I wanted to get a good idea of what the United States used to look like, many years ago in its raw state. 'It's less than an hour away, just head north on road 52,' he said. Right after my lunch, I decided to fill my gas tank, take his advice, and head north to the grassland.

It didn't take long before I arrived at the park—it was beautiful. The rolling hills and shoulder high shafts of green grass swaying with the wind were dreamlike! This was a paradise. I got out of my car and walked towards an outcropping of white sandstone buttes that I had spotted in the distance. Strangely, at the time, I was the only person in the area. I had the whole expanse of beauty to myself. The solitude and the wind were my only companions.

Once I reached the stone towers, I climbed a few feet up one of the towers and sat down, trying to take in the expansive beauty of the area. Wherever I turned, all I could see were miles and miles of green rolling hills. This was heaven on earth, I thought. There were black birds circling all around the white towers and I even saw a golden eagle fly overhead and then disappear up into the stratosphere.

As I leaned back against the stones, the warm sun caused me to relax enough to fall asleep. Exactly at the moment I was dozing off, I began to hear the sound of voices. Thinking that there were other tourists in the area, I opened my eyes, and looked around. I didn't see anyone. So I closed my eyes and again fell back to sleep.

It must have been only a few seconds that had passed when I suddenly heard the distant sound of horses. I opened my eyes and looked in the direction of the sound. About a half-mile or so away from me I spotted about, I would guess, ten to fifteen Indians! I knew these were Indians because of their dress and the long poles a few of them were carrying. At the tips of their poles were what looked like tied feathers that were blowing in the wind. They were walking alongside of about three horses, and riding on the horses were Indian men.

This was just like an Old West movie. The costumes couldn't have been better designed! As I sat there, I kept thinking to myself, how fortunate I was to be seeing this group of Indian men and their horses moving along the tall grass, just like they must have done more than a hundred years ago. The horses would sometimes snort, and a few times one of them would make a whinnying sound. It was fantastic!

I noticed that they moved from the south and were headed north. As I watched this procession, I began to think that this was not on some level normal. I thought this because as they slowly passed my area, one by one, beginning with the first in line, the figures began to fade away! Horse and man, just fade away until they had all disappeared!

This caught me off guard and I was totally awestruck! I sat there on the sandstone cliff and began to sob, as I'd never done before. I instinctively knew that I had seen and witnessed the ghostly apparitions of Indians. I had never in my life seen anything like this before. I was, after all, a 22-year-old white boy from Los Angeles. I never expected to see anything like this. I was from a big city on the West Coast. I was very surprised. It was a privilege to have been given the gift to witness this. I cried and knew enough to thank the sky and earth for the opportunity. It just came naturally to do this. I knew then, and believe today, that what I experienced that day was a true gift.

I've spoken to just a few people about this. In college, I mentioned it to an anthropology professor, and she introduced me to a member of the Sauk/Fox tribe from Wisconsin. He cautioned me to not make fun of, or to be a braggart about, what I had seen. It was a definite blessing that I had been given and I need to hold on to it and carry this vision with me throughout my life.

The reason why I want to now tell you about my experience is because I believe that others might find something in my personal story, which might open up their eyes. There are still powerful, spiritual areas of history that will not go away. These are tucked away in areas of the United States that are not hard to find. They are there; you just have to open yourself up to them and they will come to you. I know they will."

BLACK CANYON OF THE GUNNISON EXPLORING THE CANYON

While the people of the Ute bands knew of the Black Canyon of the Gunnison for hundreds of years, to many explorers it was an obscure geographic feature. The Spanish were the first Europeans to canvas western Colorado with two expeditions, one led by Juan Rivera in 1765, and the other by Fathers Dominguez and Escalante in 1776. Both were looking for passage to the California coast, and both passed by the canyon.

Fur trappers of the early 1800's undoubtedly knew of the canyon in their search for beaver pelts. They left no written record of the canyon, though, probably because they couldn't, in fact, read or write.

By the middle of the century, exploration of the American West had captured the nation's attention. In turn, expeditions came to the Black Canyon searching for railroad passageways, mineral wealth, or in a quest for water. Eventually, explorers came to see the canyon, not for commercial wealth, but for the renewal and recreation that it offered.

Today, you can walk in the footsteps of some of these hardy and inquisitive forbearers. The canyon still offers a rugged and demanding experience, even as it did more than a hundred of years ago.

RITA MANSON'S (ANGLO) STORY

Rita and her best friend, Jeanette, were seated in Rita's living room while I conducted the interview. Rita shared photos and personal stories unrelated to ghosts, regarding her husband and their life together. Jeanette was very interested in the subject of ghosts, and would occasionally interject with her own personal opinions. It was obvious to me that these elderly ladies were the best of friends, and at one time during my visit, Jeanette informed me that she had even once dated Rita's husband, Bruce, when they both had attended high school, so many years ago.

That being said, Jeanette remained quiet once Rita began her personal story. Rita's personal story that follows offers insight into the spiritual mysteries that many Native Americans know exist within the wild and rarely traveled areas of North America. Rita and her husband, Bruce, so many years ago were witnesses to such an example of this, and as you'll read, were never the same after their experience.

— Antonio

"Both my husband, Bruce, and I were born and raised in Montrose. Bruce died six years ago at the age of 75. The story I'll be telling you took place when we went camping one week into the park. We were both in our early fifties, and still very active and physically fit.

The national park is a birder's wonderland. Both Bruce and I were avid birders and even helped the park with counting migratory and non-migratory birds that nested, and yearly visited the park. My favorites were the raptors, such as hawks and eagles. Bruce enjoyed the park's resident birds such as the American dippers, ravens, and jays.

Well, after hiking into the backwoods for several hours, and after having finished setting up our camp for the week to come, we decided to take a short walk into the woods. If you know the park, our camp was located off the North Rim Road, not far from Grizzly Gulch. Isolated, and yet very nicely situated for our bird data gathering needs.

Bruce and I went for a short hike and eventually came upon a meadow. It was midday. When we entered the meadow, I began to have a strange feeling that took over me. I knew something was about. It was a sunny day, and I had no health problems, but I suddenly began to feel weak and an oppressive heaviness began to affect my breathing. I was gasping for air. Bruce took hold of me and laid me down on the grass. I began taking shallow breaths as he shook me and spoke, 'Rita, talk to me, talk to me!' Soon, I came to and began to sob like a little girl. I don't know what it was that had affected me so severely, but whatever it was came and quickly left my body. I composed myself and mentioned to Bruce, 'That was the strangest thing I have ever experienced.

There was no reason that I could think of, no allergic reaction, or anything, which would have caused me to have such an unusual attack of that degree. We held onto each other for a few minutes until I felt well enough to continue. But I did notice that once we walked out of

143

that meadow, I felt as if a large boulder had been lifted off my shoulders. Somehow, I felt that there was something on the level of the mystical, or spiritual, that dwelt in that area, and that I should never go back into it. I totally recovered and felt very good afterward. As we continued on our hike, I remained confused and perplexed as to the reason for having experienced such a reaction for the remainder of that day.

Later, after we had finished our campfire dinner, I decided to write in my journal. I entered our tent and lay on top of my sleeping bag, and began to jot down my thoughts. Bruce stayed outside. The night was very peaceful, not even the wind stirred. After about an hour, we went for a short walk to a mound of boulders, climbed the largest of these, and drank a cup of wine from a bottle I had brought along. We gazed up at the night sky, and Bruce pointed out several constellations from the blanket of stars that stood out in the darkness.

I was not in the least thinking about ghosts, or anything spiritual. But from the corner of my eye, I noticed the movement of someone's outline, or shadow, walking about the trees—just about twenty feet from where we were sitting. I turned my head and spotted a short man about four feet tall looking in my direction. He was clearly standing there, just staring at me. His left arm was bent at the elbow, with his left hand on his waist. His right hand was holding something small, resembling a bag.

I softly spoke to Bruce to look in the direction I was staring at, 'Do you see that man over there, by the trees? Look, over by that tree with the broken branch?' He said no, there was no one there he could see. Thinking my imagination was playing tricks on me, I said, 'Bruce, I think this wine is stronger than I imagined. I've had enough for tonight. I'm starting to see things. Here, you can finish the rest of mine. I'm going to turn in early.' Bruce remained on the boulder while I walked back to the tent and went to bed. After just a few minutes, I heard what I thought was Bruce walking the short distance north of our camp. I called to him, but he did not answer. I got up out of the tent and heard footsteps coming from nearby pine trees. I grabbed my flashlight and walked over to the trees. I called again to Bruce and this time I heard his voice, but it came from the opposite side of our camp.

'Bruce,' I called, 'I'm over here, over here!' I waved the flashlight attempting to get his attention. I was unable to see him, but I could tell by the distant sound of his voice that he was quite a distance away from where I was.

Just at that moment, I heard a noise coming from behind me. I looked up toward the treetops and that's when I saw the same figure of the small man I had spotted earlier. I noticed what I could only describe as a very weak greenish light, and within this light was the short man, standing on one of the limbs, or appearing to hover, suspended in midair!

I was terrified! As I turned to run, I somehow tripped and fell to the ground. But as I fell to the ground, I hit the trunk of a tree and received a nasty gash across my left eye and upper lip. I turned over on my back and placed my hand to my head. As I sat there for a few seconds, I felt the blood running down my arm. Then I looked up and in the darkness, I saw a hand reach down to take hold of my right arm. The strength this person had was obvious when, with just one pull, I was on my feet.

I looked at my arm and saw the hand and arm of the ghostly being still holding onto me. A wave of fear surged over me, as I took a couple of steps back and gazed directly at the face of the spirit. All I remember was its unnaturally large eyes, and the smile that was filled with two rows of cream-colored teeth that were outlined in dark lines!

Terrified of the apparition, I screamed, and it immediately disappeared! I quickly turned around, and ran in the darkness towards my tent. I had not taken more than a few feet when again, I tripped over something, and fell to the ground. I lay on my side, stunned. I somehow managed to turn over on all fours, and began to crawl my way back towards camp. Yelling Bruce's name, he soon located me then lifted me up. I was a mess, covered in wet earth mixed with blood. It took me a few seconds to gather my composure, but when I did, I quickly told Bruce about what I had experienced.

Confused and unsure of what to believe, Bruce helped me to our tent, and then helped dress my wounds. Because it was so dark and the weather unstable, we decided to spend the night in camp, and in the morning we'd leave for town. We both spent the night huddled together.

I kept explaining to Bruce that what I had seen was not in my imagination, but something real, and definitely not anything close to a living and breathing human at all! Eventually, I fell asleep and in the morning, I looked in the mirror and saw how swollen my face really was. After seeing a doctor in Montrose, I was given sedatives and had my two small cuts stitched up.

The drive home was interesting in that Bruce confided in me that he had stayed up most of the night, worried about me and oddly enough, he had kept hearing the strange sound of what he thought sounded like a cross between a wolf's howl and a person's laughter. It really frightened him. Bruce was not a man to frighten easily, but this unearthly sound really did frighten him.

In the few months following my ghostly incident in the park, I've mentioned what I experienced to a few people. But everyone, without exception, stated that they felt compassion for what we went through but could not believe that it was anything that had to do with a ghost. Following that, I once attended a forestry workshop and was introduced to a Ute man. I felt compelled to mention my ghostly experience to him and he answered, 'Sounds like something the Crow Indians of Montana would be experts in. They have a mythology within their tribe about the dwarfs that inhabit the outlying hills surrounding their reservation. Their stories about the small spirits that live in those hills go back generations, and they tell about the discovery of a few small, fully developed skeletons of human-like beings. I'd keep away from that area of the park. Something in your spiritual makeup is attractive to them. It's a 'medicine' that they might want to tap into. You might want to talk to a person of the Crow Tribe, but I don't think they would offer you much information because they do not talk openly about their traditions to outsiders. It's rare for them to even hint at this subject at all.'

Since that time, I have not ventured onto the north side of the canyon. I tend to stay within other areas of the park, but even then, not without a bit of trepidation. I know what I saw was real and not spiritually positive. I'll keep the pleasant thoughts and memories I have regarding the good times I shared years ago in the canyon with my husband. As for the others, I hope one day they will fade away with time."

TOWN OF MONTROSE

Montrose is considered to be the gateway city to the Black Canyon of the Gunnison National Park and the Curecanti National Recreation Area. To the east of town is located the immense Blue Mesa Reservoir. The area in and around Montrose is known as the Uncompahgre Valley. This valley is scenically beautiful and peaceful in its setting. Many outdoor activities are available including the usual hiking, fishing, hunting, and camping. In addition, local interesting places to visit are the Ute Indian Museum and the Montrose County Historical Museum. The Historical Museum is located in the old train depot. Free pamphlets are available throughout town, describing easy directions for a self-guided, historical, walking tour of downtown. Each fall, Montrose sponsors two very popular festivals: the Native American Lifeways Festival and Council Tree Pow-Wow. These are both must-see events that honor the area's Native American heritage, in particular the Ute people. Throughout the surrounding area are smaller towns, which offer their own festive celebrations, such as Cedaredge, which holds the Apple Harvest Festival, and Paonia's Cherry Harvest Festival.

Interestingly, Montrose has two wineries that specialize in, but are not limited to, the growing of two grape varieties, Chablis and Zinfandel. Lastly, a not-to-be-missed event held in July is the town's hot air balloon celebration.

UTE INDIAN MUSEUM

The Ute Museum, built in 1956 and expanded in 1998, resides directly in the center of traditional Ute territory. Annually, between 18,000 and 20,000 visitors pass through the museum. This museum is noted for exhibits that display one of the most extensive and complete collections of the Ute people's culture. Within the museum's walls are housed the Montrose Visitor Information Center, classrooms, offices, a gallery space and gift store with traditional and modern day Native arts and crafts. Dioramas and cultural programs, in addition to the peaceful Chief Ouray Memorial Park, make a stop here at the museum a must. It's a special place to visit.

The museum displays recount to the visitor how historically the Utes would migrate from the surrounding mountains in the summer to the river valleys in the winter. These resourceful Native people utilized the abundant available plants and animals lying within the Uncompahgre River valley for sustenance, clothing, and shelter.

Within the museum's grounds are located the Chief Ouray Memorial Park containing the crypts of Chief Ouray's wife, Chipeta, and her brother, John McCook. In addition, a stately and impressive monument of stone and bronze dedicated to Chief Ouray is just a few steps away. There is also a memorial to the Spanish conquistadors who ventured through the area in 1776. The museum's property encompasses the chief's original 8.65-acre homestead where both he and his wife, Chipeta, lived.

Chief Ouray died in 1880, and his remains were buried at a hidden location. This was in accordance with the Ute's traditional manner of caring for their dead. Forty-four years later, Ouray's remains were disinterred and his remains were reburied at the tribal cemetery in Ignacio, Colorado. Today, the grounds are well maintained with easy-to-traverse footpaths that meander among cottonwoods and beds of native flowers. Authentic replicas of Ute teepees also dot the grounds.

CAROL JEAN "C.J." BRAFFORD'S (LAKOTA) STORY

I conducted my interview with Carol directly outside the museum's front doors, on a sunny patio to the right of the entrance. Shaded by the large cottonwood trees that landscape the grounds, Carol felt comfortable enough to describe her spiritual experiences to me. I also described my own experiences from interviewing other museum employees, in other states, and their reported similar spiritual experiences with Native artifacts and remains. Apparently, museums' non-Native administrators are gaining more insight into the importance of having a more sensitive approach towards sacred objects, but there is still much they need to learn.

After reading Carol's story, it will become clear that crafters, artists, and the individual makers of baskets, jewelry, and drums, etc., placed much importance and spiritual significance and focus on their creations. To treat these objects as nothing more than 'simple artifacts' would be doing the creators of these important, 'living symbols' a great disservice. These symbols remain alive, and contain an energy that transcends years, generations, and time. They must be respected.

That being stated, to possess any item containing any amount of human remains, no matter how insignificant you might think, is

a big, universal immoral, 'no no'! Speaking in the spiritual sense, it is also a most dangerous thing to do.

— *Antonio*

"I began my work at the museum as Museum Director in 1997, and I've held that position since. So as of today, that makes a full eight years that I've been at the museum. Prior to beginning my work at the museum I worked at the Grand Teton National Park Museum in Wyoming. I held the title as Museum Curator, and was directly in charge of the museum's Native American collection. The collection was known as the David T. Vernon collection. There were a variety of artifacts contained within the collection that included such things as human remains, sacred bundles, etc. There is even a Crow Indian bundle that contains a human skull. The Crow people, as a specialized item for divination, historically used this bundle. Spiritually, these items are forbidden by the tribes to be displayed and are considered too 'dangerous' for anyone outside of the tribe to handle.

During my life I've seen several entities, or ghosts. I'll tell you about them in a short while, but first I'd like to describe some other experiences that I've had.

As you can tell, so far, I've involved myself in many areas of museum work. The Ute Museum does not have a large collection, due to it not having the available space large enough to display and store them. Another of the bundles that I did see at the national park museum was a Pawnee Morning Star bundle. To my knowledge, there are only three of these bundles in existence. This bundle caused me to have an unpleasant, personal, and emotional reaction, because of what it contained and historically how it had been used.

Traditionally, this Pawnee bundle required that a Lakota, or Sioux, female be sacrificed. I always felt strange holding this particular bundle because of what it contained and its heavy weight, being wrapped in a large buffalo hide. Unlike other bundles, which are much smaller, this bundle was definitely out of the ordinary in its size. Additionally, it also contained a 'paddle or club.' This club was used by the Pawnee to club to death a young girl, who, as I mentioned, would be used as a sacrificial victim.

I myself, belonging to the Lakota Nation, had very mixed reactions when, due to my position at the museum, I would on occasion need to hold the actual bundle and the weapon in my hands. You might ask why would I need to actually hold such an item in the first place? Well, due to the federal law known as the Native American Repatriation Act, that states: "Whereas all Indian artifacts being held within museums are mandated to be reassessed for their religious and tribal significance, and if found to be of such significance, are to be returned to that particular tribe, in accordance of the procedures set forth in the law."

My job required me to systematically gain access to the collection and make a decision as to whether or not each item filled the criteria for repatriation. Videos were made during my investigations, for the purpose of documenting and providing to each tribal nation's representatives the evidence they needed for the purpose of disclosing to them, whether or not the items were something significantly relevant to their tribe's history and culture.

A consultation meeting would then be held following the tribe's response to this video. This was a procedure that had to be done. And my position at the museum deemed that I was the one to do it. I must explain that I personally was very cautious and a bit fearful when the time came to examine the bundles. I remember that the Pawnee bundle was the last bundle to be examined, and I was given detailed instructions as to how to proceed with the opening of it. After all, this was something that contained human remains—Indian remains.

In the back of my mind were the words of my grandmother who years before, taught me to be knowledgeable of our history, and to gain as much information of our culture as I could. During this procedure, I kept those words in my mind, and I believed I was respectfully following her instructions. My upbringing instructed me to follow our tribe's method of spiritual cleansing, to pray and sprinkle water before beginning such a non-spiritual examination as this. I know that prayer is a very powerful and protective force, and I wanted to have as much protection as possible.

Well, when the time came, I was alone in the room when I conducted my cleansing ritual. I was respectful and sincere in my focus. Suddenly, someone pounding loudly at the room's window shook my attention. The person was yelling, 'Help, help, help!' I found out later that a young girl had drowned in the lake by the museum, and the person who was pounding at the window was attempting to get help. Now, this might have been simply a coincidence, but the timing, the manner in which this turn of events took place, makes me think it was not. After all, during the moment that I was opening the bundle, the bundle that historically and spiritually needed a young girl to be ritually sacrificed, a young girl just a few hundred yards away was drowning to her death. To this day, I still reflect on that terrible event as being a message. The girl was a non-Indian, an Anglo, but I can't stop thinking about how young Lakota girls were sacrificed when this bundle was in use. Thus, was this girl who drowned a sign to me of symbolic sacrifice?

So, I'm torn between two worlds, the spiritual and the contemporary. I do understand how difficult it is for a non-Indian to see these worlds as I do, but none-the-less, it is a fact for me.

I've got another story regarding the spiritual world and a Ghost Dance shirt that is stored in the Coulter Bay Museum in Wyoming. This museum is again located within the Grand Tetons, as is the other museum I just spoke about. The Coulter Bay Museum houses a collection that the famous Rockefeller family owned. In this museum I would occasionally spot unusual white colored lights that would bounce, or fly, about the rooms. At times, these lights would take on a human shape. For personal reasons, I'll not go into any further description of these lights, but I will say that within the museum I would always 'feel' that I was never alone. I had many other paranormal things take place at that museum, but this is all I'll say about that for now.

I'll now tell you my story regarding the Ghost Dance shirt. I knew that there was an entity that I had experienced at this museum that was attached to this Ghost Dance shirt. I believe that the owner of the shirt was always watching me. It even followed me home. I would see it standing right by my window. Initially, I was not scared at all by it. However, the situation soon started to take a turn for the worse, when I began to spot this entity inside my home. During that period, I would have dreams of an elder, who would approach me and caution me by stating, 'Do not touch the Ghost Dance shirt!' I found that dream odd, but I didn't think much more of it. I went into the museum storage room where the Ghost Dance shirt was kept, and must admit that I did touch the shirt, even after having had the dream cautioning me not to do so. It was right after doing this that the presence of the entity began to make its appearance at my home.

During that same period, I had a girlfriend named Debbie, from the Shoshone Fort Hall Indian Reservation, who came to spend some time at my home. During her visit, she approached me with a concern she had. She told me that, 'I need to tell you that there are spirits in your house. I can hear them walking about the house and turning the knobs on the doors.' Shortly after Debbie's visit, I had a couple of friends of mine who were planning on visiting and spending the night at my house. They were from the Nez Perce Reservation. When I returned from work later that day, I found a note they had left detailing their hesitance about staying in my home. They stated that there was something in the house that was of a spiritual nature, something that made them very uncomfortable. They ended up choosing to stay at a local hotel instead.

My two children are both sensitive to spiritual things, and when they both began to inform me that, 'He's here again,' I decided to contact and pay a visit to an Oto medicine man. I told him of all the experiences that I, and others, had been having at the house—the footsteps, everything. He did what he had to do, and then he sent me home with a special rock, as a spiritual protection. I know that what was in my house was due to my personal 'nonsense' having caused the negative spiritual things to take place by touching the shirt. I honestly do believe that the spirit world is a powerful one, and it is not to be ignored and fooled with. Most people don't understand this. They can't comprehend how, in this modern day, such things can wield the power to influence our daily lives. They can and they do.

Here at the Ute Museum I have had several visitors individually approach and tell me that there are spirits in the museum. They state that they can 'feel' the presence of someone watching them as they walk about the rooms. The response I give them is that this land was very important to the Ute people. Utes lived here; they died and are buried directly on the property. Spirits are very strong; they wander and sometimes linger in places that once were very familiar to them.

Now, I do know that Chipeta, wife of Chief Ouray, wanders about the grounds. I won't go into much detail about this, but people have seen her. They regularly see her. Also, another occurrence that visitors have reported within the museum takes place in the far-rear exhibit room. What is commonly heard are the ghostly sounds of the beating of a drum, the ceremonial drum that is kept under glass in that room. Ceremonial singing of songs and the chanting of voices of Native Americans are also heard in the room. The drum that I mentioned, which we have on display, is a Bear Drum. That drum was actually used during the Bear Dance. The Bear Dance is very significant to the contemporary three bands of the Ute Tribes. Each spring the tribes come together and have a Bear Dance. When I personally first heard the disembodied drumming coming from the back of the museum, it startled me at first. At the time, I was alone in the museum. This took place one night at about 8 p.m. After listening to the drumming for a few seconds, I got up off my chair and started to walk towards the sounds of the beating drum. When I got half-way to where the drum is displayed, the beating suddenly stopped! I was not the only person who heard the drumming. I had a colleague who also reported hearing the drumming. In order to make the pounding sound, it is necessary to use a drumstick, but what was equally strange is that the museum does not display a drumstick with the drum.

For the most part, strange goings-on is not very common at the museum. I am certainly aware that, prior to my arrival, the museum did have for a period of time Native American human remains that were displayed. I was told that these remains were removed, given their proper rites, and buried."

TOWN OF LA JUNTA

La Junta, situated on the southeastern plains of Colorado, is a small town with a population of about 9,000. The town's name, when translated from the Spanish, means 'the junction.' The Comanche National Grassland lies to the southwest of town and the Koshare

Indian Museum and Kiva is just northeast. This museum contains a collection of Native American artifacts and produces 'Indian' dances to the public. The museum began as a Boy Scout troop's project in the 1930's. Today non-Indians—Boy Scouts to be exact — perform the dances. Continuing nine miles northeast of the museum is Bent's Old Fort National Historic Site.

BENT'S OLD FORT NATIONAL HISTORIC SITE

"At a distance it presents a handsome appearance, being castle-like with towers at its angles...the design...answering all purposes of protection, defense, and as a residence."

— George R. Gibson, a soldier who visited the fort in 1846

Congress established this historic fort March 15, 1960, and its reconstruction was completed in 1976. The reconstruction was based on original drawings, historical accounts, and archeological evidence. Historians and archeologists studied what remained of the original fort, and during the nation's bicentennial, the National Park Service took the daunting task of re-creating the large fort as close to its original condition as possible.

Erected in the 1833 by two brothers, Charles and William Bent, and their business partner Ceran St. Vrain, the fort was one of the significant centers of fur trade on the Santa Fe Trail, influencing economies around the world. The fort was the leading industry west of the Mississippi in the early 1830's. For 16 years, Bent, St. Vrain and Co. managed a prosperous trading empire.

The fort was located on the Arkansas River, the international boundary between two countries—Mexico on the south side of the river, and the United States on the north. Strategically located on an established road, it helped pave the way for the occupation of the west by the U.S. Army, and was an instrument of Manifest Destiny and the invasion of Mexico in 1846. William Bent was known to the Cheyenne as 'Little White Man.' His fairness and respect for the culture was the reason for the company's excellent reputation among the Plains Indians. The fort remained as the only permanent structure to be seen for hundreds of miles around.

"It is crowded with all kinds of persons: citizens, soldiers, traders to Santa Fe, Indians, Negroes, etc. The Indians were Arapaho, a fine-looking set of men, with mules to trade"

—George R. Gibson, *account from his 1846 journal*

In the decades after the 1803 Louisiana Purchase, even as the earliest explorers crossed the continent, America's economic frontier expanded westward. Trappers went into the Rockies for beaver, Plains Indians showed their willingness to trade buffalo robes, and the first wagons rolled between the Missouri River and Santa Fe, initiating regular

commerce with Mexico. When traders Charles and William Bent and their partner Ceran St. Vrain sought to establish a base, they wanted to locate where they could take advantage of all these trades. So, in 1833 they built a fort (then called Fort William) on the north bank of the Arkansas River, the boundary between the United States and Mexico. It was close enough to the Rockies to draw trappers; near the hunting grounds of Cheyenne, Arapaho, Kiowa, and other tribes; and on the Santa Fe Trail, near a ford across the river.

While dining at the fort, the separation of social classes was evident. The laborers cooked in their quarters or ate from a community cooking pot. In the 1830's, beaver pelts (called "hairy bank notes") could be bartered for trade goods. As beaver numbers declined, buffalo hides became the basis of exchange.

When Bent, St. Vrain & Company planned a new trading fort in a region with limited timber, the traders turned to adobe, a building material long favored by Mexicans. Clay, water and sand, with straw or wool as binders, were mixed in pits, formed into 18" by 9" by 4" bricks, and dried in the sun. Although Mexican laborers, usually women, had to regularly maintain the adobe plaster, the bricks proved reasonably durable in the dry climate. The fort was hardly the only sign of human life in the area— the high plains had long been home to thousands of Native Americans. But for travelers two months on the trail, it was a greatly anticipated haven, the sole place between Independence and Santa Fe where they could refresh themselves and their livestock, repair wagons, and replenish supplies.

The Bent's Mexican trade grew rapidly as their caravans plied the route from Independence and Westport to company stores in Santa Fe and Taos. There, goods such as cloth, hardware, glass, and tobacco were exchanged for silver, furs, horses, and mules. Thousands of beaver pelts passed through the fort in the early years, but as the market for beaver declined in the 1830's, the Indian trade became a mainstay of the business. The fort's traders swapped American and Navajo blankets, axes, firearms, etc., for buffalo hides and horses taken in raids—no questions asked. The Bents' reputation made their traders welcome in most villages and drew growing numbers of Indians to the fort. Before long, the company dominated the Indian trade on the southern plains. The Bents were so effective as peacemakers, especially with the Southern Cheyenne, that in 1846 the fort (by then called Bent's Fort) was used as headquarters for the Upper Platte and Arkansas Indian Agency.

That year, the quickened beat of military operations stepped up the pace of activity beyond that of the seasonal trade. America was going to war with Mexico, and the fort's strategic location on an established road made it the ideal staging point for the invasion of Mexico's northern province. Storerooms were filled with military supplies; soldiers were quartered at the fort; military livestock stripped the land. Later, a growing stream of settlers and gold seekers disrupted the carefully nurtured Indian trade. In the face of polluted water holes, decimated cottonwood groves, and declining bison, the Cheyenne moved away. Escalating tensions between Indians and whites and a cholera epidemic was sweeping the area. Also, William Bent's first wife and three brothers had died. But the cholera epidemic finally killed the trade. After the death of Charles in 1847, St. Vrain tried unsuccessfully to sell the fort to the U.S. Army. It is thought that William Bent tried to burn the fort in 1849 before moving to his trading houses at Big Timbers, some 40 miles down river, near present-day Lamar, Colorado. He constructed Bent's New Fort there in 1853.

HAROLD ROONEY'S (ANGLO) STORY

I conducted Harold's interview in a quiet, local La Junta restaurant. As we were conversing, unbeknownst to me, a waitress who had been eavesdropping on our conversation came over to our table and said, "I can tell you some of my own experiences that I've had at the fort if you'd like, and why the last supervisor left the place. I used to date the guy. He'll never set foot there again after what we both had happen to us over by the horse stalls. I guarantee you that." Concluding Harold's interview, I did interview the waitress for her story. But prior to finishing her interview, she broke down and wept stating, "I'm sorry but I can't go on. I'll have to end this here. I changed my mind. I'm sorry." As much as I gathered from the little information the waitress gave me, her experience was too traumatic to retell. But what I can say here is that it did involve being held in a locked room of the fort for several hours and being subjected to a very frightening barrage of not so pleasant spiritual experiences. As for Harold, well, his story although definitely not on the same level as the waitress', remains none-the-less jaw dropping.

— *Antonio*

"I currently live in La Junta and have lived here all my life. My wife and I are schoolteachers, and have both taken groups of students to the fort on several day trips. I'll be retiring from the school district in just a few years and I'm planning on writing my own book on the area's history. There are many sites of importance in this southeastern corner of the state; sites that have played a significant role in Colorado's history and, in my opinion, have not been covered in any major way. This, I believe, is very needed. I plan to do this, do the research, and put it in final book form. My retirement will most likely provide me with the time to devote to this personal project.

As for the experiences I've had with ghosts, well, I do recall one very, very notable one that took place at the fort during the late portion of the month of September. The morning was very cold and it was during a school field trip. I had a few students with me who had been studying the history of Bent's Fort for the entire semester. Some of the students had previously visited the fort with their parents, but the majority had not. Although the fort is located in very close proximity to the town of La Junta, and is marketed extensively to tourists, the actual residents of town, ironically, do not show much interest in this major historical site that lies right at their back door.

"She had drawn the image of a man, who was seated in a chair."

As I was saying, I was with a group of my students on a field trip, and they were excited to put to the test all they had studied months before of the

159

fort's history. The day was not an unusual day given the time of year. It was cloudy, drizzly, and thinking back, perfect for sighting a ghost or two.

I turned the students loose, while I stood at the entrance and chatted with one of the interpreters who were dressed in period costume. We were scheduled to be at the fort for half a day, including a lunch break. Everything went well, and one student even brought along her drawing pencils and pads. The fort is an architecturally beautiful structure. Many people feel drawn to its massive adobe style of design.

After a few hours, we gathered for our lunch break during which the student with the artistic talent shared with everyone her colorful drawings. One picture in particular stood out from the rest, in that she had drawn the interior of a room, located on the second floor. She named the room, the 'barrel room,' but in fact the room is named, the 'Billiard Room.' She so named the room because of an obviously placed wooden barrel, which stood in one corner. But she had drawn the image of a man, who was seated in a chair, which another student recognized as being the same man she had seen seated in a chair in another area of the compound. That room was located directly below the Billiard Room, in the 'Trappers' and Hunters' Quarters.' What caused such a stir among the students was that while the student was drawing the man in the Billiard Room, several other students claim to have seen the same man seated in the room below! They compared times and came to the conclusion that it would be impossible for the man to be in both rooms at the same time. Being young, their imaginations ran wild, and they immediately claimed to have seen a ghost in the fort.

I asked the students to calm down and rationally think about this situation. I asked the student who drew the man to describe her impression of him and to tell us all the information he related to her about the fort. I imagined he was another interpreter, and although the interpreter I was speaking to at the entrance to the fort did not personally inform me of his presence, I assumed he had to be an employee.

The student stated that when she asked him if it would be all right to draw and reproduce his image together with the room, he turned to her and just nodded his head, indicating with the gesture his approval. Sensing that he must be 'in character,' she did not speak any further to him and continued with her sketching. The other students who claimed to have also seen the same man in the room below stated that he was in their words, 'weird.' I asked, 'How so?' They responded that as they had entered the dimly lit room, taking notice of him seated at a table, they respectfully saluted a 'hello' to him. He had focused his stoic gaze on them and had slowly nodded his head. The students found this response to be odd, but also thought he was a character who was acting a role for the visitors' benefit.

The oddest thing about both the artist's and the students' recollection of this man was that he had a very 'authentic' appearance. He wore a red tunic, or long coat, and his pants were of a dark blue, heavy material. His shoes were light colored and rough in appearance. In fact, the man's overall appearance was 'rough.' He had a short beard, and under his stout and wide brimmed hat, his hair was short. But the most unusual and unmistakable trait was the color of his face and hands. They were pale, almost a gray/white color! The man never spoke a word to any of the students, giving them the impression that not only did he dress the part, but actually went so far as to apply professional makeup to his face and hands in the process of being truly authentic.

As the teacher, and being the more mature, rational thinker, I felt that my responsibility was to locate the interpreter I had spent the morning conversing with to inquire as to who this individual employee, character actor was. I also wanted him to visit and personally meet with the students, which I'm sure they would have appreciated, and answer their questions about the fort.

I approached the interpreter, and mentioned the man in the red tunic, and he said, 'We have no one else on the property that is dressed in the manner you're describing. I'm the only person here in costume. The only other employees at the fort are in the corral area, and I guarantee those guys would never 'play dress up.' Not for any amount of money.' I decided to walk over to the park's administration office, located at the entrance to the fort, and speak to the officer on duty about this situation. After introducing myself, and giving him the details, he stated,

'As far as I'm aware, no one else is providing the service of interpreter that your students claim to have seen.'

Now, whether or not an actual ghost was seen by one or ten students at the fort that morning, is a matter of opinion, but I can say with full confidence that the students were absolutely, emotionally affected by what they saw. That man, they believed, was a ghost; and try as I might, I could not sway them in the least. In all honesty, I had no evidence to offer them to the contrary.

My own thoughts regarding that experience are that if indeed my students saw the man, giving descriptions of his dress and facial features in full detail, and were not in any way thinking of such things as ghosts or goblins prior to visiting the fort, then what is the final answer? What is the explanation? I don't know where to go with this. I do believe that there are things unknown to us regarding the hereafter. No one can prove the existence of ghosts, but can anyone disprove them?"

CITY OF PUEBLO

With a population of 102,000, Pueblo—Spanish for 'town'—is situated on Interstate 25, along the Arkansas River, and at the east edge of the Rockies. To its west are the Wet Mountains and Lake Pueblo State Park.

To its east lie the vast plains.

In 1872, the Denver & Rio Grande Railroad staked a mark on the city that characterized the city, reforming the city from an agricultural-based economy into one of an industrial steel-base one. This new economic focus eventually developed Pueblo to become Colorado's third-largest city. In fact, due to the abundance of coal in the area, and steel mills, Pueblo was originally known as Steel City. Although the steel mills no longer remain, the town developed a master plan, working within a focus, and an infrastructure of innovative and progressive people-friendly guidelines.

An example of this is the $50 million Riverwalk project that includes retail shops and numerous entertainment outlets. This project has revitalized the city. In addition, the Pueblo Raptor Center is another project that houses rescued wild birds such as owls and eagles.

Pueblo also offers its residents something that is a rare sight indeed in the state—a swimming beach. In addition, Pueblo citizens enjoy their own zoo, complete with an antique carousel, and impressive restored Victorian neighborhoods. Also, the Sangre de Cristo Arts & Conference Center offers year-round activities. There is also an ongoing revitalization of Pueblo's Union Avenue Historic District, and a must-see spot is the completely revamped El Pueblo Museum, exalting the integrity of the many diverse cultures and people who have played a role in Pueblo's success.

Today, Pueblo shares many unique big city characteristics with Colorado's two larger cities in the area of arts, cultural events, restaurants and outdoor activities. In the fall, Pueblo sponsors a celebratory Chile & Frijole Festival, resplendent in the colors, pride and joy of its Hispanic population.

STEVEN KAKEMOTO'S (JAPANESE) STORY

Steven and I met for the purpose of this interview within a hotel lobby in Pueblo. Currently retired from his archeological work, Steven is today working on completing his book entitled, "Pit House Fire Rings of the Eastern Colorado Plains." Steven's face carries the lines of his profession, caused by years of working outdoors, amidst dirt, sunlight and wind. Steven joked about the number of added years the Colorado weather has forced on his 'young' 67-year-old face. "Kind of sexy. I'm a magnet for senior Japanese ladies," he told me.

As I began to touch on his personal story that he had experienced in Pueblo, he stopped me, then added, "This story I'm going to tell you is pretty interesting, but when you have more time, I'll tell you the stories about what I saw when I spent a year in Peru. Now you talk about ghost stories! The supernatural things that I saw digging in those mountains would scare the living daylights out of you!"

I added, "Yeah, Steven, I bet they might, but for the sake of argument, I can tell you that those mountains known as the Rockies, to the east of where we're now sitting, also have a fair share of their own scary moments." Steven answered, "When I begin my own book of Peruvian Ghost Stories, I'll look you up."

— Antonio

"I'm a retired professor of biology, and I've lived in Pueblo all my life. Having now lived here for 67 years, I've heard lots of stories about ghosts and haunted areas from local people. My own personal experience with a ghost took place when doing archeological excavations at what remained at Fort Pueblo, which I soon discovered was not much.

Briefly, the fort was constructed of adobe brick and built in 1842 on the northern side of the Arkansas River. Trappers established the fort, and in 1854 the Utes attacked and completely killed everyone within its walls. My job was to excavate and record any artifacts that could be found at a circumscribed, designated area of the fort. I began with this work in the spring of 1987.

Beforehand, I was told a story that the fort had a paranormal history of being haunted. That is to say, people reported such activity as a headless woman who is seen walking among the ruins. This story's legacy began at the time that the fort was actually inhabited. Whether true or not, as a historian, I took note of this. Well, when I began my work, I had a rotating staff of eight graduate students who I supervised at the site. The students would stake grid lines and take copious notes as instructed to do so, as dictated within the archeological process. This is very time-consuming work, and I would be the first to agree that it is often boring, but very necessary.

About a week or so into our project, we began to uncover little objects of merit. Such artifacts as bottles, metal spoons, clay pipes, and bits of broken pottery, or shards were placed aside. After a little more than a month of digging, we discovered the usual arrowhead or two, but soon we were filling a small paper bag with numerous arrowheads. Given the history of the fort's demise, this was evidence of a major battle that had been fought against the trappers and other inhabitants. Well, about this time is when things started to get a bit uneasy, in terms of the supernatural.

Due to the warm spring weather, at times we were digging late into the night. Well, it was one of these nights that two students began to strangely report that they felt someone was watching them as they did their work. One even reported that she had heard the disembodied, unmistakable voice of an elderly man say, 'Leave us alone.' Another student who understood a few words of the Ute language approached me to say that she had heard a voice speaking in an Indian sounding language, possibly Ute.

One day, as I was in the excavation pit, I glanced to my right side to reach for my small hand pick, spotted the pick, and noticed it move on its own! It gave a quick half-turn away from my reaching hand. After I immediately turned completely around, I heard a very deep voice make a laughing sound! This sent a shock of fear through me. I knew that I had just experienced something very unusual; something supernatural!

I decided to contact a friend of mine, Patricia, who worked as office secretary for the Catholic Pueblo Diocese.

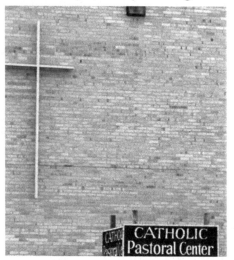

I thought she might offer some insight, or explanation on some level, regarding the occurrences that we had experienced. When I informed Patricia about this, she said she would inform a priest who she knew might have some answers.

Just a day later, I received a phone call from Father Tom. After introducing himself, he stated that he was also aware of the stories that had been told regarding the fort grounds being inhabited by spirits. Further, that he would like to offer his services the following Tuesday morning to bless the area, if I would be open to it. At that split second, I was unsure as to my answer, but I found the words to say, 'Yes, of course. Tuesday morning would be fine.'

That following Tuesday, Father Tom, myself, and three students were at the excavation pit. Two of the students were the women who had first approached me and spoke to me about their experiences.

The priest did his rite of blessing the area, then asked us to place a crucifix within the area where we would be working. We did this and since then we did not have any further problems.

Whether this blessing actually worked or not is difficult to prove, but all I can report is that for the remainder of our work, we did not have another supernatural experience at the site."

SITE OF TAYLOR

The town of Taylor is so small that it doesn't even merit a 'dot' on most maps. But, rest assured, Taylor does exist. Today, Taylor's only 'inhabitants' are just a sparse sprinkling of structures, mostly very old homesteads that have fallen into disrepair. Located on state Highway 145, within the area of Taylor Mesa, not many 'living' individuals can call this lonely place home.

It's anyone's guess when Taylor was homesteaded. Most likely ranchers or farmers must have attempted to carve an unsuccessful living from its soil. Today, Taylor's uneventful history has been long forgotten.

NICANOR DOMINGO'S (HISPANIC) STORY

I met with Nicanor at his home in the town of Dolores. His 88 years of living a sometimes-difficult life have clearly left their mark on his weathered, but noble face. Nicanor still keeps a small chicken coop with six hens and one very old rooster in his backyard. Nicanor preferred that I conduct the interview in Spanish, the language he converses best in. I obliged his request, and as it turned out, was rewarded with one of my most memorable interviews.

Nicanor openly spoke of his childhood, his years in the army, and present, pending death. His doctor, he mentioned, informed him not long ago that he has inoperable lung cancer, and won't make it through the end of this year. Not appearing to be swayed by this information, Nicanor stated to me, "Oh, doctors—what do they know. The only one who can give, or take, life is God. I'll let Him decide for me when I need to die — not a doctor."

— Antonio

"I was born in 1918 and raised in Dolores, Colorado, but every opportunity my brother and I got to visit my grandparents' little ranch in Taylor, well, we were overjoyed. I still remember my father hitching up the mule wagon and off we'd go. We'd stop and visit with friends and a few relatives along the way, and sometimes spend the night. When we arrived at my Grandpa and Grandma's house they were always very happy to see us. Upon our return trip home, our wagon was loaded up with canned peaches, meats, and vegetables. Those were happy and simple times for us. But make no mistake; making a living from the land was backbreaking work. I worked with my father on our own small ranch for many years, even after his death in 1967.

Today, there's nothing left of the village of Taylor, nothing but broken-down barns and what's left of the few houses that once were people's shelters. It's sad to see, but time does pass us by, and then leaves us with only memories to remember. But that's enough about my history. If I continue on like this, I know that I'll begin to bore everyone who's reading this story. So now I'll tell you about my story that took place at my grandparents' ranch in the early 1960's.

When I was about 18 years old, I had a best friend named David. He and I would go fishing, hunting and just do a lot of things together. David's family knew my grandparents very well. One day, my grandparents invited David and me to spend a summer month at their ranch. I think it was August. Anyway, I told my grandmother that we would do that. Then she asked us if we could take care of the ranch and animals while they both went away to visit my aunt in Alamosa, Colorado. We agreed to do that too, and felt great about being alone for a whole month. We were both very knowledgeable about ranch living and caring for chickens, cows, and horses. This was before telephones and television. We didn't even have any electricity—we used kerosene lamps!

When we arrived, we divided the chores between the two of us, and soon settled into a routine. It felt great to see how we could accomplish the responsibilities of ranch living. It was hard work, and didn't leave us with much time for playing around, but knowing that my grandparents were also going to give us a little pay for taking care of the ranch was really great.

Well, David and I would finish doing what we had to do for the day at around 6 p.m. After that we had free time. One of those days, I decided to quit early and took the rifle and went hunting for some rabbits up in the woods behind the ranch. David decided to stay at the house and play cards with a friend of his who was visiting from Dolores. I told them that I'd be back before sundown, and asked David to get the wood stove going at around that time, because we were going to have rabbit for dinner. Then off I went. Remember, it was early in the day, and there was still plenty of daylight. I walked about a mile or so into the woods. There were maybe about three other families that lived in Taylor at the time, but none of their properties bordered the rear of my grandparents' property, so it was open, wild land for as far as anyone cared to hike.

I had already shot two rabbits, so I decided to turn around and return to the house. I knew I'd find at least one or two more rabbits on my way back. Suddenly, I heard a loud noise coming from my left. I thought it might be an elk or bear; it was that loud. I stooped down, laying low in the ground. The gun I had was a simple rifle that was fine for shooting rabbits, but to shoot an elk, or bear, it was not going to cut it. My rifle was no match for those large animals.

I heard the branches breaking and something coming, something large, making its way towards where I was. Then they came into view, a pack of about eight or ten coyotes that were walking in a single, long row. They were walking in a single line, but most unusual was that they were swinging their heads from side to side! I stood still.

This didn't last very long because they seemed to be focused on a direct course of travel. They passed by me without ever giving me any indication that they knew I was crouching there—just a few yards away. I was definitely confused by them. Coyotes are very wary of people, and I, thus far, had crossed paths numerous times with coyotes in my life — usually having to chase or shoot them for killing livestock. So I found this behavior to be very, very strange.

I finally did make it back to the house that evening, and managed to shoot another rabbit for dinner. I described the coyotes to David and his friend, and both of them began to laugh, and their ribbing went on into the night. So, I just decided not to tell anyone else about my experience from then on.

That night, I needed to get out of bed and head for the outhouse. As I was making my way back to the house, I saw two strange balls of light in the distance bouncing about the trees. One was slightly larger than the other, which was about two or three feet round. They weren't very bright, but just bright enough to be visible. I walked to the front door and stood looking at them from the safety of the inside of the house.

They moved faster than I thought. Soon they were flying by the side of the house and then across the dirt road that led up from the main road to the house. This all took place within about four or five minutes.

169

Very quickly as the balls moved to the main road, they made a curve upward, and disappeared into the sky. I felt very strange and couldn't figure out if I was going through some weird kind of mental sickness of some sort. In the morning, because of the fun the guys had made of me earlier in the day, I decided not to tell them about the two balls of lights.

I rose up, early as usual, and went to the chicken coop to feed the chickens and gather eggs. We had a few newly hatched chicks, so I needed to crack dried corn into smaller pieces in an old, metal hand-grinder to feed them. As I was doing this, I heard someone at the chicken coop's door calling my grandfather's name. I knew it wasn't David, or his friend, because I saw through the wire mesh that there were three Indians standing outside—a man and two women.

I stopped what I was doing and walked over to see what they wanted. The women were dressed in long skirts and the man was carrying a large bag. They said that they were on their way to meet some relatives in the town of Mancos, and wanted to know if I could help them with something to eat. They said that my grandfather knew them, and he would always give them some food. The man said that they had even camped out on the property a couple of times before.

I told them that my grandparents were not home, but that I'd give them some leftover rabbit and corn stew, tortillas, and a few boiled eggs. They were happy with that. They also told me they were not Utes, but Jicarilla Apaches. They spoke very good Spanish, and in a short time we were conversing about my grandparents, and how welcoming they had always been to them. Then, before they left, one of the women took a beaded necklace from around her neck and placed it into my hand. The other woman reached into her pocket and brought out a thin strip of leather that had a small piece of abalone shell attached to it, which was also a necklace.

At that point I felt compelled and secure enough to tell them about my two experiences with the coyotes, and the balls of light. They became very still. The younger of the two women gave a strange look to the man. He said, 'Be careful, and do not tell anyone else about what you have seen. Those things are spirits, and the spirits are powerful beings. Keep to yourself the offerings they are giving you. Stay inside at night. They want to use you. If you do this, you'll grow to a very old age, but you'll need to remember these things. Remember your experiences, because the spirit beings will be following you throughout your life.' I couldn't think of a response, so I simply answered, 'Yes, yes I'll do that.' They soon said goodbye, and continued on their way walking down the road to Mancos.

When my grandparents returned three weeks later, they had brought gifts; for me a pair of black leather shoes, and for David, a long-sleeved shirt. When I had the opportunity to be alone with my grandparents, I told them about their three Indian friends who had paid their home a visit in their absence. They immediately answered, 'Nicanor, what Indian friends? We have never had any Indians visit and stay with us!' I described to them the Apache man and two women, and they said that they had never had any Apache Indians stay with them. I answered, 'Well, maybe they confused you with someone else.'

I didn't know what to make of all that I had experienced at my grandparents' ranch that month, but it did leave me with a lot to think about in the following years to come. I never told anyone aside from my immediate family about the coyotes, the balls of lights and the three Indians. I don't know what these 'signs' were all about, or why I was told to keep quiet, but now that I'm an old man, I don't think it will do much harm for me to tell you about it.

These things happened to me more than 70 years ago, and I still remember how it felt to see them. I remember my youth spent at my grandparents' ranch, the sunlight, the work and good times. But one thing that I'll never forget are the spirits I saw, and the three Apache spirits that visited me that day. And you know, I still have the necklaces they gave me."

CITY OF DENVER

Colorado's capital city at an elevation of 5,280 ft. is also referred to as the 'Mile High City.' Contained within its city limits can be found an array of entertainment, shopping, and performing arts. At a glance,

Denver's metro area covers over 4,500 square miles with a current population of over 3 million.

Historically, the Denver area was the gathering place of several Native American Nations including the Lakota, Ute, Cheyenne, Apache, Crow, and Arapaho.

Due to all the riches that were extracted from within the mountains of Colorado, Denver became a very wealthy place to call home. Very ostentatious mansions, tree-lined avenues and boulevards were, at the time, commonplace. Just one of Denver's notable personalities was the quick-witted 'unsinkable' Molly Brown, who entered American folklore by miraculous and unpredictable chance when she survived the sinking of the ocean liner, the Titanic.

Denver's International Airport is the largest commercial airport in the world, and the 18th busiest in the world.

The city's excellent outdoor amenities, city parks, museums, gardens, and natural attractions, together with a very fine urban trail system—perhaps the best in the nation—and uniquely diverse neighborhoods enhances the richness of the whole community named Denver.

WEMBLEY PARK DOG TRACK

Wembley Park was a greyhound-racing track located four miles north of downtown Denver. The track featured conference facilities and numerous racing events throughout the year. It closed in 2008.

RAY SANDOVAL'S (HISPANIC) STORY

Ray and I met at his home, where the interview was conducted. Ray expressed his curiosity for all things paranormal. He showed me his collection of videotapes, DVDs, and books he has collected over the years, all on the subject of ghosts and such. I was already familiar with several of these items in his collection. I openly expressed my thoughts to Ray regarding the importance of maintaining a skeptical and cautious attitude when viewing or reading anything related to the field of the supernatural.

Because there are so many disingenuous individuals who claim to be 'experts' in the field, they easily coerce sincere people seeking answers, believing anything these 'experts' offer as 'fact.' I'd like to think that I assisted Ray in his personal journey of spiritual development.

Foremost, I sternly suggested that if he wished to pursue a positive focus of understanding the paranormal, he would first need to remove the Ouija board he so highly prized from his home. Such tools as this 'open doors,' and the great majority of these doors, so to speak, lead to terrible, negative consequences.

I hope I assisted Ray on some level. Given Ray's personal story that follows, I can sense that he is a gifted and insightful individual who has the ability to 'tap into' this area of study.

— Antonio

"My family has lived in Denver for three generations. I was born and raised in Denver. In the year 1967 I joined the army, and at the end of

my military service, I lived in Fremont, California, for a total of eight years before eventually returning to Denver. My own personal ghost story took place about ten years ago, during the month of July, right over in the area of the dog runs, by a grove of trees. I had been working at the track for four years, as a member of the park's maintenance team. Before starting my employment at the park, I was a cook at a local Denny's restaurant. The restaurant I worked at was located close to my apartment, but because of a chronic illness, I was forced to quit my job and seek other possibilities of employment — hopefully one with health insurance coverage. I was told about an opening at the dog track, and after submitting my application, was hired on a part-time basis. I began as a full-time employee one year later.

Before having witnessed my ghostly experience, I had never seen or experienced anything like that before. I have to say that the whole experience has convinced me that there are things we, the living, have to accept. We need to respect the spirit world. I've definitely changed my view of the afterlife after having had my own experience at the park.

My experience began one night during the month of July, at around 10 p.m. I was already working full-time, and because I was a fairly new employee, I was given the least desirable shift, between 8 p.m. and 4 a.m. I was in the area of the track that I described earlier, cleaning up a large area of ground.

At the time, I was busy with my work and was wearing a set of earphones, listening to music on my portable CD player. Suddenly, something caught my eye. A small, strange ball of light came shooting over from behind my right side, and zoomed past in front of me. Thinking it must be someone shooting a firework, I took a few quick steps, sought cover, and stooped to the ground, and quickly scrambled behind my maintenance vehicle.

I removed my earphones and waited to hear the ensuing exploding sound. Instead, I witnessed another flying orb that came and disappeared in the same area. It both traveled and disappeared without making any sound. I was totally surprised and left wondering, 'Where did they come from?' and 'What were they?' I knew I had not imagined the strange lights that I had just seen. No other employee was in the area with me at the time, so I was unable to confirm with another person what I'd just seen. I kept this information to myself for a few weeks, and hoped that would be the end of the flying lights.

About two months later, another incident took place that made the flying lights I'd seen before seem like child's play. One evening, as I was sitting in my truck, and at about the same time as my first experience, I noticed the movement of lights coming from the area where the previous ones had traveled. These new lights were moving back and forth, from tree to bush and back. They were about three feet from the ground and would leave a trail of light as they moved. There were about three to four of them. It was difficult for me to tell how many there were because they would disappear behind each tree.

Because I was at a distance from them, I didn't feel as apprehensive as I had the first time I witnessed them. This time I took the opportunity to study the lights and I even enjoyed the show. The little light tails they'd leave as they traveled through the air only lasted a few seconds, and resembled the tail of a comet. Suddenly, I heard my name called out, 'Ray, what's that?' A fellow employee and friend named Armando was calling to me from inside one of the buildings. Armando was also looking at the lights as he was standing at a window. I made a gesture with my hands for him to come outside and see for himself. We both stood next to each other and watched the light show, for just under a minute or so.

After it was over, we decided to cautiously take a walk over to the trees and attempt to discover what evidence we might find, if any. We searched the area, and with our flashlights looked up and down the trunks of the trees, under the bushes, and along the tree limbs. And discovered nothing at all.

Armando was from Mexico and he mentioned that in the small town where he grew up, there are lights similar to these that have been spotted for many years in the surrounding hills and mountains. The people in his town believe that the lights are the souls of Indians who are continuously maintaining a watchful stronghold on their lands. I myself didn't have any explanation for the lights, so without another explanation all I could do was to agree with Armando's explanation. The following morning, after ending my shift and getting into bed, I had the strangest dream I have ever had.

I dreamt that a strange woman visited me. This woman appeared strange because of the dark, violet light that surrounded her figure. In my dream, she was weeping loudly and for some unusual reason, I approached her. The woman walked quickly away from me and I ran after her. I quickly caught up with her as she ran to a grouping of trees, similar to the trees where I had witnessed the flying lights, and I grabbed her arm. I could feel the icy coldness of her skin as she violently struggled for me to let go. Just then, I heard in the distance, the voices of many people crying, coming from all around the trees and bushes. My attention was quickly focused back on the woman whose arm I was holding. She suddenly fell to the ground and stopped struggling. It was then that I noticed how wrinkled and age-spotted her arm was, giving me no indication whatsoever of having any life. I was just holding onto a dead arm! I felt a heavy feeling come over me, something like an overwhelming sense of sadness. I dropped her arm and suddenly awoke from my dream, crying. I opened my eyes and stared at the ceiling of my room for several minutes, thinking over and over about the dream. Going over the whole dream in my mind, I stayed awake for an hour or so, before falling back to sleep.

I haven't seen any more of the flying lights, or know of anyone else who has had the experience that Armando and I witnessed. I don't know what to think about the dream's meaning other than perhaps in years past, an Indian massacre might have taken place in that area. That's what Armando suggested to me when I described my dream to him. Until now, both of us have kept our experiences with the flying lights to ourselves. I don't expect the flying lights, or any other strange things will start up as before, but you never can tell. I've also not had another strange dream about the ghost woman, so I hope they've settled down, or even moved on."

BUFFALO BILL MUSEUM

Born in Oakley, Kansas, and laid to rest in Lookout Mountain within

the Colorado town outskirts of Golden, the museum pays a lasting tribute to this legendary man, who died in 1917 at his sister's house in Denver.

KIMARY A. MARCHAESE'S (ANGLO) STORY

I interviewed Kimary outside the museum walls where we sat on a picnic table, surrounded by the magnificent, panoramic vistas that surround the museum's perch-top location. Kimary was very knowledgeable, sharing her own personal religious beliefs and describing to me how they have provided her with the strength to withstand any demonic or evil influence.

After our interview was completed, I was given a short but adequate tour of the museum itself. The museum contains a better-than-average collection of artifacts and related memorabilia, much of it significant to the history of not only the west, but also the nation. I would highly recommend that if the opportunity ever comes your way, that you

definitely make it a point to visit this museum. The museum staff, and a ghost, or two, or three, would appreciate your visit.

— Antonio

"My position at the museum is Exhibit Coordinator and Artist. I was born in California and raised in Hawaii, and arrived in Colorado in 1978 to attend college. During the period that I was attending school, I obtained a job at the museum, and have since been employed at the museum for a total of 14 years.

Admittedly, I was not familiar with the stories of ghosts, which I discovered later exist in the museum, but that soon changed. During my first month of work at the museum, I had a conversation with the museum's curator who is named Jan. Jan expressed to me her concern regarding how uncomfortable she felt during those times when she would be working alone in the building. As we talked a little more, Jan informed me that these uncomfortable feelings originated from the strange events she herself had experienced within the building. Small items would move about with a seemingly will of their own, and sometimes she would even hear the 'clinking' of spurs, as if a cowboy would be walking the halls. Finally, she added that she was always aware of feeling the presence of Buffalo Bill's spirit, who would be watching her every move.

Another employee named Keith Allen also worked at the property. Keith was a city employee of Denver's Parks and Recreation. Sadly, six years ago Keith was killed in a car accident. Keith was one man who took a keen interest in the paranormal experiences that visitors would regularly report having had at the museum. He informed and described to me on several occasions the things he himself would see on the property. Because Keith not only worked, but also lived on the property, he had the advantage of spending a fair amount of time discussing the topic of ghosts with the public. Keith lived within the building named 'Pahauska.' Today, the structure is used as the museum's gift and snack shop. Pahauska, in the Native Lakota language, is a word that translates to 'long hair.' Long Hair was the name given to Buffalo Bill by the Lakota. Keith was a museum interpreter of Buffalo Bill's life, and would dress the part of Buffalo Bill, in full costume.

Many of these experiences that were reported to Keith would take place at Buffalo Bill's actual graveside. That grave is located just a short walk to the south of the museum. The most frequent spiritual events that were reported to him were the sounds of a man's booted footsteps wearing spurs, 'clinking' about the graveside. Employees and visitors within the museum itself have reported these same sounds. Keith told me that the visitors stressed to him that they were absolutely telling him the truth; that they were not making such a thing up. Keith stated to me that the serious tone in their voices was very convincing.

One evening, Keith had his own funny encounter, as he was returning to the museum from an event in town. For the fundraiser, he was required to dress in an interpretation of Buffalo Bill's full costume. As he got out of his car, and walked toward the Pahauska building where he lived, he heard the sound of voices coming from the area where Buffalo Bill's graveside is located. Keith decided to walk up to the site to see what was going on. Arriving at the graveside, he told me that he heard the loud screams and shouts of teens as they scrambled into the woods. Keith had unknowingly surprised these naive teenagers, who by coincidence had been conducting a séance in their attempt to contact the spirit of Buffalo Bill! When these teenagers spotted Keith approaching them wearing his full costume, they apparently believed that Keith was Buffalo Bill's spirit and scampered willy-nilly into the woods!

An unusual and unique tradition that the public has been engaged in for many years is to leave coins on Bill's grave. For the purpose of discovery, the museum staff has researched this unusual habit, and found that years ago someone began to toss buffalo nickels upon the grave's stone. Today, since the buffalo nickel is no longer being made, regular nickel and other coins are tossed. This tradition is a curiously odd one, and seems to be thoroughly enjoyed by the public. The museum benefits from this by regularly gathering up the coins that are added together with the money that is raised for the general museum education fund.

If you happen to look at the reverse of an original buffalo nickel, you'll spot the side view portrait of a Native American. A very good friend of Buffalo Bill's was a Native American called Iron Tail. Iron Tail was employed and performed within Bill's Wild West Show. It is assumed that this Indian man's likeness was the model that was most likely used for the nickel's portrait.

Another item that is tossed onto the grave are bobby pins. The tradition of doing this dictates that single women who toss bobby pins on Bill's grave will soon find a husband. I personally know of a group of six women who visited the museum. They walked to the graveside and all but one woman tossed a bobby pin. Within the year, all were engaged to be married—all but one!

A local newspaper got wind of this and ran with the story. The paper soon sponsored an event at the museum that coincided with the anniversary of Buffalo Bill's death. The women were invited to return to the graveside with a handful of bobby pins. The women complied, at which time bobby pins were distributed to the gathered crowd for the purpose of tossing pins on the grave. I personally got into the action that day, and also tossed a bobby pin. I don't know if it will do any good, so you'll have to check back with me in about a year's time to see if it actually worked.

Strangely, most of the ghostly events the public experiences tend to take place at closing time. Of course, as I stated before, some of our employees who work alone within the museum do report unusual activity. I also have, and do work alone many times at the museum. Personally, I'm not afraid of spirits, because my personal religious beliefs

tell me not to be. I do, however, believe that such things do exist, but truthfully, I'm not scared. I know that nothing evil or negative is in the building, so that gives me comfort."

ALBERT HALBERSTAM'S (ANGLO) STORY

Due to having given short notice for the interview, this story is another one of a few I've had to conduct on the spot, inside a vehicle. I met Albert mid-way as he was leaving for a job assignment, and it was necessary to make adjustments. Fortunately, the Halberstam's car had sufficient space for Albert and me and my recording material. Admittedly, spirits do have a practice of attaching themselves to objects and places, but thankfully Albert's young daughter has not carried any negative effects from her own encounter at the museum. As for Albert, he's not saying.

— Antonio

"I was born, raised, and still live in Denver. Close to three years ago, my wife, Wendy, and I decided to take our nine-year-old daughter on a weekend outing to the Buffalo Bill Museum. We were not ready to, or expecting to, have a ghost manifest itself to us, but that's what actually took place. Our experience happened down in the basement, where the museum's stuffed buffalo is displayed.

As Wendy and I were taking our time strolling through the numerous displays and reading the informational descriptions, our daughter, Christine, let go of my hand and made a beeline directly towards the display of the stuffed buffalo. The stuffed buffalo is roughly about five feet tall from hoof to shoulder, and is surrounded by a wood fence. Because of its realism, I could understand how it might be very attractive to both children and adults. As was the case, my daughter ran right to it.

Keeping a close eye on our daughter, we watched her fascination with the display as she took her time scrutinizing each inch of the animal. At the time, Wendy was marveling at a glass case where a number of Native American artifacts were displayed. I decided to walk into one small room where I heard what I thought was the recorded voice of a man describing something. His voice had the effect of being very sure of itself, and direct. Somewhat commanding.

Upon entering the room, I found it to be empty. I quickly glanced around the displays, hoping to find a button that would enable me to press it and listen to the pre-recorded tape. Nothing.

I thought this was very unusual, because I had actually heard the voice of a man talking in the room. Stranger still, while this thought was going through my mind, I began to feel a sudden weakness come over me, almost as if I were about to faint. Then the lights started to flicker off and on. As an unusual coldness came over the room, enveloping my shoulders, I quickly walked out of there and approached my wife who was looking at a display of rifles. 'I don't know what's going on, but I suddenly don't feel very well. I'm going to step outside for a little fresh air,' I said to Wendy.

As I walked over to the buffalo, to ask Christine if she wanted to accompany me outside, I spotted her standing and staring at the bottom of a ramp that led up to the first floor. I asked her what she was looking at and she answered, 'The tall man with the hat.' I looked down the ramp, and not spotting anyone, I asked her, 'Christine, where is he? I don't see him.' She answered, 'Daddy, he's waving to us, over there, see?'

I got the weirdest feeling that is difficult to explain. I imagine it must have been fear because I took hold of my daughter's hand and walked over to Wendy. I said, 'Honey, I think we need to go outside. I'll tell you what's going on after we're outdoors.' Wendy gave me a strange look of apprehension, but didn't argue. As we exited the museum, I explained to Wendy what I had experienced in the room, and about the man in the hat Christine had seen. Not wanting to appear alarmed, we spoke in soft tones to

Christine and asked her to tell us all about the man she had seen.

Christine responded in her innocent voice, 'He told me that buffaloes are dangerous, and I should never go out to the corral alone. I told him we don't have a corral, and he walked away. That's all he said.'

Not wanting to give her any ideas, or scare her, we didn't press her with any further questioning. I glanced at Wendy and she smiled back at me, indicating that she understood. We decided to head back home and not mention the man with the hat to Christine again. Before we headed to the car, I told Wendy that I was going to use the bathroom.

Instead of going to the bathroom, I walked over to the front desk of the museum's entrance and spoke to a woman. I asked her if there was a costumed man wearing a hat that was walking about the place. She answered that there was no one fitting that description, or any man dressed in a costume in the museum. 'Are you sure?' I asked. 'Yes, yes,' she answered. Then hesitating a bit, while looking at me straight in the eyes she said, 'Why, did you see our ghost?' 'Nah,' I said, 'just wondering.' Then I walked away.

Well, that's all I can tell you about what I personally experienced, and what my daughter saw at the museum. It's not that frightening, but it's still a little scary, don't you think?"

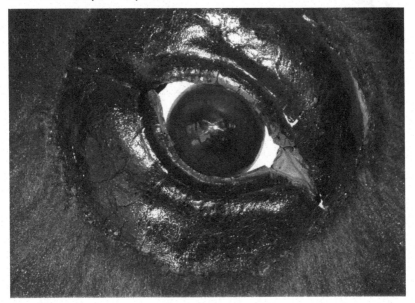

NEW MEXICO

here is something magical about the landscape of New Mexico that must be savored. Although the desert areas might appear harsh and hostile at first glance, a closer examination will find it teeming with plant and animal life, revealing unexpected beauty. It is possible to unlock some of its secrets and experience some of its surprises just by getting off main roads and taking the time walk, to look, listen and explore any number of lonely pueblo roads. Perhaps, the desert might be coaxed to reveal its mysteriousness when taking an evening stroll during a full moon when the sagebrush is alive with the sudden, darting shadows of who-knows-what. There's no need to be alarmed by the mournful cry of the wind, or the slithering sound of an occasional rattlesnake making its way along the desert ground. After all, these are just what you'd expect to find in the desert and mountains of New Mexico. But, wait! ... has anyone ever mentioned the other realm of life, that dimension that exists beyond the shadows of a lone flickering

candle, the unfamiliar eyes that gaze out from between the cascading bouquets of wilted casket flowers, the shadows that adhere to memory as cemetery mud to a shovel, or the nightfall that sometimes blesses and sometimes curses? Come walk down that old reservation road, listen and be alert for what might frighten, but what will most definitely make its presence known to you. There, look at that clump of sagebrush over by that ancient cottonwood tree, where the arroyo suddenly drops down from sight. Did you see that shadowy Indian woman giving off a glowing aura of green light? She's calling to you, extending a long skeletal finger motioning for you to follow her down into that dark arroyo. Now she's grinning a large smile exposing teeth so large and yellow they appear to be horse-like. You say you don't see her; you don't believe? Well, just read the following stories and see if these Native New Mexican stories are simply nothing more than campfire smoke.

ACOMA PUEBLO

The 'People of the White Rock,' or Acoma, Ah'-ku-me, are located on a sandstone mesa 367 feet above the surrounding desert valley. Acoma is also known as Sky City, and is one the oldest continuously inhabited

Native American villages in the United States. These pueblo people have a history of producing some of the finest examples of red-and-black-on-white pottery to be found.

The pueblo's first contact with Europeans took place in 1540. These Spaniards were initially a part of Coronado's expedition.

In the year 1599 the barbarous Spanish territorial governor, Juan de Oñate, slaughtered over 800 pueblo inhabitants who were defending their homes from his forced demand of tribute and supplies. The hundreds who survived were equally brutally mistreated. Today, close to 6,000 pueblo descendants live on the reservation, and over 30 families still occupy the Sky City Village year-round. Sky City Casino, owned and operated by the Pueblo of Acoma, also provides the revenue needed to develop the quality of life for these proud and historically rich people.

ROBERTA WHIRLWIND'S (ACOMA) STORY

Without giving any additional information as to her residential location within the pueblo, Roberta's interview was conducted after hours, within one of the pueblo's school rooms. Roberta spoke of experiencing many spiritual things aside from this one story. Roberta stated, "Jealousy spurring attacks of witchcraft from family to family and from friend to friend has damaged a few relationships on the pueblo. It's so sad to comprehend how this all got started, but you know people are people and just 'cause you're Indian doesn't shield you from some negative, universal human traits. Money and its controlling power can be a strong force to combat. Some of us forget this until it becomes too late."

— Antonio

"My ghost haunting happened to my mother and me on the reservation when I was nineteen years old. The last thing we ever expected to experience was a ghost. But that's exactly what took place one summer day. I remember at the time, I was in our living room watching a soap on the television. My mother was in the bedroom caring for my baby brother when our two dogs began to bark. I thought a stranger was walking up to the house. I waited for a knock on the door, but there was none. I got up to look out the window. I looked around the yard, but saw no one. Soon the dogs stopped their barking. About an hour later, again the dogs began to bark.

This time there was a knock at the front door. My mother asked, 'Who's there?' and a familiar friend's voice answered, 'It's me, Sonia.' Sonia was a seventeen-year-old school friend of mine who lived several miles away. I got up to open the door to let her in. I asked, 'Didn't you tell me you were going to Albuquerque with your father today?' Sonia answered, 'Yeah, but my father's plans changed.' I spotted dirt and dust on both her left leg and forearm, and her hair was also dirty. I asked her about this and she said, surprisingly, 'Oh, really? I'm sorry.'

Sonia then turned her attention away from me and began to speak with my mother about how pretty my mother's dress was. I thought her behavior was strange because Sonia was not that much of a talker, and she never spoke to me about such things as dress patterns. I was especially suspicious of her when she began to talk to my mother about how much she missed her own mother, who had died when she was only two years old. Sonia was not the type of person who would even hint at discussing her mother's death. I know it was an emotionally painful subject for her, so I would not ever bring it up. But now here she was in my house, talking easily to my mother and me about her mother. This was too strange for me. I knew that something was not right with Sonia. I asked her if she wanted a drink of pop or water. She refused, saying, 'No, thanks. I'm not thirsty.' Again, I thought this was strange behavior because it was a hot summer day and she looked like she had been walking for a long while.

Sonia and my mother spoke for about an hour in our kitchen while I continued to watch television. I didn't feel like joining their conversation because one soap followed the next, and I didn't want to miss my stories. But soon, Sonia said that it was time for her to leave. I asked her if she wanted to wait for a ride home from a neighbor's son, who would be returning home from work in an hour. But she refused, saying, 'I need to take care of many visits before I leave to go home.' I looked at my mother, who made a hidden sign to me with her head, indicating to let her go on her way. Right before Sonia left our house, she smiled, and said, 'It makes me happy to see you both again. I think of you all the time.' I don't remember how I answered her, but I think I said something like, 'Take care of yourself, and don't fall down any more.' Sonia smiled and walked out the door. My mother and I watched her as she walked down the road and dis- appeared in the distance. My mother spoke first, 'I don't know what it is, but I got a strange feeling from Sonia. Is she doing all right? She's not on drugs, is she?' I said, 'I don't think so.'

I didn't hear from Sonia for two days, until I met a friend driving on the road on the way to buy some groceries. As our cars approached each other, he waved at me to stop. He asked me if I had heard that Sonia and her father had been in a car accident on their way to Albuquerque, and that Sonia had died. I was shocked! I told him that she had just visited us two days before. He looked at me strangely and said, 'Are you sure it was two days ago, because the accident happened at 10 a.m. two days ago.' I knew that Sonia had visited my house at around 3 pm that day, several hours after the accident! I decided to keep Sonia's visit a secret, so I acted confused about the dates. I said good-bye to my friend and instead of driving on to the grocery store, I turned the car around and drove straight home. I cried all the way home. I cried so much that I had to stop the car and pull myself together. Sonia's spirit had paid me a visit and I didn't even realize it. I miss her so much. Whenever my mother and I go to church we always say a special prayer for her. It's been over seventeen years since my friend visited my house. I have not experienced any more visits or noises, or anything like a haunting. I know she is at peace, but I still miss her very much."

SANTO DOMINGO (GUIWA) PUEBLO

The Santo Domingo Pueblo is best known because of its people's skill in jewelry-making. They produce some of the finest examples of this art to be found, and are rivaled only by their traditional art of pottery making. The Native name of this pueblo is Giuwa. The people are friendly but generally considered the most conservative of the pueblos in terms of customs and ceremonies, which they closely guard. This cautiousness has helped the pueblo maintain a high degree of religious and tribal unity.

In 1886, a disastrous flood leveled a major portion of the pueblo that included the original adobe church and homes. Four years later, the community constructed a new church, which stands today in the pueblo's central plaza. History records that Spaniards led by Oñate in 1598 and de Vargas in 1694 were intent on claiming the pueblo and its land for the Crown of Spain. Obviously, the pueblo resisted such audacity. Today, the pueblo is proud to declare its historic role against the Spaniards in the Great Pueblo Revolt of 1680. They are to be admired and appreciated.

Present day finds the inhabitants of Santo Domingo Pueblo continuing their craftwork, and moving into the modern world of computers and various facets of technology.

JOSEPH NIGHTWALKER'S (SANTO DOMINGO) STORY

I conducted Joseph's interview one day during a two hour drive from Santa Fe to Taos. With the tape recorder placed between us on the seat, he freely described his and his wife, Ruby's experience at a bed and breakfast in Santa Fe. Take from his story what you will, but remember that sometimes all our attachment to what used to be our home, can prove to be so strong that even after death we find it difficult to move on.

— Antonio

"My experience with a ghost took place in Santa Fe six years ago. My wife, Ruby, and I wanted to get away for a couple of days, and wanted to stay in an upscale hotel. Because of our last minute plans, we found out that all the hotels were booked up. Our second choice was to look into staying at a bed and breakfast. Santa Fe, among other things, is a city known for its excellent accommodations. An employee at the Hotel St. Francis recommended that we contact the 'Adobe Guest House' on the south of town. Ruby called, spoke to the owner, Antonio, and booked the room. The bed and breakfast was very nice. The large house had four rooms; our room was located down a long hallway at the front of the house. During our check-in, Antonio handed us a sheet of paper that described the history of the house. Then he showed us to our room. As Ruby unpacked the suitcase, I started a fire within the kiva fireplace. We got comfortable and I began reading the informational sheet that we were given at check-in. A family named Martinez built the house in the early 1920's, and it was the first adobe house built in that part of Santa Fe. I read that the house was bought from the Martinez family by the first female archeologist of New Mexico, Dr. Burtha Dutton. The two men who now owned the house bought it from Dr. Dutton. I remember these details because, being an artist myself, I knew about Dr. Dutton and the stories about her association with the well-known artist, Georgia O'Keeffe. So these two names certainly are not easy for me to forget. I put the sheet of paper back on the nightstand, and my wife and I took a short nap.

About 45 minutes later, Ruby and I woke up and drove into town for our dinner reservation. After dinner it started to snow, slow at first, then harder and harder. We walked around the Santa Fe plaza, window-shopping, but when we saw how heavy the snow was falling, we decided to call it a night and drive back to the B&B. When we got back to the room, I looked out the window and saw about a foot of snow covering the ground. I also noticed that there were four other cars parked in the parking spaces. There was a full house at the B&B. Ruby and I got into bed, and we quickly fell asleep at about 10 p.m.

I was awakened suddenly from my sleep when I heard the sound of breaking glass coming from down the hallway. I looked at my watch and saw that it was 3 a.m. I turned to see if the sound had also awakened Ruby. She was sound asleep. When I didn't hear any more noise, I thought that I had imagined it. I closed my eyes, and soon I heard the sound of footsteps walking down the hallway towards our room. I kept quiet. As the footsteps got closer, I heard them stop at the other side of our door as the doorknob slowly began to turn. By this time I was wide-awake and was fully aware of what was going on. I kept my eyes focused on the doorknob, but because of the darkness, I only heard the knob turning, but couldn't see it actually turn. Then the strangest thing happened. I saw a white misty figure come right through the door! It didn't have any particular shape; it was just like drifting smoke. I decided to wake Ruby, so I hit her side with my right elbow. As she woke up, I whispered to her to look in the direction of the door. The smoke then started to change into the outline of a small woman! Ruby saw the same thing and spoke, 'It's a ghost, Joseph!' Then she pulled the covers over her head. I guess I found my courage, because I yelled out to the image, 'Get away, and get out of here!' The ghost took two steps towards our bed. I grabbed my pillow and threw it at the ghost, then reached over and turned on the light. As soon as I turned on the light, the ghost disappeared!

Both Ruby and I slept with the light on the rest of that night. In the morning at the breakfast table, I asked the owners of the B&B, Antonio and Hank, if the house was haunted. They looked at each other, then at me and answered, 'Not that we're aware of. No one has ever mentioned anything about ghosts in the house. Why do you ask?' As Ruby and I told them about our experience the night before, the other guests seated at the table began to tell their own similar experiences hearing loud sounds.

Although the others didn't mention seeing any ghosts, they all said they heard the sound of breaking glass, and a few even mentioned hearing footsteps in the hallway. Ruby got nervous talking about the ghosts, and asked us to change the subject. We finished our breakfast and went back to our room. Some of the guests returned to their rooms, while others drove off to explore the sights of Santa Fe.

After a few minutes passed, there was a knock on our door. I opened it and Antonio was standing there asking if he could talk to us. I invited him in. He started to tell us a little bit more about the house. He had a nervous smile on his face, and then apologized for not being totally honest with us at breakfast. As he put it, 'I didn't want to upset the other

 guests who might be a bit sensitive about such a subject.' But now he wanted to set the record straight and admit that the guesthouse was haunted, and yes, there have been several other guests who have seen ghosts in the house, including himself. He said the previous owner, archaeologist Dr. Dutton, kept a collection of American Indian artifacts in one room of the house. During her many archeological digs throughout the Southwest, she would return to her house in Santa Fe with stone axes, pottery, and various other samples of pueblo culture. In fact, in one room of the house she kept several medium size cardboard boxes stacked one on top of another, with actual Indian skeletons! He added that our room was not the room where the skeletons were kept, so we could feel safe about that, but that our room used to be Dr. Dutton's bedroom. He also mentioned that Dr. Dutton was still very much alive, and living in a local convalescent home— shocked Ruby and me. He said that throughout the seven years of owning the property, both he and his partner had witnessed many ghosts in the house. Antonio said there were many times when he would be in the kitchen and notice a shadow of a person walking from the hallway into the living room. He'd investigate only to discover there would be no one there. Other times he'd hear his name being called from an adjoining empty room. When he would walk to the room, he'd see the fleeing image of a shadow! Antonio's partner, Hank, also later spoke to us about similar instances he had experienced in the house. Antonio mentioned that guests to the B&B had the common experience of hearing ghostly footsteps and the breaking sound of glass. Ruby asked, 'What have you done to rid the house of these ghosts?' Antonio said that he and his 75-year-old father had conducted a cleansing ritual in the entire house, and since that time, the appearances of ghosts had stopped. But now he was unsure of the reason why the ghosts had decided to return. We talked a little more

about several things before he left to make the beds in the guests' rooms.

My wife and I felt a little better after having this conversation. We left to do a little shopping in town, and when we returned to the house, we noticed the faint scent of burnt sweet grass incense. Antonio once again knocked on our door, this time to inform us that he and his father had once again blessed the whole house. That night was spent without any further visits from a ghost. The prayers and incense had chased whatever was still in the house.

A few days after Ruby and I returned home to our pueblo, we got a phone call from Antonio. He mentioned that we should read the local newspaper, because on the front page was an article about the recent death of Dr. Burtha Dutton. Apparently, Dr. Dutton had died at a local convalescent home, less than a mile from her old home, now the B&B. But what we should take notice of, Antonio said, was the date of her death. She died the same night that the ghost of the white woman had visited my wife and me! Was the ghostly woman who visited us that night in Santa Fe the ghost of Dr. Burtha Dutton? I don't know how this could be proven, but we were in her bedroom, in her house, on the night that she expired. It just makes sense to us."

SAN JUAN (OKEH) PUEBLO

This particular pueblo has been inhabited since 1300 and is a well-known center of art. The Native name is Okeh. The Spanish explorer Coronado first made contact with this pueblo in 1541. The ensuing years of hostility and the 'harsh lash' of Spanish rule resulted in discontent and resentment. In 1680, Popay, a religious leader from San Juan, led the Great Pueblo Revolt of 1680 against the Spanish. During this revolt, approximately 400 Spanish were killed, and the survivors were driven south to El Paso. For twelve years following the revolt the pueblos lived their lives in peace. But, for several reasons, the revolt did not gain lasting unilateral support from all the pueblos. This lack of unity made a reconquest in 1692 by another Spaniard, de Vargas, possible. At San Juan, numerous ceremonies are performed throughout the year based on solar and lunar cycles. Among the more important of these dances is the Deer Dance, which assures abundance for the pueblo. This dance is performed in the month of January or February. Other important dances are the Basket, Cloud and Buffalo. Of utmost importance in these dances is the teaching of personal responsibility to the gathered onlookers.

Today, San Juan Pueblo is slowly increasing its economic base, and generating needed income with its enterprise, Okeh Casino.

DELORES THUNDER CLOUD'S (SAN JUAN) STORY

The bond between a parent and child is historically one of the strongest to be celebrated. As you'll read in Delores' story, even death has no permanent stronghold in this regard.

— Antonio

"My experience with a ghost took place when I was only fourteen years old. My younger brother, Vincent, and I had been living in my grandparents' house in San Juan. Five years before, both our parents had died when my mother lost control of their truck returning from a shopping trip to Albuquerque. They were both thrown from the truck and died at the scene. I was ten years old, and my brother was seven. We were given the choice of moving to Arizona and living with my mother's Navajo relatives, or staying in San Juan. We chose to stay in San Juan, and moved in with grandpa and grandma and their little dog, Pretzel.

Living in San Juan with my father's parents was wonderful. Grandmother had very bad arthritis that made it difficult for her to get around without help, and grandfather had a leg removed due to diabetic complications, which kept us from leaving the pueblo. But Vincent and I always looked forward to the many ceremonial celebrations that were held there year-round. We were happy and had many childhood friends. My grandparents had a two-bedroom house with a small-screened porch. In the summer months, we moved grandpa's bed out to the porch, where he would spend the nights sleeping in the cool air with Pretzel lying next to him on the floor. Vincent and grandma each had their own bedrooms, and I slept in the living room on the couch.

One Sunday morning when everyone else was at church, I was taking a shower, and had left the bathroom door open. Pretzel started to bark. For some unknown reason, I felt that someone was in the house. When I looked through the hazy, glass shower door, I noticed a figure standing in the bathroom doorway. This surprised me, and I felt embarrassed. I assumed it was my grand- mother and I said, 'Sorry, I forgot to close the door. Could you close it for me?' I saw the figure moved away, into the hallway. I said, 'Grandma, is that you?' There was no response. Pretzel was barking even more. I remember feeling immediately terrified. I stood frozen and felt very helpless in the shower with the warm water falling on my body. Again I said, 'Grandma, please answer me. Is that you?' When she did not answer, I decided to get out and see who was in the house. As I turned off the water and wrapped a towel around me, the thought hit me—there is a stranger in the house! I started to get scared. I thought how was I going to leave the bathroom and confront this person? Did he have a knife or gun? I was trembling! Somehow I got the strength to walk slowly out of the bathroom and into the living room. Pretzel came running to me with the hair on his back standing straight up, as if he were a scared cat! I looked in all the rooms, the closets and under the beds. No one was in the house, or on the porch. I returned to the bathroom and finished drying myself, then walked to the porch, sat on my grandfather's bed, and waited for everyone to return from Sunday Mass.

When they got home, I wasted no time in telling my grandparents about my experience. They listened to me, but I could tell they were thinking I must have imagined it all. Soon, I started to believe the same thing. But I never took another shower with the bathroom door open again. A few nights later, I again experienced something. This time, I knew we had a ghost in the house. I was asleep on the couch in the living room when I was suddenly awakened by the noise of someone in the kitchen. I heard the sound of dishes being moved around, then silverware being dropped on the floor. I kept still. The sounds were not very loud; they were gentle sounds, as if someone didn't want to make a lot of noise. But I could hear them very clearly. Because I was drowsy, I soon fell back asleep. Then I was awakened by footsteps coming from the kitchen to the living room. By this time I was wide-awake! The footsteps were slow and they sounded as if there was dirt or sand on the floor being dragged by the shoes. The footsteps started to come over to the couch and I was scared. I closed my eyes and pretended to be asleep. The footsteps were right at the side of the couch! I could 'feel' the presence of someone standing next to me. Even though I wanted to look at who was standing in the living room, because I was so afraid I kept my eyes closed tightly. Then I felt the pressure of someone sitting next to me, and one couch cushion moved as if someone had sat down. I was terrified, but still did not move a muscle. Something inside me told me that if I opened my eyes, I would be frightened to death by what I would see. In just a few seconds I felt a hand stroking my hair! I can't describe how this affected me. I was so scared that I began to softly cry. The ghostly fingers then took hold of some strands of my hair and lifted them up off the pillow. I could feel this actually happening. This scared me so much that I let out a scream and pulled the covers over my head! My grandmother yelled at me from her bedroom, 'Are you alright, Delores?' In a few seconds she came into the room, and when I explained what had happened, she told me not to worry and gave me a small crucifix to hold. She also lit a candle and placed it on top of the television. The comfort of the candle's light and crucifix gave me a feeling of safety. I soon fell asleep, holding that crucifix close to me.

Well, the visit of that ghost soon became a common thing. I would experience the nightly visits at least twice a week. I knew I would be getting another visit when I would start to hear the dishes in the kitchen begin to rattle. Then the footsteps would begin, and come to where I would be sleeping. I know this might sound a little strange, but I soon got used to these visits. I never stopped being scared, but I was expecting to hear the noises. I always slept with the crucifix, and this gave me the courage to make it through another night. But one night was different. The dish sounds and footsteps started-up as usual, and as the ghost started to play with my hair, I turned over on my left side, away from the ghost, and faced the wall. Right after I did this, I felt a warm breathing on my exposed right ear. It was as if someone's lips were right next to my ear, breathing in and out, in and out! I froze. Then I heard the familiar soft words of my mother say, 'I love you, Dolores.' I immediately opened my eyes and turned to face whoever was in the room with me. As I did this I saw the white, shadowy image of a woman standing directly in front of the television. I knew it was my mother. Her image slowly began to fade. I started to make out the television as it appeared behind her image. Soon she was gone. I cried and cried calling to her not to leave. But it was no use. Grandmother came into the room and I told her my story. She cried with me while she held me in her arms. Grandmother comforted me and explained the wonderful thing that had just happened to me. I never had another nightly visit from my mother again. One visit was enough to let me know she loves, and is watching over me. Because I experienced this many years ago, I know it would be a good thing for me to now tell my personal story to others. So many people suffer the loss of a loved one. They think that they are gone forever, but I know this is not so."

NAMBE PUEBLO

Located just north of Santa Fe, this spectacularly beautiful pueblo is known for its landscape and waterfalls. In the Native language Nambe means, 'mound of earth,' or 'people of the round earth.' Although very much Hispanicized due to intermarriage with local residents, Nambe is in the process of revitalizing its cultural, traditional Native life.

Spanish records note that contact with Nambe's Native population took place in the early 1600's, at which time an initial church was built. Fires, revolts or decay destroyed that church and the following two churches. Although little recorded history remains of this pueblo, the traditional Nambe arts of weaving, pottery and jewelry-making are being produced with enthusiasm and pride.

CARLOS TWO BEARS' (NAMBE) STORY

Carlos and I met for his interview at a local hospital where he is currently employed as a staff I.C.U. nurse. We located an empty room and the interview began. This story is interesting for the fact that his personal experience with something spiritual was to prove to be for Carlos the beginning of many more experiences to come. Carlos stated, "Something shook my soul to its core in 1992 and I believe opened the door for my life to change in a new direction. I'm not scared; I deal with death constantly working in my profession. I see it almost daily."

— Antonio

"My ghost experience took place when I was working in Albuquerque in 1992. I was working as a visiting nurse with a local hospital and had a caseload of about twenty-two patients. My job was to do the usual routine of charting a patient's vitals, such as blood pressure, monitoring medications, and noting any changes related to physical and mental health. Over time, my patients grew to enjoy my visits, and I got to know them quite well. One of them was a widowed woman, Juanita, who had been living in a board-and-care facility on Albuquerque's west side. Juanita was a likable lady of eighty-two who had suffered a stroke on her left side at age seventy-seven. She had adjusted to her illness, and had made good improvements, but because she was without a family to care for her, she had been living at the board-and-care facility for five years. The residents of this facility all had private rooms and were well cared for. The mental picture I keep in my mind of Juanita is of her wearing her favorite purple hand-knitted cap that a friend gave her on her birthday. She loved that hat, and always made sure to have it on when I'd pay my bi-weekly visits.

One day I received a sad call from my supervisor informing me that Juanita suffered a heart attack and died in her sleep. Given her age and illness, I was not surprised by the news, but nonetheless, it was difficult for me to continue my weekly visits to the board-and-care facility knowing she would not be there. The owners of the facility discovered her body in the early morning and, not wanting to alarm the other residents, kept her death a secret. The residents were told that Juanita had been taken to live with a cousin. Since the residents were for the most part incapable of much reasoning due to dementia and other chronic illnesses, none asked further questions of her whereabouts. Juanita's body was removed while all the residents were entertained in the backyard. In just two days, a new referral was made from the hospital, and a new patient, Mildred, was admitted to the facility. I, together with the facility owner, accompanied Mildred from the hospital to the board-and-care, and to her room. She was never told about the previous occupant, except that her name was Juanita and she had gone to live with a cousin. That was all.

The following morning when I paid the facility a follow-up visit, the administrator took me aside. She informed me that something strange had happened in the early morning to their new resident, which had shook her up quite a bit. Mildred was sitting alone in the living room watching television. I was told to encourage Mildred to talk about her 'visitor.' I asked her to tell me how she had spent her first night at the board-and-care. She told me a story that I will never forget. She said someone shaking her bed awakened her in the night. When she opened her eyes, standing next to

her was a short Hispanic woman. Mildred asked her what she wanted and the woman said, 'You are in my bed. You need to get out of my bed and find another room.' Mildred responded, 'No. You're mistaken. This is my room, and this is my bed, and if you don't leave I'll call the staff!' Then Mildred said the Hispanic woman waved her finger in her face and said, 'This is my bed and I'm going to tell the owner how upset you've made me.' After saying this, the Hispanic woman disappeared! I asked Mildred, 'What you're telling me is that you think you saw a ghost. Is that it?' Mildred responded, 'Yes, that's what I saw. A ghost in a purple hat, and I want a room change today. I'm never going to set foot in that room again. It's haunted.' I have to admit that I started to get goose bumps. I assured Mildred that a room change would be made that day. I never disclosed any information about Juanita, or about Juanita's death, to Mildred. I definitely could see the fear in poor Mildred's eyes.

After leaving Mildred, I spoke to the administrator, and she said that someone knocking on her bedroom door awakened her in the night! When she got out of bed to answer the door, there was no one in the hall. Then she heard Mildred's voice yelling for help. After comforting, reassuring words from the administrator, Mildred spent the night on the living room sofa with the light on. None of the facility's residents made contact with Mildred during her admittance. There was absolutely no way she could have conjured up such a story. And what would have been her purpose? There were two other rooms available, so moving Mildred to another room would not have been a problem.

Juanita's old room was turned into an office. The staff did not want to run the risk of having another new resident complain about having an angry ghost shake their bed during the night, or being awakened by a ghost knocking on a bedroom door. All I can say is that experience in the summer of 1992 gave me a very creepy feeling that has stayed with me to this day."

POJOAQUE (PO-SUWAE-GEH) PUEBLO

In the native language, Po-suwae-geh or Pojoaque (using the Spanish pronunciation) translates to 'drinking water place,' or 'gathering place.' Archaeological studies show the pueblo being inhabited as early as 500.

In the early 1600's, San Francisco de Pojaque, the first Spanish mission, was founded. Pojoaque was historically a major-sized settlement, with a very large population. However, following the Great Pueblo Revolt of 1680, the Spaniards, led by Don Diego de Vargas, significantly reduced its population, and it was ultimately abandoned. The pueblo was again settled in 1706. Five families established homes and by 1712

the population increased to 79. In 1890, a smallpox epidemic combined with encroaching non-Indians once again pressured the Native inhabitants to abandon the pueblo.

In 1933, only 40 descendants of the original population again settled the pueblo. In 1936, the pueblo became a federally recognized tribal reservation with over 11,000 acres. Today's current tribal enrollment exceeds over 265 members. Pojoaque is venturing its efforts into developing its economic base with several tribally-owned businesses: Cities of Gold Casino, and Poeh Cultural Center and Museum.

SANTUARIO DE CHIMAYO

In 1816, Don Bernardo Abeyta had a miraculous vision of a light, which shone from within the earth. As he brushed away the dirt, he discovered the crucifix of Nuestro Señor de Esquipulas. In time, Don Bernardo and the residents of El Potrero, then a separate community, finished the massive adobe chapel honoring the six-foot crucifix. In the rear, to the left of the main chapel, is a smaller room where 'El Posito' or the 'little well' is located. Here, healing sand is removed by the faithful to be rubbed on the body, in hope of a cure. Adorning the walls of the santuario are many of the cast-off crutches and personal prayers of the pilgrims who make the journey of sacrifice to the Santurario de Chimayo each Easter. Estimates of yearly visitors are in excess of 300,000. Known as the Lourdes of the Southwest, the Santuario de Chimayo is revered by pilgrims who believe in the miraculous healing power of dirt scooped from the floor of its chapel.

KATHERINE BLUE WATER'S (POJOAQUE) STORY

We both met in a Santa Fe city park on the eastern end of town. Seated on a bench, as the interview was progressing, Katherine's two young sons were playing a short distance away. Katherine stated, "I've told my sons about their uncle and I try to keep his life as real, using my memories as I am able to. I think they have an appreciation for this. At least at Christmastime our little family tradition to honor my brother has now become theirs."

— Antonio

"On Good Friday morning in 1987, I decided to join the group of pilgrims who make the yearly walk north to Chimayo. The night before my walk, I stayed at a friend's house in Santa Fe. I packed some snacks and two jugs of water for the walk. I figured it would take two days of walking to get to the Chimayo Santuario by Easter Sunday. I woke up at 6 a.m. and walked to St. Francis Drive, which leads north to Chimayo. Groups of pilgrims were already on the road from as far south as Albuquerque. People carried homemade crosses, flowers and large pictures of loved ones. Some sang songs and some prayed the rosary. I carried my food, water, a walking stick, and a picture of my brother. I had decided to make the pilgrimage in my brother's honor. My only brother had died two days before Christmas the year before. His death was sudden and unexpected. I wanted to make this pilgrimage as my personal sacrifice to his memory.

During the first day of the walk, there were several times when I felt like giving up. It was hot and my feet were sore. But I knew I had to continue. There was just no way I could stop. I could see the determination to finish the walk on all the other pilgrims' faces as they walked past me. There were even older people on the road. I knew it must have been very difficult for them, but they were still at it. As I arrived at the area of the highway where the Tesuque Pueblo begins, I noticed that my strength was getting weaker and weaker. I walked a few more miles, and then I decided to stop at the Camel Rock Rest Area. I

Camel Rock

was hot, tired, hungry and thirsty. I ate and drank some of my supplies, then lay out under a shady tree and took a nap.

I had a strange dream. I dreamed that my brother was walking with me on the pilgrimage. In my dream, I was unaware that he had died. We spoke to each other as if nothing unusual had happened. Another strange thing about my dream is that when I spoke to him, I was unable to recognize the sound of my own voice. It was weird. I sounded as if I were speaking in a can. My voice sounded very muffled.

I also remember that, during the dream, my brother spoke to me about needing a feather for the new hat that he was wearing. I didn't recognize the hat, but he asked me to find him a nice feather. I don't know why this was so important to him, but he kept telling me to find him a feather. I attempted to respond to his words, but as I said before, my voice was confusing to me. Whenever I opened my mouth to say anything, my words came out all mixed up. When I woke up and realized that I had a dream about my brother, it made me sad, yet at the same time a feeling of happiness came over me.

I got up from under the tree and continued on my walk to the santuario. This time I felt renewed, and even though I had blisters on my feet, I knew I would finish the walk. Right before nightfall, Michele, a friend of mine who was driving, located me and took me to her home where I spent the night. I told her about the dream and the strange feeling it left with me. That night I had no trouble falling asleep, and in the morning, Michele drove me back to where she had picked me up on the highway to begin the remainder of my walk. I walked for hours

and hours, all the while praying to myself and thinking of my brother. It seemed to me that everyone on the pilgrimage was in a happier mood that day.

Groups of people were singing religious songs and several cars were stopping, offering to give us burritos and cold drinks. Nothing unusual happened that day to me. As we had planned, my friend Michele once again located me and took me to her home for the night. I got to bed at about 9:30, but this time I had another dream of my brother. In this second dream, my brother appeared very thin and asked me to bring him water from a nearby stream. The interesting thing was that he wanted me to bring him water in his hat. He handed me his black hat and asked me to dip it in the stream, and fill it with water. I did as he asked me, but when I returned it to him filled with water, he said he could not drink the water because it was not his hat. I spoke and told him that it was his hat. He responded that his hat had a beautiful feather on the brim, and this hat did not have a feather, and therefore it was not his hat. I awoke with a dry throat. I tried to speak, but the words were very difficult to pronounce. I got out of bed, walked to the kitchen and drank two tall glasses of water. I don't know what was going on, but I knew I had to get back to sleep in order to be rested for the following day of my walk.

The next morning after breakfast, Michele again dropped me off at the spot on the road where she had picked me up. I walked and walked until I finally got to the little village of Chimayo. People were everywhere — pilgrims, tourists and locals. There must have been over a thousand people. I tried to get into the santuario, but because of all the people, I was being squeezed and

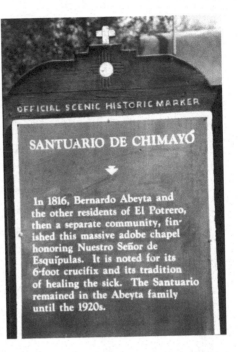

OFFICIAL SCENIC HISTORIC MARKER

SANTUARIO DE CHIMAYÓ

In 1816, Bernardo Abeyta and the other residents of El Potrero, then a separate community, finished this massive adobe chapel honoring Nuestro Señor de Esquipulas. It is noted for its 6-foot crucifix and its tradition of healing the sick. The Santuario remained in the Abeyta family until the 1920s.

pushed so much that I decided to wait for a few hours and rest under a tree, just below the hill of the santuario. It was cooler and because I was so tired, I lay down on the grass and took a short nap. When I awoke, the crowd had thinned out and I did manage to get into the santuario, and squeezed my way into the small side room where the Chimayo dirt is kept. People bring small paper and plastic bags to fill with handfuls of dirt. I had also brought my own little bag, but I searched and searched and could not find it. I decided to use an old sandwich bag that I had in my backpack. I opened up the small bag, and then reached my hand into the hole in the floor. When I dropped my fistful of dirt into the bag, I noticed something unusual. Mixed with the dirt was a feather! As I examined the feather, I knew this was a sign from my brother! I held the plastic bag up to the light and started to cry. Even though they didn't know why I was crying, people around me began to hug me. I dropped to my knees and thanked God and my brother for giving me this sign.

When I got back home to the pueblo, I told my mother about the feather and my dreams. I showed her the feather in the bag of dirt. She walked over to her bedroom closet and brought back a box. She opened the lid and pulled out a brand new, black cowboy hat. She told me that my brother had hinted to her that he wanted a hat before he died, so she and my father had bought him one, to present to him as a Christmas present. But because he suddenly died two days before Christmas, my parents decided not to tell anyone about the hat, and kept it hidden in their closet. Mother then took the bag of dirt, opened it and removed the feather. As we both started to cry, she placed the feather in the hatband and said, 'Now your brother has his hat.' Since then, we don't spend a Christmas without bringing out my brother's hat from the closet, and hanging it in the living room, next to the Christmas tree."

TESUQUE (TETSUGEH) PUEBLO

In the Native language 'Tetsugeh,' means 'place of the cottonwood tree.' The pueblo is located just a few miles north of Santa Fe and, despite continuous contact with European culture throughout much of its history, prides itself as being one of the most traditional of all of the pueblos. Its role in the Great Pueblo Revolt was in leading the first attack on Santa Fe. Archaeologically, the pueblo existed before 1200. Tesuque is not a large pueblo, but it more than makes up for its small size by having stubbornly resisted the Spanish and Anglo–American invaders. Traditional ceremonies continue to play an important role in the pueblo community, as does the art of pottery, which is considered very collectable. Today the enterprising Tesuque community is bolstering its economic base by focusing on tourism, gaming and farming.

DANIEL HIGH MOUNTAIN'S (TESUQUE) STORY

Daniel's story is one that reminds us to be respectful and cautious of those things that we might not be too familiar with. And when stepping into the realm of the spiritual, this rule of conduct cannot be over-emphasized. Daniel has learned this and as he stated to me, "I won't ever step foot into another cemetery unless

I absolutely have to. I don't want to be that shaken up again, ever!"
                                                                    — *Antonio*

"My experience took place in the state of California. I was visiting two old friends from high school who were living in Sacramento. Right after graduating, they moved from New Mexico to California, found work in the computer field, and got married. They always were pressuring me to follow them to California and get a job working with computers. Eventually, their phone calls and stories of making lots of money led me to drive to the west coast to see for myself. It was October, and I was planning on spending two weeks at their condo. On Halloween eve a neighbor who was having a birthday party for a girlfriend invited the three of us over. There were about twenty or so people invited. As the evening went on, one of the dinner guests started telling ghost stories. We went around the room as each person took a turn telling a ghost story. Some of the stories were really dumb, but one guy told a couple of stories that gave us all the creeps. This guy, Randal, was involved with a group of ghost hunters. He told us about how they would go into haunted houses and graveyards looking for ghosts. The guy looked like a hippie from the 60's, long hair and beard. He surprised me when he spoke because he spoke like an educated college man. Anyway, after Randal told his stories we asked him if he had any pictures of ghosts. He said he had a three-ring binder filled with pictures of ghosts in his car. We asked him if we could see them. 'Sure,' he said. So we waited until he returned with the photos. I didn't know what to expect.

When he returned, we got to see photos of fog-like images hovering over tombstones, on staircases, in homes, and in people's front yards. The pictures were taken during the day and night. Some of the photos showed the faint images of facial features, but most were just large smoky-looking forms. Randal told us that his ghost hunting group was going to be doing some research the following night, Halloween, at a local cemetery. He asked if any of us would like to come along. Most people said that they had parties to attend, but for some reason, I said that I would like to go. Normally I don't go for such things, but I told him that I would be ready for him the next night at 9 p.m. Two others said that they would also go, so it was a date. The three of us were told to bring a tape recorder with new batteries, and a brand-new unopened cassette tape.

The following night, we drove to the Old City Cemetery on 10th and Broadway. When we walked up to the cemetery gates, I saw in the distance, among the tall stone markers, several bright lights. Randal said that his group was already preparing, and those lights were from a television crew that had also been invited. I felt a bit uneasy, but ready for whatever ghost things might take place. We were told to feel free to ask questions, and to keep an eye out for any strange movements or lights. Randal introduced us to the members of his group. Some of his friends showed us sensitive recording instruments that were supposed to measure electromagnetic fields and energy disturbances. Randal asked us to get our recorders ready. I unwrapped my tape and checked the batteries. Everything was working. Randal then asked us to walk among the graves and find a quiet spot where we 'felt energy.' Once at the spot, we were to turn on the tape recorder and walk away. I felt strange doing this. I located an old, fancy looking gravestone under a big pine tree, and turned on my recorder, then placed it on the grave, and walked away. I didn't feel any 'energy'— it was just a grave I chose at random. I watched as the others looked at their meters and took flash pictures. I didn't see anything unusual.

I was invited to have some coffee just a few yards away from the main area of activity. I kept my eyes on the tree where I had placed my recorder. I made sure that no one went by that area. At about 10:30 I decided to go and check my recorder. I saw that the tape had finished recording on side one, so I turned the cassette over, pressed the record button, and walked away. After another hour, I picked up my recorder and brought it back to the area where we were all gathered. We each took turns playing back short ten-minute portions of what we had recorded, but nothing unusual was recorded. When I played my tape, like the others, it was filled with silence.

Well, that was enough for me. I was kind of bored with this ghost hunting stuff. I told everyone that I was going to have to get back home. When I left the cemetery and got into my car, I put the recorder under the passenger seat and drove home. I kept thinking to myself what a waste the night had been. The next morning I got in my car and drove to a local cafe for breakfast. As I was having breakfast, I decided to go to my car and bring back the tape recorder. I had a pair of small headphones that I used, so the people sitting at the other tables wouldn't think I was weird. Like the night before, all I heard was the low hissing sound of the blank tape. But after about 20 to 25 minutes of listening, I started to hear something strange. I re-wound the tape and increased the volume. What I heard made my hair stand on end! At first the sounds were very low voices, then a long high- pitched whistle started up. The voices were so low, I couldn't make out what was being said. I know that no one walked up to my tape recorder the night before, and I certainly did not hear such noises in the area. I was just a few yards away! After these sounds stopped, two very clear human voices started up. A female voice spoke, 'No pictures. I said, no pictures!' Then a male voice said, 'Get out, out, out, get out, get out!' Wow, I actually caught spirits talking! I took off my headphones, and turned off the tape recorder. It scared the you-know-what out of me! Each time I re-played the tape, I got more and more shaken up by the voices.

I quickly finished my breakfast and drove around town trying to make sense of the recording. I didn't play it again until later that evening when my friends returned from work. Even they agreed that hearing the recording was scaring them. When I returned to New Mexico, I contacted a lawyer friend who worked in Albuquerque, and asked him if he could recommend a sound lab that could enhance the sounds on the tape. One-hundred-and-fifty dollars later, I got my original cassette tape, and a new enhanced tape with all the sounds and voices in a much clearer form. I can only listen to this new tape for a few minutes without having to turn off the recorder and put it away. It's a scary thing to hear. I've been thinking about contacting Randal, but I don't believe that bothering the ghosts would do anymore good."

MESCALERO APACHE (INDEH)

Far and wide the Apaches roamed over the region known today as the Southwest. They ranged from Texas to central Arizona, from far south in Mexico to the peaks of Colorado. For centuries before the first

Spaniards and other explorers, the Apache people knew the secrets of the mountains and the deserts as no other people have, before or since. Proud always, and fierce when need be, the Apaches bowed to no one except their Creator. They lived off the land, and cared for no possession

except their land. The Mescaleros took their name from the mescal cactus. In earlier days the mescal, a desert plant, supplied the Apaches with food, beverage and fiber. Literally, it was their staff of life.

A time of violence came to the Apaches in the last century. Before it ended, the Mescalero and other Apache bands had lost much of their Southwest empire. The Mescaleros were more fortunate than some other Native American groups, who were also dispossessed. They could still live in sight of their sacred mountain, White Mountain, which was, and remains, the source of their wisdom. Today, the Mescalero Apache Indian Reservation is located in the south central part of the state of New Mexico, in Otero County. Executive Order of President Ulysses S. Grant established it on May 27, 1873. Subsequent Executive Orders and Acts of Congress have altered the area and defined the boundaries, fixing the gross area at 720 square miles of 460,661 acres, all of which is in tribal ownership status. The United States never specifically obligated itself by treaty, or Act of Congress, to set apart a reservation for the Mescalero Apache Indians. The Executive Orders that set aside these lands use the term 'Mescalero Apache Indians, and such other Indians as the department may see fit to locate thereon.'

The Lipan Apache survivors who suffered severely in many of the Texas wars were taken to northwest Chihuahua, Mexico, in about 1830. They later were brought to the United States, and placed on the Mescalero Reservation about the beginning of 1903. In 1913, after the capture of the famous spiritual leader, Geronimo, approximately 200 members of the Chiricahua and Warm Springs bands of Apaches were being held as military prisoners. They were subsequently moved from

Fort Sill, Oklahoma, to the Mescalero Reservation. The Mescaleros numbered about 400 persons when their reservation was established. Chiricahua and Lipan bands became members of the Mescalero Apache Tribe when the tribe was organized formally in 1936, under provisions of the Indian Reorganization Act.

Today the population of the reservation exceeds 4,000 enrolled members. Several families have relocated off the reservation, where they have found employment. Most of the tribal families live in or near the community of Mescalero, but there also are settlements at Three Rivers, Elk Silver, Carrizozo, Whitetail and Mudd Canyon.

The visitor who comes to the Mescalero Reservation today expecting to see braves and women in buckskins and blankets is likely to be disappointed. Changes have occurred in their ways of life over the last hundred years. In that time the Mescaleros, while striving to adjust to a dominant culture so different from their own, have survived stresses that might have destroyed people with less fortitude. Their adjustment to the complex ways of the white man's society is not yet complete. The Mescaleros have come far along the new road, however, and the trail should be smoother from now on. The tepee and the buckskin garments are gone from the reservation now, except for the four days over the Fourth of July holiday when the tribe observes the ancient 'Coming of Age Ceremony' for Mescalero maidens. Gone, too, are the raids against enemy forces. Almost gone is the mescal gathering when the cactus is ripe for harvest. The deer hunt still takes place, but with rifles rather than bows. The Mescalero tribal members of today live in houses, shop for their food and other necessities in stores, drive to the stores in automobiles, and dress much as their neighbors do. The Native American language is largely spoken, although almost all of the Apaches speak the English language fluently. A few also speak Spanish. Typical Native American names have gradually vanished except for a few of the older generation. The Mescaleros are free to enter into marriage with whom they wish, thus the varied surnames now common on the reservation. Modern first names common to the general public are given. Tribal members work for their living, as do their neighbors. Contrary to belief, the Mescalero Apaches are not receiving an annuity from the U.S. government. Not for many years have the Mescaleros, or any other Indians, received food, clothing or gratuity payments from the federal government. The Mescalero Apache Tribe owns Ski Apache, the largest, best-developed ski area in the Southwest. Also owned by the tribe is the Inn of the Mountain Gods, a luxury resort complex. The Inn opened for business on July 10, 1975, and its reputation as one of the Southwest's finest facilities has grown rapidly. The Inn plays a major role in the economy of the tribe, and indeed all of southeastern New Mexico.

ALICE GOOD MEDICINE'S (APACHE) STORY

I conducted Alice's interview on a sunny and hot day on the grounds of the Catholic St. Joseph Mission Church, located within the reservation. Initially we met for the interview at a nearby gas station then decided, at her urging, to move to the nearby church grounds where she felt more comfortable discussing matters of the spiritual world. I was most impressed by Alice's calm demeanor and asked, after hearing her story, how she had found the strength to deal with her unsettling encounter. She smiled and simply raised her finger and pointed to the church saying, "I don't attend church regularly, but I am a believer."

— Antonio

"Before I begin my story, I first have to tell you that this is going to be the last time I'll ever tell anyone about my experience. Apaches don't like to talk about these things, and I don't like to talk about ghosts either. I'm just going to tell this story because I think it's important for people to know that ghosts do exist, and we all should be most respectful of those who have passed on.

Eight years ago, my husband Casey and I bought a house from a man in the resort town of Cloudcroft. Casey works as a ranger for the forest service, and a fellow ranger told him about a very nice home that a guy was selling at a great price. At the time, we were looking to buy a house and when we heard about this property, we decided to check it out. Casey phoned the owner and made an appointment the next day for the both of us to have a look. Following the directions the owner gave Casey, we entered a small canyon filled with tall pine trees. The house was located on three acres of land at the end of a dirt road. Just a few other homes were in the area. It was in a pretty isolated area. We found out that the rear of the property bordered the Mescalero Reservation. We both wondered why the asking price for the property was so low. We spotted the house, and as we drove up to the front door, we kept saying to each other, 'Why is the price so cheap; there must be something wrong with it.' We met with the owner, who looked very thin and sickly. He told us that he had cancer and needed to sell the house as soon as possible because of the medical bills that needed to be paid. He gave us an inside tour of the house, but when he started to have difficulty walking, he asked us to walk outside on our own. As Casey and I toured the backyard and inspected the hot tub, water pump and septic system, we knew there would be no question about buying the property. When we entered the house, we told the owner that we would talk to our bank that same day, and as far as we were concerned, it was a done deal.

A few weeks later, we moved into the house and began cleaning and removing trash left behind by the owner. Before we moved in, the owner told us that he was only going to remove what he could, and we could keep what he left at the house. We found several boxes filled with old receipt books, and lots of photographs taken of women's hairstyles. One box had scissors, combs and everything that a beauty shop would need. In the basement we found one big box filled with bottles of hair dye and blow-dryers. We put most of these things in the pick-up and dropped them off at the Indian Employment Training Center on the reservation. I kept a hair dryer and some brand new hair curlers that were still in their original plastic bags. Casey found some tools in a crawl space, dusted them, and hung them in the garage. There were other smaller boxes that we could see with a flashlight, way in the back of the crawl space. Because of where these boxes were located, and all the dust, we decided to leave them where they were until we finished with the other more important chores. Everything else, we got rid of.

We installed new rugs in the living room and the three bedrooms, and then painted the whole inside of the house. The owner had left a washer and dryer as part of the sale of the house, and I had to move these away from the wall in order to paint. When I moved the dryer, I spotted some sheets of papers and envelopes that the owner must have misplaced. I picked them up and read them aloud to Casey. They were personal letters addressed to the previous owner of the house from another man named Gary. The ex-owner of our house had been in love with Gary and these letters mentioned that Gary had AIDS. They were touching letters about Gary's illness and his battle with AIDS. In one letter Gary mentioned that he was looking forward to visiting for the Christmas holiday. There were birthday cards and other letters with poems and things like that. Casey told me to put the letters in a box and keep them for the owner. Casey said, 'Who knows, he might call or pay us a visit one day.'

About a month after my husband and I settled into the house, we began to feel some strange things. Casey and I always sensed that someone was in the house watching us. As we were alone in the house watching television, there were times when we would both hear a voice call out from another room. We would hear, 'Hey!' being called out to us. We would get out of our chairs to investigate who was in the house, but there would never be anyone in the rooms or in the yard. Other times I would hear my name being called, and when I would turn to look, I clearly spotted the shadow of a man standing in the next room, then quickly fade away! Casey also saw this same shadow walk from the bedroom to the bathroom at night. In the kitchen, knives would be removed from the wood knife block, and in the morning, I would find them spread out in the sink! In the bedroom a strange thing took place.

One day as I went to look for a record album, I opened my closet door, and discovered that all my record albums were warped! Like an intense heat had melted them. The strangest of all these experiences took place one night. Earlier in the day, Casey called to tell me he was going to be late coming home. I decided to soak in the hot tub out back that night. While I was soaking away, I noticed something moving at our upstairs bedroom window. I looked up and saw a tall man standing at the window, staring down at me! This terrified me and I froze! I just kept staring at this figure until I heard Casey's truck come up the driveway. When I saw Casey come into the bedroom, I yelled for him to open the window, so that I could talk to him. When he opened the window I yelled, 'Who's that guy standing next to you?' Casey looked to his left and said, 'You see someone standing next to me, where?' I yelled back, 'Right there. Don't you see him?' After I said this, the ghost walked slowly away from the window, and disappeared. Casey never saw anyone in the bedroom with him. I decided then and there to move out of the house. I told Casey, 'That's it, the house is haunted and we're out of here!' He agreed with me, and we contacted a real estate company. By the end of the month, it was sold. I didn't want to haggle with the price, so when the first offer was made we took it!

A year later, I was driving through Cloudcroft when I decided to stop and pay the new owners of the house a visit. I was curious about what they might have experienced. I never told the realtor or the new owners about our ghost experiences, so when I visited the new owners, I acted as if I had nothing else on my mind. I met with the wife, and sure enough, our conversation soon turned from talking about the garden and pesky deer to ghostly shadows and voices coming from empty rooms. All along I acted as if this was all new to me. Then after a couple of minutes, I began to feel nervous, and I asked her if we could continue our conversation outside. I felt much safer talking outdoors. She told me that her husband was seeing shadows of a strange man, and feeling the touch of a hand that would sometimes touch his face.

She herself would hear voices calling her name, and one time she heard a noise, which sounded like someone breaking dishes in the kitchen. Then she stopped, and said she was going back into the house, to bring back something they recently discovered in the basement. She came back with a white envelope and a ceramic jar. She gave me the envelope and told me to look inside. I noticed that on the outside of the envelope the name 'Gary' was written in pencil. When I looked inside I saw folded tissue paper. She asked me to unfold the tissue. When I did this, I saw that there was a lock of brown hair taped to the back of a small photograph of a thin man about fifty. I got the shivers and gave the envelope back to her. I asked her where she had found the envelope. She said that one day she was cleaning the closet shelves in the bedroom and discovered it on the highest shelf. Before I got around to telling her about the love letters I had found in back of the dryer, she started to tell me about the green ceramic jar on the table before us that her husband had found in the basement. One day as he was in the basement, he spotted a group of small boxes in the crawl space. He used a long pole to pull them towards him. They were covered in thick dust, so he decided to carry them outside and open them in the fresh air. The first box contained old stuffed animals. The other smaller box contained the green jar. She told me the jar had a taped seal around the edge. Her husband used a knife to cut through the thick tape, and when he opened it, they found a small, clear plastic bag filled with what they thought was white sand. The bag was tied with a red cord and a hand written label was attached to the cord. On the label was written, 'Cremains of Gary Bullock.' Right before me on the table was this jar and the ashes of Gary Bullock! That was enough for me. I told the wife that I was getting scared. I needed to go and be on my way. I also told her that she needed to get rid of the jar and ashes. I said I would visit her again sometime, but I've never gone back to that house again. And I never will!"

CITY OF SANTA FE

Santa Fe, founded in 1610 by Spanish missionaries, translates to 'Holy Faith' in Spanish, and is the oldest capital city in the U.S. Santa Fe is located on a high plateau at the foot of the Sangre de Cristos, 'Blood of Christ,' Mountains. Native Americans had been well established in the area, constructing notable structures and trade centers, centuries before Europeans ventured into the region. Today this well-known city is regarded as one of the nation's premier art centers.

SOFITA BECERA'S (HISPANIC) STORY

I conducted this interview with Sofita Becera in her living room, which also served as her bedroom. The simple items of decoration displayed about her home provided clues to Sofita's modest taste. Handcrafted crocheted doilies and other needlework rested upon Sofita's well-worn furniture. Placed at the foot of her yellow/green sofa was an oblong hand-woven rug which Sofita's best friend, Belinda Ortiz, had given to her as a wedding present many years before. What

remains dominant in my memory, however, was Sofita's religiosity. On a wooden table her deceased husband had made over twenty years ago stood a statue of the Virgin Mary. In front of the statue was a small bouquet of plastic flowers and a votive candle which flickered continuously throughout the interview.

Born on August 12, 1899, Sofita was nearing 93 years of age, but had the spunk and vitality of a much younger woman. She wore thick-lensed glasses because of cataract surgery performed eight years earlier. Sofita's story concerns a molcajete, a carved, stone tool developed by ancient Native American people several hundred years ago in the valley of Mexico. It is shaped like an average-sized melon with the center hollowed out. A smaller stone is used inside the hollowed-out portion of the molcajete to crush or grind herbs and spices. This stone mortar and pestle is so useful that it remains a popular tool with people on both sides of the border dividing the United States and Mexico.

— Antonio

"In 1921, I was twenty- two and had married Daniel the previous summer. We had a small house about two miles east of the Santa Fe plaza. In those days, two to five miles was not considered very far to travel, and those of us without horses would walk, carrying supplies of food or firewood. It was not an easy life, but the good times made up for

Unlike a metate—a long, flat stone used by Native Americans throughout the southwest to grind corn into a flour-like powder—the molcajete is rounded, bowl-shaped.

217

the bad. My good friend since childhood, Belinda Ortiz, would join me at mid-day after I had done the cleaning and fed the chickens and goats. Belinda and I passed the time talking about what was going on in our neighborhood, things like who was romancing whom.

During one of these afternoon visits, Belinda and I went outside to rid my yard of a stray dog that was barking and chasing my chickens. Three young neighborhood boys came by, saw our trouble, and started throwing stones at the mongrel. Once rid of the dog, I asked the boys why they were so covered in dirt. They explained that they had been exploring in the nearby hills, and had discovered a small cave behind a grove of trees against the side of the mountain. They had gathered some sticks to enlarge the opening and peered inside. With the help of the afternoon sun, they saw several pots and a quiver of fox pelts containing arrows. I told them they must have uncovered a burial site, and should not have touched or taken anything, because they must respect the dead. They listened with wide eyes, and then said they did not want to return, but they were afraid that others might disturb the cave. Belinda suggested they take us to the cave so we could help them cover it up. The boys agreed, and off we went.

About six miles into the Sangre de Cristo mountain range, on the eastern edge of the city, we crossed a small stream, and entered a grove of trees. There we found the cave. The opening was about four feet high and one foot wide. We peered inside and saw the small painted pots, a woven grass mat, and the quiver of arrows— just as the boys had described. In the back of the cave, I saw a large dark mass of fur and a bony foot protruding from underneath the fur and knew this was a burial cave. I realized that the corpse must have been a man and a hunter, because he was wrapped in a bearskin and had his hunt weapons with him. I kept this knowledge to myself as I made the sign of the cross. I turned to Belinda and the boys and said, 'We will have to seal this up, so go down to the stream and bring mud and stones.' While they were all busy at the stream, I looked inside the cave again. This time I saw a roughly carved molcajete. I reached in and grabbed the molcajete and the small grinding stone that lay beside it. I thought this would fit in my kitchen perfectly, so I carried it some distance away and covered it with grass and leaves. I felt it was worthless compared to the pots or the fox quiver. We diligently worked with our hastily gathered adobe building materials, and soon the sun had caused a dry, thin crust to develop on the surface of the  moistened mud. We placed large branches with lots of leaves in front of the sealed entrance, and agreed that we had done a good job. I instructed the boys to return home on their own, but Belinda and I stayed behind.

After they had gone, I told Belinda about the molcajate. She was not very happy about what I had secretly done, but after she saw it, she agreed that it would do no harm to put it to use once in a while, after all those years lying unused in the cave. I retrieved the molcajete and we went home. I scrubbed it clean of all mud, and placed it on the kitchen table to surprise my husband. When Daniel saw it, he admired its beauty, but asked nothing of its origins. Instead, he suggested I grind some chile for the following day's dinner. So the next day, I did as he had suggested and crushed some dried, red chile pods for dinner. The molcajete performed very nicely, but later that night, while I was sleeping, I was awakened by a loud banging sound. I shook my husband out of his sleep and told him to listen, but the sound had stopped. The next night, I was again awakened by the same sound, but this time I recognized it as the sound one rock makes as it is hit against another—a 'click–click' sound. Immediately, I knew it was the molcajete. I got goose bumps on my goose bumps, but I kept still and eventually, after what seemed an eternity, the sound stopped.

The next morning, I told Belinda about the sounds in the night. She said it was my own fault for taking what was not mine. I agreed and asked her to return the molcajete to the cave. She refused, insisting I should do it myself. But I was too frightened, so I carried the stone to the back of the house, and left it there beside the back door. From time to time, I would hear the familiar sound, but I dared not tell Daniel its history. I just endured the night poundings, and the guilt that would overcome me. Out of fear, I could not bring myself to return the molcajete to its rightful resting place.

One November night, as a soft snow dusted everything, I heard the molcajete again. It had been several months since the last time I had heard it, but as usual, the clicking sound awakened me from my sleep. I got out of bed, went to the back door and carefully peered through the window. I saw the freshly fallen snow glistening in the bright light of a full moon. Then I looked down to where the molcajete stood, and was surprised to see the materialized prints of a barefooted person pressed into the snow! The footprints made their way from the molcajete until they disappeared behind a large cottonwood tree. Although snow covered everything else in the yard, the exposed molcajete, which I was using as a doorstop, had been brushed clean, and fresh human footprints surrounded the molcajete. Since that night I have heard the clicking sounds of the molcajete only twice; on the day that my good friend Belinda died, and on the day that Daniel was laid to rest. But I was no longer afraid. I guess I've come to accept the spirit that dwells in or around the grinding stone as something that I will have to live with. I now consider the molcajete as if it were a chair or table, something taken for granted, but useful when needed. I believe this 'stone friend' will stay with me, and provide companionship until I leave this world."

Author's Note: In September of 1991, Sofita suffered a massive heart attack and died at home, surrounded by her son and two neighbors. Later, her son contacted me and informed me that his mother had

The actual Molcajete of this story

mentioned to him that she had wanted me to have the molcajete. I accepted the gift with nervous apprehension, and assured her son that I would take care of it and that eventually I would place it in a location that befits its history.

LA RESIDENCIA

La Residencia was a nursing-home facility located at the corner of Paseo de Peralta and Palace Avenue. Today, it is part of an updated, remodeled hotel property. Prior to October 1983, the building housed the original St. Vincent Hospital, which provided for the health care needs of Santa Fe and northern New Mexico. Many of the city's health care workers who served there believe it to be haunted, specifically nurses

who completed residence work at this facility for their New Mexico nursing licenses. The following narrative is an interview with one employee of La Residencia—the Nurse Coordinator.

LORAINE BACA'S (HISPANIC) STORY

I met with Loraine within the facility's cafeteria. Amid all the noise of kitchen staff preparing the room for the soon-to-be-served lunch, Loraine described her unsettling experience. She stated, "I believe this building is one of the most haunted places in Santa Fe, if not the most haunted. Just ask anyone who has ever spent any time here if they've heard or seen something. I bet they'll all say 'yes.' If they will tell you 'no,' I know they would be lying!"

— Antonio

"All the nurses who I now work with and have worked with in the past are very much aware of the ghosts that dwell at La Residencia, but the basement holds its own special, grisly power. I personally can attest to this. You couldn't pay me a sack of gold to walk into that basement—day or night. When staff members ask me to accompany them to the basement, I tell them, 'The day I go back into that hell, is the day I turn in my resignation!' The basement has many rooms and hallways, and it's very dark. The state museum offices, which are located in the building next to La Residencia, use one large hallway as a storage area. Native American artifacts, such as stone tools, pottery and grinding stones, are kept in that space. I imagine these items, and others stored in large, sealed crates, have been excavated from burial sites. Considering how non-Native Americans treat living Indians with disrespect, it would not surprise me if there were skeletal remains down there in cardboard boxes. I am convinced that there are a lot of upset spirits in that basement. Other employees have reported hearing loud banging noises and voices coming from the basement at odd hours of the day and night. No one—except for new employees—ever ventures to the elevator and presses the 'B' button. In the past, the 'seasoned' staff members used to initiate new employees by escorting them to the basement and leaving them there to find their way through the dark maze of hallways to the stairway—without the aid of a flashlight. The only available light would be the green glow from the exit signs. Eventually, the initiates—pale as a ghost—would reach the upper floor, where we would welcome them.

One evening, I was selected to accompany a new nurse's aide to the basement for this eerie 'rite of passage.' We rode the elevator down and, arriving at the basement, I sent her off with the usual instructions: 'Find the stairs and meet us on the third floor.' She hesitated, and then said, 'I'll do it.' As the elevator door squeezed shut, I shouted, 'Good luck,' and then went upstairs to wait with the others. We waited and waited. Nothing happened. The aide did not arrive within the expected time, and we began to worry for her safety. Imagining all sorts of disasters—a broken leg, a hit on the head—another nurse and I decided to investigate. Once in the basement, we called out the aide's name. No response. While the other nurse held the elevator door open, I shone a flashlight around—spotting dusty chairs, boxes and crates. Elongated shadows flickered and fluttered against the walls. I definitely wanted to be somewhere else. I called the aide again, and this time I heard a weak response. I followed the sound of her voice—down one hall, then to the left. Finally I located a room. I called to her again. 'I'm here, down here on the floor,' she said. She was in one of the storage rooms, crouched in the corner, in almost total darkness. She told me she had lost her way, and then became confused and scared. I hugged her and she took my hand. Then I yelled to the other nurse, that I had found our missing aide.

As we turned to make our way out of the room, the beam of my flashlight caught something on one of the walls. I thought it was water, but as we looked closer, we saw that it was blood. It was fresh and it glistened in the light. It covered over half of the concrete wall and seemed to be oozing from the wall itself. I could even smell the unique, iron scent of hemoglobin. There was no doubt in my mind—this was blood! Well, after a scream or two—who's counting—we high-tailed it out of the room toward the elevator. 'Press the button! Press the button!' we yelled to the startled nurse. When we reached the others upstairs, I told them what we had seen. Everyone got so scared that no one even considered the possibility of returning to the basement—ever.

However, the following day, after much deliberation, two nurses talked me into taking them to the room where we had seen the blood. Down we went with flashlights in hand, along the dark hallway, my stomach in knots. We found the room, and I said, 'Right in there, on the wall by the door.' We aimed our flashlights, but the wall was dry— clean as sun-bleached bones. There was no trace of blood on the wall or on the floor. I remember saying, 'Let's get the hell out of this place!' Two days later, I asked one of the maintenance men, who had worked in the facility when it was St. Vincent's, if he was aware of any strange happenings in the basement. He told me he had heard stories from other employees, but didn't pay them any mind. When I asked him about the room where I had seen the blood, he told me there used to be a small furnace in that room where the hospital surgery department cremated amputated limbs and organs. I just about died on the spot.

As you may have guessed, there have been no more initiations in the basement."

TOWN OF TAOS

There is evidence that man has lived in the Taos area as far back as 3,000 B.C. Prehistoric ruins dating from 900 A.D. can be seen throughout the Taos Valley. The Pueblo of Taos remains the link from these early inhabitants of the valley to the still-living Native culture.

The first Europeans to appear in Taos Valley were led by Captain Alvarado, who was exploring the area for the Coronado expedition of 1540. Don Juan de Onate, official colonizer of the province of Nuevo Mexico, came to Taos in July 1598. In September of that year he assigned Fray Francisco de Zamora to serve the Taos and Picuris Pueblos.

Long established trading networks at Taos Pueblo, plus its mission and the abundant water and timber of the valley, attracted early Spanish settlers. Life was not easy for the newcomers, and there were several conflicts with Taos Pueblo before the Great Pueblo Revolt of 1680 in which all Spaniards and their priests were either killed or driven from the province. In 1692 Don Diego de Vargas made a successful military re-conquest of New Mexico and in 1693 he returned to re-colonize the province. In 1694 he raided Taos Pueblo when it refused to provide corn for his starving settlers in Santa Fe.

Taos Pueblo revolted again in 1696, and de Vargas came for the third time to put down the rebellion. Thereafter, Taos and most of the other Rio Grande pueblos remained allies of Spain and later of Mexico when it won its independence in 1821. During this long period the famous Taos trade fairs grew in importance so that even the annual caravan to Chihuahua delayed its departure until after the Taos Fair, held in July or

August. The first French traders, led by the Mallette brothers, attended the Taos Fair in 1739.

By 1760, the population of Taos Valley had decreased because of the fierce attacks by Plains Indians. Many times the Spanish settlers had to move into houses at Taos Pueblo for protection from these raiders. In 1779, Colonel de Anza returned through Taos from Colorado, where he had decisively defeated the

Comanches led by Cuerno Verde. de Anza named the Sangre de Cristo Pass, northeast of present Fort Garland, and also named the road south from Taos to Santa Fe through Miranda Canyon as part of 'El Camino Real.' In 1796-97, the Don Fernando de Taos grant was given to 63 Spanish families.

By the early 1800's Taos had become the headquarters for many of the famous mountain men who trapped beaver in the neighboring mountains. Among them was Kit Carson, who made his home in Taos from 1826 to 1868. In July 1826 Padre Antonio Jose Martinez began serving the Taos parish. He opened his school in Taos in 1833 and published textbooks for it in 1834. He printed El Crepusculo, a weekly newspaper, in 1835 and was prominent in territorial matters during the Mexican and early United States periods in New Mexico.

After Mexico gained independence from Spain in 1821, the Santa Fe Trail became the important route for trade between the United States and Mexico. A branch of the trail came to Taos to supply its trading needs.

From 1821 to 1846, the Mexican government made numerous land grants to help settle new sections of New Mexico. During the war with Mexico in 1846, General Stephen Kearney and his U.S. troops occupied the province of New Mexico. Taos rebelled against the new wave of invaders and in 1847 killed the newly appointed Governor Charles Bent in his Taos home. In 1850 the province, which then included Arizona, officially became the territory of New Mexico of the United States.

During the Civil War, the Confederate army flew its flag for six weeks over Santa Fe. It was just prior to this time that Kit Carson, Smith Simpson, Ceran St.Vrain and others put up the American flag over Taos Plaza and guarded it. Since then, Taos has had the honor of flying the flag day and night.

The discovery of gold in the Moreno Valley in 1866 and later in the mountains near Taos brought many new people to the area. Twining and Red River, once mining towns, are now prominent ski resorts.

The Carson National Forest contains forested lands in the Sangre de Cristo and Jemez Mountain Ranges. It was created from the Pecos

River Forest Reserve of 1892, the Taos Forest Reserve of 1906, and part of the Jemez National Forest of 1905.

A narrow gauge railroad, the Denver and Rio Grande Western, was built from Alamosa, Colorado, to twenty-five miles southwest of Taos in 1880. In later years it was nicknamed the Chili Line and eventually connected with Santa Fe. A surrey and four horses joggled passengers from the station to Taos. During World War II, the train was discontinued; Embudo Station on the Rio Grande is all that is left of it today.

The next invasion began in 1898, when two eastern artists came to Taos and depicted on canvas the dramatic mountains and unique peoples. By 1912, the Taos Society of Artists was formed by these and other artists who had been attracted to the area. New Mexico became a state in 1912 as well.

World Wars I and II came and went, and members of the three cultures of Taos—Indian, Spanish and Anglo—fought and died together for their country.

In 1965, a steel arch bridge was built west of Taos to span the gorge 650 feet above the Rio Grande, thus opening the northwestern part of New Mexico to easy access from Taos.

TAOS (TUA-TAH) PUEBLO

Taos Pueblo, home of the Taos-Tiwa Indians, is the site of one of the oldest continually inhabited communities in the U.S. The name Taos is a Spanish version of the native Tua-tah, which translates as 'in the village.' Taos Pueblo is the northernmost of New Mexico's nineteen pueblos; it is located seventy miles north of Santa Fe, the state capital, two miles north of the world-famous art colony of Taos, and some fifteen miles from the internationally renowned Taos Ski Valley. The pueblo is at an elevation of 7,000 feet.

The origin of the pueblo in its present form goes back many hundreds of years before the Spanish arrived in 1540. It goes back some 300 years before Marco Polo traveled to China in the 13th century. Had Columbus discovered the 'new' world even 500 years before he did, back when Europe as we know it was young and 'America' was not even a vision, and had he proceeded immediately to the great

Southwest after stepping ashore on a remote island off the Atlantic Coast, he would have found in place in Taos a vibrant and established culture. The pueblo was here long before Europe emerged from the Dark Ages and made the transition from medieval to modern history. Regiments of Spanish conquistadors from Coronado's 1540 expedition were the first Europeans to see Taos Pueblo. The Spaniards reportedly were in quest of the Seven Cities of Cibola (the Fabled Cities of Gold) and they believed they had finally found one of the cities of gold when they saw Taos Pueblo from afar, perhaps with the sun shining upon it. What the Spaniards saw was not a city of gold but two massive, multi-storied structures made of shaped mud and straw and with soft, flowing lines which came to be the distinctive architectural style of the entire southwest.

Taos Pueblo looked very similar to the way it does now, divided into north and south houses by the westerly flowing Rio Pueblo de Taos. In 1680 a massive revolt against the Spanish was conceived in Taos and launched successfully by the united effort of all the pueblos. The Spanish were driven back into Mexico and all of the territory of New Mexico, including the Spanish capital of Santa Fe, was again in Indian hands. This was an event truly distinctive in the annals of American Indian resistance to the opening of the 'new world.' It remains today the only instance where extensive territory was recovered and retained by Native Americans through force of arms. Taos, the seat of the rebellion, returned to its traditional, full independence for a period of almost two decades. The Spanish returned in 1693 with a large army, but Taos itself remained the center of open rebellion for some five years after the southern pueblos were once again subjected to foreign control. This distinctive military success is especially noteworthy in light of the fact that the traditionally peaceful, agrarian-based pueblos achieved it, a tranquil society that initially welcomed the foreigners with open arms.

The pueblo's Native religion and culture survived not only the turmoil of the last decade of the 17th century—a hundred years before the birth of the United States of America—but also the 1847 rebellion of the pueblo against the new American government that replaced the Mexican and Spanish dominance. Taos Pueblo has retained its old ways to a remarkable degree. The rich cultural heritage of the pueblo is exemplified not only in the exquisite architecture but also in the annual seasonal dances. Visitors to the pueblo are welcomed to observe the dances, but are not allowed to take photographs of them. The current reservation economy is primarily supported through the provision of government services, tourism, arts and crafts, and ranching and farming. In 1980, the tribal council established a Department of Economic Development to generate tribal revenue and job opportunities and to assist local Indian businesses. Many opportunities for development are available to the pueblo, some of which include increased capitalization of tourism, labor-intensive clean-industry plants, and office rentals.

ALFRED J. MONTOYA'S (TAOS) STORY

I met Alfred at his Taos adobe home situated within eye's view of the mountains that rise from the east. Alfred was very forthcoming with his story and we both shared with each other personal thoughts and beliefs regarding the spirit world. I know you'll appreciate Alfred's story and at its end, his personal comments.

— Antonio

"I was born on the Taos Pueblo Reservation in 1950. The beautiful mountains, which surround the pueblo, are the Sangre de Cristos (Blood of Christ). The Spanish gave them this name because, during some sunsets, the light that reflects from the sky onto these mountains colors the mountains red. These mountains are sacred to the pueblo people and are honored in a very special way. I always enjoy hiking into the mountains and being at peace with our Mother Earth. I do some hunting of deer, elk and bear, and a lot of fishing. As a member of the pueblo, I don't need a hunting license to hunt these animals; however, outside of the pueblo land it's required. I prefer to stay here in our mountains where I feel free  to do as I wish without restrictions. It was in these sacred mountains where I had my first experience with spirits.

In the fall of 1974, the forest service employed me. My job duty was to clean up areas where irresponsible hikers and campers had tossed paper, bottles, cans and other trash in the forest. The crew of guys I was with used horses to travel about the area. One day we were instructed by our supervisor to ride up to Blue Lake, which lay deep within the mountains, and clean up the area. I was busy with some other work at the time and was excused from heading out early. The others in my crew, including my supervisor, left in the morning, and I was to meet up with them later in the afternoon. Eventually, I reached the lake at about 3:30 p.m. that afternoon. I scouted the area and spotted horse tracks and footprints all about the ground. I knew that the crew had done their job of cleaning up the area, so I decided to head out in the direction the crew might be, in order to later meet up with them. I had been instructed by my supervisor earlier that day to locate and follow an old crude barbed-wire fence. By following the fence, I would travel in the direction the men would be going. This was a short-cut route. I gazed above the mountain tops and noticed that the clouds were traveling fast. The cold night would soon come, so I attempted to hurry as best I could. Luckily, I had packed a few food supplies and a bedroll on my horse before leaving for the mountains. All I knew was that the place where I would meet the others was what we called in our pueblo language, 'place of the onion grass.'

Ultimately, I did locate the barbed wire fence. It branched out in two directions; one went east, the other west. I sat on my horse for a few minutes, trying to decide which way to go. Trying to make sense of everything was difficult, especially since the forest was pretty thick with growth. I decided the best option was to follow my instincts and head in the direction I thought was north. I began to notice that things were not right. I knew I was getting lost because, after about five miles of riding, I began to travel down a ridge, which was unfamiliar to me. To make matters worse, the sun would soon be giving way to the night, so I needed to locate my friends. Before long, I reached an area that I recognized from other previous visits to the area. Immediately I knew I had gone too far and had missed the trail. I reached a stream and followed it north. I needed to hurry because the sun was now behind a ridge and a cool breeze was settling in. Suddenly I turned to my right and I saw a beautiful big buck, about a ten pointer! The buck had his head lowered and was drinking from the stream. My horse made a noise, and the buck raised his head. He faced my direction and I could see his big, dark eyes gazing at me. I always carried a pistol with me, so when I saw this buck out in the open, I knew the opportunity for fresh deer meat was just a few feet away from me. I slowly reached for my gun, brought it into my line of sight, and had the buck in my view. Something inside me made me lower the pistol. I decided not to shoot. I put my pistol away and then looking right at those big black eyes, I held up my hand and in the Indian way said, 'Good-bye, my brother. We will meet again someday.' As I rode my horse away, I took a short glance behind me and noticed the buck just stared at me. I soon reached the meadow area known as 'the place of the onion grass.' Since it was already dark, I thought it would be best to make camp for the night. I could join up with my buddies in the morning.

It didn't take long for me to make a fire and roll out my sleeping bag. I led my horse a little way to a grassy area of the meadow and left him to graze for the night. It was definitely a dark night. As I ate some of the food I had brought with me, I gazed up at the stars and felt at peace. I asked the Creator and Mother Earth to protect and watch over me. I threw more wood on the fire and listened to the cracking and snapping noises it produced as the wood was consumed. I rose from where I was seated and went to get my horse. I returned to the camp and tied my horse close to where I could keep an eye on him. Throwing more wood onto the fire, I decided to make some coffee. There I was in the cold darkness with both hands wrapped around my coffee mug. Everything was peaceful and soon I felt sleepy enough to climb into my sleeping bag for the night. I watched the fire dance before me and very soon my eyelids became heavy. Before I closed my eyes, I heard some noise to my right. I sat up in the sleeping bag and turned my head in the direction of the noise. The flickering light of the fire illuminated the area I was looking at. There, from the forest, came into view a man dressed in old, traditional-style Indian garments. He was dancing but had his back towards me. He came closer and I kept still. He had an odd manner of dancing which I was not familiar with. Soon he was across the fire from me. Al- though I heard no music, no drumming sound, he danced and sang with a rhythm all his own. He danced in a backward motion. I was unable to make out his facial features because his head movements were

so quick and sudden. I just saw a blur. It was very difficult to focus on his face. The song he sang was unrecognizable to me. Even the words he sang were strange. I was interested in knowing who this man was, but at the same time I was scared. It was very odd to see this man out here in the forest before me. Because of his clothes, I knew he was from another time, long ago. As he danced, he raised his arms and soon began to motion towards the darkness. He motioned as if calling someone to join him in his dance. It was strange to see this faceless man dancing and motioning as he did.

Then from the direction he was facing came another figure, a woman. She slowly entered the lit area and began to dance with the man. Unlike the man who sang throughout his dance, the woman remained silent. She danced in a forward direction, taking steps left then right, left then right. I was frozen with fear and amazement. I was as still as I could be. She was also dressed in old-style clothes. She wore traditional leggings and moccasins, and her hair was done up in the traditional pueblo woman manner. Over her back she wore a manta (a shawl worn over the shoulders and back). Although I was able to make out all the details of her outfit, her face was a blur also, and she was not someone I recognized. I kept quiet as they both danced in unison. I was mesmerized.

Suddenly, they made their way away from my camp and fire and moved towards the stream. It was at this point that I heard them both laughing. They soon disappeared by the stream and into the darkness of the night. During this 'spiritual performance' I was unable to move my arms, legs or other part of my body. My eyes saw the vision and my ears heard the sounds. My focus was centered in simply observing and nothing more.

After they left me, I was alone with my thoughts. I knew what I had

just witnessed was a spiritual sign. I was left mentally numb. I just sat there in a void. Then again, I heard some sound coming from the north. I turned and saw what appeared to be flashlights coming my way through the forest. Great! I thought. My buddies had seen my fire and located my whereabouts! There were three lights and they moved around in the darkness, coming closer and closer towards my direction. I was so relieved and happy that they had found me. After what I had just seen, they couldn't have come at a better time. As the lights came closer, they suddenly stopped about a hundred yards away. I threw more wood into the fire and waited. Expecting to see my friends' faces any second, I sat back in my sleeping bag.

Out of the forest came three male figures, three men whom I did not recognize! As they got closer I saw that they had three horses with them. When they got to about fifty yards from me, I saw that they were Indians and were dressed in white-man's clothes: Levi jackets, jeans, etc. Once they were close enough for me to hear their voices, I heard them speak in mumbling tones. I was unable to make out what they were saying. As soon as they spotted me, they stood still. I don't know why or how, but immediately I knew I was being visited by more spirits once again. As soon as this thought came over me, I closed my eyes and prayed. When I opened my eyes, the men were opposite the campfire. Then, suddenly, in an instant, they had moved to another area of my camp, horses and all! Then, in a blink of an eye, they were back where they were before, all seated and gazing in my direction. Altogether, they extended their fingers towards me and pointed in a way that made me think I was something funny to them. They spoke, but all I could make out were mumbling sounds. At one point, one of the men bent forward to get a closer look at me. I looked at their horses and then at the fire, which separated us. The man who had his eyes focused on me then let out a big laugh. I was scared.

I must have passed out because when I came to, I found myself out of my sleeping bag, on the ground, several feet away from where I had been by the fire. I was on the cold ground shivering. The last thing I remembered was being in my sleeping bag, and now here I was freezing on the open ground several feet away. I got up and walked over to where the fire was. It was out, but there were still some hot glowing coals in the pit. I threw more wood on top of the coals and soon I got a fire going again. I took my loaded pistol in one hand and a flashlight in the other and walked around the area where I had seen the three men. There was no sign that the ground or grass had been disturbed. I noticed that the sun was lighting up the sky before it made itself known above the mountains. As the light made the ground around me more visible, the only tracks I could find were the ones I had made coming into the meadow. There were no others. The grass was wet with dew and undisturbed. I soon packed up my horse, cleaned camp, and rode up the ridge away from the meadow. I couldn't erase from my memory what had happened to me just a few hours before. I was comforted by the morning sunlight that warmed my face and by the songs of the birds flying in and out of the trees.

Up in the distance I spotted my friends riding down the ridge. I heard them let out a yell and call out my name. I knew immediately these people were not spirits, but living human beings! As we met up with each other, my buddies had a shocked expression on each of their faces. 'Hey Alfred, you look pretty pale,' one guy said. 'What happened to you?' I began to describe the night before to them. They freaked out! They were quiet throughout my story and when I was through, they began to tell me a story of their own.

They said that at about the same time that the spirits had appeared to me, they had all seen two Indian spirits! At first they heard the sound of footsteps running over the forest ground among the trees. Then a strange sense of someone watching them from the darkness overwhelmed them all. As they all sat quietly before their campfire, looking at each other, suddenly two Indian men dressed in old-style warrior outfits came out of the forest, running at full speed right by them. Of course, they all knew something unusual and spiritual was taking place. The two warriors just raced by and disappeared into the forest from where they had come. After discussing among ourselves the possible reasons for what we had all experienced, we had no answers and were perplexed. I was apparently the most puzzled of all. I guess my friends saw this and decided that I needed to have a spiritual cleansing. My friends had me face north and in the afternoon sunlight I was prayed over in the Indian way, in order to remove the bad forces I might have been exposed to. We all headed back home and did not speak about what had happened any more.

That evening, arriving at my house, I did mention my experience to my grandmother. She looked at me and listened to each word as if I was telling her something very important, something sacred. Then, after I was through, she held my hands and informed me that she had some sad news for me. I was told that my other grandmother had died the same night I had had my vision. My grandmother also told me that what I had experienced was my other grandmother's way of showing me that she was all right and was now passing into the other world, the spirit world. Grandmother further informed me that the dancing man and woman headed in a southerly direction and disappeared because, 'That's the spirits' way; they travel south. You were where our Sacred Blue Lake is located. It's the spirits' way.' Grandmother then told me that the three men, who showed themselves to me, after the two dancing spirits had left, were very different from the man and woman. 'You know, those three spirits were very powerful. It was a good thing you did not speak to them. Keeping quiet was the best thing for you to do. Otherwise those spirits would have taken you away with them. You would have been left dead in the forest, your spirit would have been lifted away, and all we would have found would be your body. We would not have known what was the cause of your mysterious death. What saved you was the campfire that kept burning between where you were and where the spirits were. It was good that you asked the Creator for a blessing and for Mother Earth to protect you that night.'

The story I have just told you is the truth. It is what I saw with my own eyes. There are people who do not believe in these things, but some do. I'm happy to know that my grandmother who passed away chose to let me know how she was and that she was headed to the spirit world. Because of the darkness that night, I could not recognize her. The dancing spirits were presented to me for a purpose; they were not bad or evil. But the other spirits, the three men... Well, I knew something was not right when I saw them.

You know, there are many other stories and incidents that have taken place in and around the pueblo. I have experienced some very strange things. There are such things as witches and evildoers, but I would rather not talk about them. To talk about them would only give them more strength and increase their power for doing bad. There are areas of power up here in the mountains, areas that feel negative to the soul. Indian people whom I've spoken to tell me that, as they travel through the forest, they can sometimes feel the presence of eyes gazing at them from between the trees. Some have even told me that they feel the presence of someone following them, something that moves from behind the trees, and hides among the shadows. There are a lot of things that have happened to people around here. Most people prefer not to talk about them. Perhaps it's best not to. We'll leave it at that."

LARRY C. TIBBETTS' (ANGLO) STORY

This interview was held within the restaurant's dining room. Having to frequently stop and restart the interview while Larry attended to immediate business situations was for me, well worth the story. It's not uncommon for the purchasers of a new property to discover personal items that were forgotten or even purposefully left behind by a previous owner. But what Larry discovered in his restaurant's basement was indeed a shocker for both Larry and his fellow staff.

— Antonio

"The Garden Restaurant began in this building thirteen years ago. Before that it was an indoor flea market, and before that it was a grocery store. I've personally been associated with the restaurant since it began. Currently, the Garden Restaurant serves breakfast, lunch and dinner, and we have a bakery. We're located on the Taos Plaza, so it's easy to locate and often a resting point while people are window-shopping or strolling through the many stores and galleries. It's also a popular gathering spot for locals and tourists alike.

It was either the first or second day after purchasing the property that I decided to take the stairs down to the basement and look around. I found the usual items that would be found in such an old building—cardboard boxes and trash. However, in one corner of the basement, there was a cardboard box, which, surprisingly, contained a complete human skeleton. Pulling back the cardboard flaps, I could see the rib, hand, spine, leg and arm bones, a disorderly mass of bony framework,

including the skull. The bones were surprisingly clean, although dusty. Apparently, one of the past owners of the building was into archaeology. Soon afterward, when the basement was cleaned and all the trash removed, the box, which contained the bones, was moved to the rear of the basement and forgotten.

Two years later, the restaurant changed hands. The new owners, who were devout Catholics, took notice of the box with the skeleton and decided to have a local priest perform a blessing over the bones and bless the building. An archaeologist from the local museum was also called in and revealed the origin of the bones. We were told that they were of a Native American woman. For their own reasons, the new owners named the skeleton Snowflake. After the priest was done with his blessings, the box of bones was taken somewhere in town and reburied. I've not ever had anything spiritual or unusual happen to me here in the building, but employees have. I've been told of strange noises, cold chills and other stuff happening to workers. Our two bakers, Anna and Earl, who spend most of their time in the basement where the bakery is now located, have experienced such strange things."

ANNA M. JOHNSON'S (ANGLO) STORY

"I have been one of the bakers at the Garden Restaurant now for about seven months. The ghost, or 'Snowflake' as the employees call her, has made her presence known to me in very strange ways. Although I've been scared by her,

I want to think she'll never do me any harm. I hope she is a kind and friendly spirit, at least to me. I try to do nice little gestures to show her that I would like to be her friend. For instance, whenever I have any leftover dough, I will bake her a mini-loaf, and place it away from the other employees' view. I usually place it on top of a shelf and in the back, away from view. Strangely, when I look for it in a few days, it will be gone. I'll then ask the others about the 'missing' bread and they won't have a clue. I make these personal offerings of good will to Snowflake because I don't want her to do anything mean or evil to me. I admit that when I'm alone in the basement, the last thing I want is to have a nasty ghost watching my every move. Of course I get scared. Who wouldn't? So my little bread loaves for Snowflake are my guarantee that she will leave me alone.

I know when Snowflake is around because I'll hear strange footsteps on the ceiling above me. When I'm alone down there in the wee hours of the morning, sometimes I'll hear these footsteps. The temperature in the basement reaches between 90 to 100 degrees because of the ovens. Strangely, I'll feel the presence of someone in the basement with me. It's a freaky feeling. Then suddenly, I'll feel this bone-chilling cold wind. I'll become motionless, because I already know this is the sign that the ghost is about. Suddenly, this cold wind will pass right through me! The cold air will last about thirty seconds, then slowly it passes. I experience this about once or twice a week between the hours of 9 p.m. and 5 a.m. If someone speaks of the ghost or mentions her name, it's almost a guarantee that she will give you a dose of cold air. Because I've been talking to you about her during this interview, I know she will become excited and make her presence known to me tonight. I just know it! I'm not the only person who has experienced this. There is another baker named Earl who has heard the noises and felt the cold wind.

A couple of months ago, two other bakers and I were working in the basement when suddenly we all heard the sounds of footsteps coming from above. We stopped what we were doing, and when the sounds continued, we looked at each other. Then, without any more notice, we heard a large metal object hit the floor above us. Boy, we were scared! The footsteps continued, only this time we heard a larger metal object being dragged as well. We all knew there was a burglar in the restaurant above us. Then we heard the footsteps become louder and louder. I grabbed a large knife that was on the table, and with the other two employees following behind, we made our way slowly but cautiously up the stairs. We turned on the lights but saw no one. We looked under every table and in each bathroom. Nothing was out of place. The doors were all locked from the inside. Immediately, we knew that the source of the noise was not due to any living person. It had to be Snowflake!

There are other times when I'll be in the basement and I'll hear the pots and pans making all sorts of noise. I'll go into the next room where they are kept on the shelves and hanging on hooks. I'll find several pots thrown over here and pans thrown over there. It's crazy. Sometimes I'll be busy at work listening to the radio, and then I'll hear a noise, look up and see two, three, or more pans just fly off the rack onto the floor, slide across the room, and end up at the opposite wall! I know there are such things as ghosts. If I didn't know before, I sure do now. I get scared sometimes when I'm alone in the restaurant. Although Snowflake has scared me, I know she is just upset because of all the years her bones were kept unceremoniously in a cardboard box. Her spirit must be trapped within the walls of the restaurant. I just hope she finds rest and peace someday."

SALINAS MISSION AND PUEBLOS OF THE SALINAS VALLEY

In the stones of the Salinas Valley Pueblo Ruins one can hear the faint echoes of the communities that lived there three centuries ago. Before they left the area in the 1670's, Pueblo Indians forged a stable agricultural  society whose members lived in apartment-like complexes and participated through rule and ritual in the cycles of nature. Two ancient Southwestern cultural traditions - the Anasazi and Mogollon - overlapped in the Salinas Valley to produce the later societies at Abo, Gran Quivira and Quarai. These traditions had roots as far back as 7,000 years ago and were themselves preceded by nomadic Native

Americans who arrived perhaps as many as 20,000 years ago. As the Southwestern cultures evolved, better agricultural techniques from Mexico and the migration of Tompiro and Tiwa speaking peoples from the Rio Grande spurred the growth of settlements in the Salinas Valley. By the 10th century, substantial Mogollon villages flourished here. The dwellers practiced minimal agriculture supplemented by hunting and gathering, made a simple red or brown pottery, and lived in pit houses. Later, they lived in aboveground jacales of adobe-plastered poles.

By the late 1100's the Anasazi tradition from the Colorado Plateau, introduced through the Cibola (Zuni) district and Rio Grande Pueblos, began to assimilate the Mogollon. The contiguous stone-and-adobe homes of the Anasazis represented the earliest stage of the pueblo society later encountered by the Spanish. Over the next few hundred years the Salinas Valley became a major trade center and one of the most populous parts of the pueblo world, with perhaps 10,000 or more inhabitants in the 17th century. Located astride major trade routes, the villagers were both producers and middlemen between the Rio Grande villages and the plains nations to the east. They traded maize, piñon nuts, beans, squash, salt and cotton goods for dried buffalo meat, hides, flints and shells.

By 1300 the Anasazi culture was dominant, although the Salinas area always lagged behind the Anasazi heartland to the north in cultural developments. Brush-and-mud jacales had evolved into large stone complexes, some with hundreds of rooms, surrounding kiva-studded plazas.

Besides the domestic plants already mentioned, the inhabitants ate wild plants, raised turkeys, and hunted rabbits, deer, antelope and bison. They wore breechcloths, bison robes, antelope and deer hides, and decorative blankets of cotton and yucca fiber. Turquoise and shell jewelry obtained in trading were used in rituals. The Pueblos' weaving, basket-making and fine black-on- white pottery, a technique the Salinas people borrowed from the Rio Grande pueblos, impressed the Spaniards.

The Salinas pueblo dwellers were an adaptable people who drew what was useful from more advanced groups. But strong influences from the Zuni district, the Spanish explorers, and deteriorating relations with the Apaches to the east radically altered pueblo life. In the end, cultural conflict and natural disaster devastated the Salinas pueblos. The Apaches, formerly trading partners, began raiding the pueblos both for food and for revenge for Spanish slave raids in which Pueblo Indians had participated. The pueblos might have survived the raids, but along with the Apaches and Spaniards they were hit during the 1660's and 1670's with drought and widespread famine that killed 450 people at Gran Quivira alone. Recurring epidemics further decimated the population, which had little resistance to introduced diseases. The ability of the pueblos to withstand these disasters may have been weakened by the direct disruption of their culture under harsh Spanish rule. In any event, the Salinas pueblos and missions were abandoned during the 1670's, and the surviving Indians went to live with cultural relatives in other pueblos. In 1680 the pueblos north of Salinas, in an uncharacteristic show of unity, revolted and expelled the Spaniards from their lands in New Mexico. In the general exodus of Native Americans and Spaniards, the Piro and Tompiro survivors of the Salinas pueblos moved south with the Spaniards to the El Paso area. Indian communities there absorbed them, making them the only linguistic group among the Pueblo Indians during the historic period to lose their language and their homeland.

MARIA DE LA CRUZ'S (HISPANIC) STORY

I interviewed Maria in the home where she and her husband live, now located in the city of Albuquerque. From time to time during the interview, she asked me to stop the tape recorder in order to gather her emotional strength. I could clearly see that the interview was not going to be easy for her. Maria still felt the fear of what she experienced over ten years before. The interview proceeded slowly but cautiously.
— Antonio

"My first experience at the Salinas Mission ruins took place about ten years ago, when I was seventeen years old. My mother was going to spend the weekend with her sister and brother-in- law, who lived in the town of Mountainair. She asked me to accompany her on the trip. She knew I would enjoy the visit because I would also have the opportunity to visit with their children, my cousins. At the time, we lived just about twenty miles north of Mountainair, in the very small town of Estancia. We arrived at my cousins' house at 11a.m. My mother spent the time in conversation with her sister, me, my cousin Delfina, and Delfina's boyfriend.

After dinner, Delfina decided that we should go for a ride in her boyfriend's car. I told my mother about the plan, and she said, 'Just be back before it gets real dark.' Off we went. We drove west following the setting sun, listening to music from our cassette tapes. We were having fun just cruising along. Eventually, we came to a gate and a sign that read, 'Salinas Pueblo Mission National Monument.' Neither of us had ever visited the monument, but we knew a little about it from our parents. We decided to stop and look around. There was a small sign that hung on a chain across the dirt road leading to the entrance that read, 'Closed.' We decided to take a chance and left the car parked by the side of the road. We then walked over into the site. I asked Delfina and her boyfriend to take the lead. As she held onto her boyfriend's hand, I carefully followed behind. It was a warm August night and I knew from experience that on such nights rattlesnakes liked to come out of their burrows and feed. I didn't want to take any chances on getting bitten. We kept our ears open for a rattling noise. The moon was out and shining brightly, so this gave us confidence as we walked along the road. As we got within sight of the tall ruins of the church, we noticed a soft, yellow glow coming from within the structure. We thought there must be a private party for the park rangers or a celebration of some kind going on. As we got closer, we heard the low singing or chanting of church music. It wasn't very loud, but we could clearly hear it as we approached. Not wanting to be noticed, we carefully approached the front entrance of the church and looked inside.

We could not believe our eyes! There was a misty, yellow cloud that looked like fog. This fog floated about a foot or two above the ground. Above this cloud were several twinkling lights, similar to the flames of flickering candles. It was such a beautiful thing to witness that it didn't frighten us at all. We were amazed as we gazed at the wonderful sight.

The chanting music slowly intensified; however, we were unable to make out the words. Then, from within the fog, we saw the ghostly images of people slowly emerge! Their complete forms were difficult to make out, but I could see their shoulders and small heads. I said, 'Look, you guys! People are appearing in the cloud!' Delfina's boyfriend reached down and picked up a small stone. He took a swing and threw it. It landed within the middle of the cloud and immediately the ghostly images along with the cloud and bright light disappeared! That was all it took to send us running back to the car. Rattlesnakes or not, I didn't care where I stepped. I was determined to be the first one to reach the car and get inside!

Once we were in the car, we drove without stopping until we reached my cousins' house. We told our parents what we had seen, and they reprimanded us for being so foolish. 'You should never have done what you did. Don't you know those places are sacred? There are lots of spirits that hang around the mission, and you should give thanks to God that they did not take you with them!' Delfina's father told us about the time that he and his friend saw some ghosts at the mission when they were children. 'I remember the time that my friend Luis and I were playing in an area of the mission that had some small hills. We didn't know it at the time, but those small mounds were what were left of the original pueblo houses. We heard a noise in the trees, and then a large flock of birds flew away. Suddenly, everything seemed still; even the wind stopped. Then we saw three small shadows of people running in and out of the trees. They would look at us from behind the trees, and then they would run and hide behind other nearby trees. I got the feeling that they were playing a game with us. We never got close to them because we were somewhat afraid. I was nine and Luis was ten years old at the time, and as far as I'm able to remember, the ghostly shadows weren't any taller than us.'

Today, as an adult, I'll make sure that my baby is aware of ghosts, and that they should be respected. I never make fun of spirits. I know from experience that there are things we can't explain, so we should just leave them alone."

CHACO CULTURE NATIONAL HISTORIC PARK

The cultural flowering of the Chacoan people began in the mid 800's and lasted more than 300 years. We can see it clearly in the grand scale of the architecture. Using masonry techniques unique for their time, they constructed massive stone buildings, great houses, of multiple stories containing hundreds of rooms much larger than any they had previously built. The buildings were planned from the start, in contrast to the usual practice of adding rooms to existing structures as needed. Construction on some of these buildings spanned decades and even centuries. Although each is unique, all great houses share architectural features that make them recognizable as Chacoan.

In the 1100's and 1200's, change came to Chaco as new construction slowed and Chaco's role as a regional center shifted. Chaco's influence continued at Aztec, Mesa Verde, the Chuska Mountains and other centers to the north, south, and west. In time, the people shifted away from Chacoan ways, migrated to new areas, reorganized their world and eventually interacted with foreign cultures. Their descendants are the modern Southwest Indians. Many Southwest Indian people look upon Chaco as an important stop along their clans' sacred migration paths, a spiritual place to be honored and respected.

REX HENDERSON'S (ANGLO) STORY

My interview with Rex took place at his parent's home in the northeastern area of Albuquerque. We sat in his living room surrounded by examples of Southwestern art and family photos taken several years before. Said Henderson, "My father enjoyed photography. That's why in most every room of the house you'll find at least two or more examples of his work. On the wall and on the tables you'll find dad's passion. He loved taking pictures of nature and Indian ruins."

During our interview, from time to time Rex would need to excuse himself after becoming overwhelmed when reminiscing about his and his father's relationship. "I really loved my father. I miss him very deeply," he'd tell me. Although I had heard of strange occurrences that others had experienced at Chaco, this would be the first I'd record. I hope you enjoy this particular story, not simply for its narrative, but for its view into a historical past unique to New Mexico.

— Antonio

"Let's see, I guess to date, it's been about eight or nine years since my encounter with a spirit. Coincidently, I had recently been divorced from my wife. As bad luck would have it, as soon after our divorce was finalized my father died. My ex-wife Sherry and my dad got along very well, and when she heard about his death, she took it pretty bad. Sherry was not a terrible person at all; in fact, she was the best person to have ever had come into my life. But as in most things, change comes and sometimes we just have to admit to ourselves that it's time to accept and move on.

During our twenty years of marriage, Sherry and my mother were the primary caretakers of Pop. My father was a very active man before being diagnosed with Alzheimer's, and in the end it actually wasn't the Alzheimer's disease that killed my father. What took place one afternoon was that he had, without anyone noticing, walked out the side gate of the backyard; just slipped away quietly and in broad daylight. He was in the process of aimlessly wandering the streets several blocks away before my mother noticed that he was missing from the backyard. The police report noted that a witness spotted him standing between two parked cars. She stated that my father darted out into the street as an oncoming car hit and killed him. The hospital report stated that due to

245

his massive head injuries, he died instantly. It was a very sad time for my family and me and somehow we managed to get through the sadness and depression.

My father's body was cremated and I held onto his ashes for over a year before I decided together with Sherry and my mother that we needed to either bury them or disperse the ashes in a proper place. I mentioned to my mother that I wanted to take him to the Sangre de Cristo Mountains that surround Santa Fe. In her own manner, my mother made it very clear to me that she didn't want to go along with that. Sherry spoke and said, 'Rex, when your father was able to, he enjoyed reading about southwest anthropology. Do you think he would approve if we were to spread his ashes somewhere over in Chaco or maybe even the Grand Canyon?'

I gave her idea some thought and because Albuquerque was not that far from Chaco Canyon, it was my first choice. Arizona's Grand Canyon was close to a day's drive away—much too far a drive. Chaco was closer and for personal reasons I wanted to keep him in New Mexico. We all three decided on Chaco Canyon and even though we knew it had to be against the law to spread cremated remains in a national park, we decided to do this anyway. As the morning came and with dad's boxed ashes lying on top of our jackets on the car's back seat, Sherry and I drove about four or so hours to the park. My mother was unable to accompany us due to her age. The trip would just be too much to bear. The visit would be our first to the park for both Sherry and me. As we entered the park at around 3 pm, there were not many people that were visible.

We parked the car and soon placed the cardboard box containing my father's ashes in my backpack. We hiked about a mile to an area of the park that seemed isolated enough for the purpose of spreading my father. We hiked into an area of the ruins named Pueblo Bonito. I never would have imagined how huge and spectacular the ruins would be. It was so overwhelmingly large. Admittedly on a spiritual level the area seemed so magical. We were both totally caught off guard by its beauty and solitude. We walked around for a few minutes until Sherry found the perfect spot at the base of a very tall, stonewall for depositing the ashes. Directly above this wall was a window outlined in stone and at its top was a lintel of ancient wood constructed many hundreds of years before.

It was obvious to us that we were alone. Simultaneously we ceased talking and immediately noticed how still the air was. Everything was quiet and not even a blade of grass moved. Never did we hear even the sound of footsteps, a conversation, or the voices of any noisy distant hikers. But not wanting to risk being discovered, we quickly spread my father's ashes along the base of the wall.

As soon as I had returned the empty box to my backpack, we both decided to offer a personal prayer. But before we began this offering, we noticed that the wind began to start up. And not just wisps of wind; no, this wind had a very strong force behind it. It was so strong and sudden that my father's ashes blew up and over us! Most of the ashes blew away as Sherry and I quickly ran to the opposite side of the room just to avoid being covered in the swirling cloud of ashes! For sure this was very unusual.

In all the years I've lived in the Southwest, I've not ever encountered wind coming up in such a sudden manner and with such force. Together with the ashes, bits of debris were also being blown up off the ground. A fear came over us and with a forceful voice Sherry yelled at me, 'Let's get out of here—now!' We scrambled up and over the rocks and eventually made our way into the open. Very strangely, as we walked into the area at the outside of the ruin, the air was as still as it could be. We had no doubt that this was something very weird, maybe even paranormal. This windy occurrence was not a random thing; it definitely had something to do with the intent of our visit. In both our souls, we knew it had to be. We gave thought to the possibility that if the wind was a sign of my father's presence, then why were we so gripped by fear? My father would be pleased to be honored in such a manner. No, this was not what I'd call a pleasant experience. Sherry and I were both left wondering if the spirits of the ancients were angry with us. And not much later we were to soon find out.

That evening as we drove out of the park we chose to stay at a motel in the town of Thoreau, several miles south of Chaco on Highway

40. It was just too late to continue on to Albuquerque. Here's when things got even stranger. We had an experience that proved to us that we had indeed done something that was not welcomed by the spirits. Deeply asleep in our bed, I was the first one awakened by the loud sound of a glass breaking in our room. I thought it was a glass; I still can't imagine what it was, but it sounded very much to me like a glass window had been broken. I opened my eyes and looked all about the room. Sherry soon awoke and asked me what was going on. I told her that I had heard a sound. She kept still. She kept quiet because as soon as I had answered her, we both immediately began to catch the scent of something very musty and moldy. It was an awful odor; something that gripped the back of my throat and even made my gag reflex react. Sherry immediately sat up in bed as I sat against my pillow. 'What is that smell?' she said. The smell soon became overwhelming to her. As we were sniffing the air, I noticed that the odor immediately became even stronger. I spoke, 'It smells like rotted, musky tanned leather, or very old rotted cardboard.' After saying this, we got the fright of our lives!

We both spotted a large, dark shadow, more of a mass of darkness, begin to come out from the wall. I'm not ashamed to say that this caught us off guard and made us jump against the bed's headboard! Right after seeing this, a person's arm materialized! The arm reached out from the darkness towards our bed; nothing else, just the arm, nothing else. The arm was not attached to a body— it was just an arm. Surprisingly, it made a swaying motion, something like a hula dancer would make. We both saw it at the same time and there was no doubt that this thing was a ghost! Without giving it any further thought, I grabbed and pulled away at the pillow that Sherry was leaning against and threw it at the ghostly arm—making a direct hit! I jumped out of the bed, then reached for the light switch and turned it on. The only evidence of having been visited by the ghost was the pillow on the floor; nothing else. The odor also had disappeared. We were both shaking and Sherry very much wanted to get back in our truck and drive back home that night. In a loud voice she said, 'I don't want to go through any more ghostly stuff like that again.' I left the light on and answered, 'Sherry let's just try and go to sleep. I don't think we'll have any more visits.' Without a pause Sherry spoke, 'Nope, I'm not going to stay here another minute. If you want to come with me, I'll drive us home, but I'm leaving with or without you—I'm out of here!'

In less than ten minutes, we quickly packed our few clothes in a plastic bag, got into the truck and headed home. During our drive home, we discussed the situation and both agreed, without a single doubt, that a ghost visited us, if only by an arm, it was a spirit nonetheless. The action of the wind at Chaco earlier that day, followed by the hotel experience later that night, was evidence enough for me that having innocently disposed of my father's ashes in such a sacred site, was not appreciated by 'someone.'

Today, I do remain concerned that the spirits at Chaco did not hold my father's spirit accountable. He had nothing to do with what Sherry and I did. I regret it, but what was done was done. You can't go back and change it. Frankly, as beautiful a place as it is, I never want to set foot in that park again!"

ZIA PUEBLO

The pueblo is located approximately 16 miles north of Albuquerque, and eighteen miles northwest of Bernalillo, New Mexico. It might be a bit difficult to spot, being that the pueblo blends so easily into the natural features of the surrounding landscape. Historically, the pueblo has endured much adversity, given both its documented written and oral evidence pertaining to contact with western culture and natural disasters, tragically suffering over 600 lives lost in the Great Pueblo Revolt of 1680 alone. But survived it has. The state of New Mexico adopted this particular pueblo's symbol featuring the Zia symbol in red, upon its bright yellow background for the state's flag. The official salute to the state flag is, "I salute the flag of the state of New Mexico, the Zia symbol of perfect friendship among united cultures."

Today the pueblo's inhabitants share a common practice of existence by way of farming, carefully managing livestock, and producing beautiful traditional works of art, the most popular being unpolished red-ware pottery. Most Zia inhabitants are multilingual, speaking English, Spanish and their own traditional language of Keresan. The pueblo's Corn Dance is celebrated in the month of August concurrently with the religious Catholic feast day of Our Lady of the Assumption.

MARITA O. SALAS' (ZIA) STORY

This story took place oddly enough, at a parking lot in the northern New Mexico town of Taos. I, together with a Navajo friend from college, located Marita at a local restaurant, Michael's Kitchen, where we arranged to hold the interview and have lunch. I was amazed at the personal ghost story Marita presented to me. Not only was hers an eye-opening one, but one that included the introduction of witchcraft, animals and eventual spiritual renewal. Read her story and be as amazed as I was.

—Antonio

"I've lived on the Zia Pueblo for most of my life, but today I reside on the Santo Domingo Pueblo with my husband, Martin. I've had a lot of experiences with spirits and I'm not the only one in my family to admit to this. Encounters with spirits tend to be common within the Salas family. I know it's a gift, but it's a gift that must be treated with respect or terrible things could take place. I believe that with our sharing of knowledge, others might be more open to accepting visits from our friends and families who have gone over. Saying this, there are many who are totally scared of just the thought of possibly seeing a ghost or spirit. I believe that unless you realize early on that such things are, for the most part positive, you'll be missing a great opportunity to learn. That's how I look at it.

One of my experiences took place in 1996. I'll just tell you this one story for your book. I've encountered many more, but this is the only one I'll share with you. I was twenty-two at the time. My sister Lorrina had given birth to my niece, Agatha. Before Agatha was born, my sister had gotten into an argument with a woman from the San Felipe Pueblo.

Both of these women in their younger days attended the same high school and for years they had never gotten along. Their hatred for each other revolved over a guy, of course. Lorrina and the other girl were both interested in this one Santo Domingo fella, who today has moved away and is married and living in Los Angeles. Anyway, they never got along since high school. By chance Lorrina and this now grown woman happened to meet one day at the Sandia Casino's parking lot. The other woman's father, when alive, was known to be a witch in her pueblo. The woman cursed at Lorrina and noticing she was pregnant, pointing to my sister's belly, stated in her own language, 'That baby is going to always have a fear of the dark, because the darkness will always be her worst enemy!' My sister cursed her right back in our language. Then Lorrina and her husband got into their car and drove home.

The week before my sister gave birth, she was at home and the family was gathered in the living room one night watching television. I watched as Lorrina rose off her chair and was holding onto her belly. I asked her if she was alright, and she answered, 'Yeah, it's just that the baby is kicking me.' Then my sister walked over to the kitchen to fix herself a snack. As she was bent over the kitchen sink a loud 'thud' sound was made as something hit the window before her. My sister let out a scream and said, 'I just saw a woman's face appear in the window!' My twelve-year-old brother Felix ran out the door to see if he could find a woman on the property. He returned saying, 'Nobody anywhere around the house. But I found this dead bird under the window.' Felix stood before us, holding in his right hand the lifeless body of a small bird. Suddenly, the dead bird flew out of Felix's hand, flew for a few seconds around the kitchen, and then bounced off of my sister's belly.

Then after doing this, it fell lifeless to the floor. Lorrina gave another scream and yelled, 'Get that thing out of the house—it's a witch!' My mother ordered Felix to remove the bird to the outside of the house, and to put it on top of a trash can. Felix did this and also finding an empty coffee can, placed it over the dead bird, and used a rock to weigh it down. The rock was to prevent any cat or other animal from finding it and and removing it. Although we all felt very uneasy with the unusual things that had just taken place, my father asked us to not talk about it.

Talking about it he said would give the negative forces power; so none of us spoke a word about the bird for the remainder of that evening.

During the night, after having gone to bed, Lorrina's loud crying in the middle of the night awakened us all. She was awakened from sleep and called out for my mother. My mother ran to my sister's bedroom with me following right behind her. Opening her bedroom door, we found my sister sitting up in bed with tears flowing from her eyes.

'Mother,' she said. 'I just saw Dora. She was standing right over there  by the closet door. I really did see her—honest. She was staring at me and she was holding out a red sash with dark bird symbols on it. It was a wide sash and using both her hands. Dora held out the sash so that I could clearly make out the bird symbols. Dora spoke saying I was to wear it in order to protect my baby. Mom, I'm so scared!'

Before I go any further with my story, I'll tell you that Dora was my nine-year-old younger sister who died two years before. Dora developed cancer and did not survive more than five months after being diagnosed. My sister Lorrina was describing to my mother my dead sister's spirit who had visited her that night and had given her a sign, or instructions, in order to protect her from witchcraft. Eventually we all got to bed.

The following morning my father decided to make a visit to a local pueblo artist, a weaver, and purchase a red sash. This artist was a friend of the family, who was well known for making ceremonial dancing sashes. Father presented the sash to my mother. Mother used her skill in sewing and sewed several black bird patches along the middle of the sash and also sewed between each bird, a small blue cross. After completing this, mother gave the sash to my father who walked over to our Catholic church—Our Lady of Assumption. Father, together with my brother entered the church, walked up to the altar and placed the sash upon the altar asking for a blessing. After this was done, father dipped both ends of the sash into the basin of holy water at the entrance of the church and returned home. Both my parents presented Lorrina with the sash and my sister quickly wrapped it around her waist. A sense of comfort came over her and we all immediately could sense that our family's strong faith and unity was stronger than any witch's curse.

That same day my father asked my brother to light a fire and burn the dead body of the bird. My brother removed the rock and then lifted the coffee can off the bird—it was gone! Strangely, in its place were two short black feathers tied together with a short black cord! Hearing what had taken place, my father walked over to the trashcan and, using a long stick to drop the feathers onto the ground, he covered them with sticks and paper. Then he himself struck a match and lit it all on fire, making sure every last bit of the feathers were consumed.

Four weeks and a day later my sister gave birth to my niece, Agatha. Lorrina and her husband named the baby Agatha, but gave her the middle name, which in our language means, 'little blue bird.' Lorrina chose to add the word 'blue' to Agatha's middle name because when she was born, the tiny, purple veins on her chest over Agatha's heart formed what appeared to be the outline of a bird!

Today, my niece is a happy and healthy young girl. She even dances at our pueblo's feast day and is a great student. So, everything turned out fine. When she dances, Agatha always dresses using the red sash our family gave her mother years before. It's comforting to know that when confronted with evil, my younger sister's spirit came to our family's defense. I know there is goodness in the world, and all we have to do is work towards defeating the bad that wants to take over. Sometimes we, the living, need a little help to remind us that this is so. I am telling you my story because I know that the more people know that evil has no power over goodness, in the end evil will consume itself."

LAGUNA PUEBLO

With roughly eight thousand members, Laguna is the largest Keresan-speaking pueblo. Due to having one of the world's richest uranium fields located on the reservation, many of the pueblo's men became miners with a large number earning both geologically focused degrees and learning mechanical skills outside the pueblo. In the 1970's, a resurgence of the pueblo's traditional art of pottery-making was revised.

Not unlike their Acoma neighbors, the work of Laguna artists is easily identified by its orange, yellow and red colors. Laguna Pueblo celebrates the feast of St. Joseph on March 19th and on September 19th. The feast is known for its inclusion of many arts and crafts booths, carnival rides and sporting events.

HECTOR PEÑA'S (LAGUNA) STORY

The following interview was conducted at Hector's house on the Laguna Pueblo. Aside from his talent as a jeweler, Hector also enjoys the pleasures of surrounding his home with found objects such as unusable old saddles, boots which he props upside-down on fence posts, old bottles and other cast-off objects from a long ago time in New Mexico's past. Among these items, I spotted a goat or two, a few chickens and a very friendly grey cat. Hector explained, "I really enjoy my animals; they keep the bad spirits away; at least that's what I tell myself. The chickens provide me with eggs, and if the goats could do the same, can you imagine the omelets I'd make!" Hector and I got along well and being a humorous type of guy, after reading about his frightening experience, it would surprise you to think how he or anyone else could ever retain such a positive demeanor.

—Antonio

"I've lived at Laguna for all my life. I'm going to tell you my personal story of seeing a ghost when I was visiting a Navajo friend in Arizona. My friend Larry, who is Navajo, and I were silver jewelry-makers, making rings, pendants, bracelets and necklaces. We'd travel by car all over the Southwest and even into California selling our jewelry. We didn't get rich, but we managed to pay our bills and make some change on the side. Well, it had been just over a year since Larry and I had been on the road selling our inventory. Each of us had spent the previous year at our homes making more jewelry for the following year's sales. In the month of February, I drove my truck to Larry's home in Phoenix. The following day we were to drive to California to attend a large Los Angeles trade show of Native craft people. We had attended this show several times before, so we were excitedly anticipating the good sales the show would bring.

Before I go any further into my story you need to know that the Navajo people do not like to mention such things as ghosts or spirits. They keep quiet about this. It's not something they talk about. It disturbs them, and not unlike a lot of other tribes, they are respectful of the spiritual world. It so happened that Larry's house was being remodeled and because of this, we were going to have to sleep in his brother's house in nearby Tempe. His brother was not at home so we had the house to ourselves. This was not a big inconvenience. As the evening came, Larry loaded up his inventory into my truck and off we drove to his brother's house. The house was not a very large one, just a regular three-bedroom. But his brother had converted a backyard, two-car garage into a one-bedroom apartment. I told him that because I didn't want to hear any passing traffic noise, I would spend the night in this apartment. Larry said 'Okay, go ahead. I'll wake you at around 4 am. We'll dress, get some breakfast in town and after getting on the road, we should be in Los Angeles before 1 pm.'

Well, that was our plan, but strange occurrences over the night would soon change all that. I got to bed at close to 10 pm. When I entered the small room, I immediately felt a very strange vibe. I thought it might be caused by being in the odd, little confined space of the apartment. It was a small room, nothing very weird, but I had no other explanation. I decided not to concern myself too much with this, and instead entered the shower and after drying myself, I quickly got under the covers. Just five minutes after going to bed, I heard what sounded like a shoe falling to the floor. I looked around in the darkness and didn't notice anything that would make me think I was not alone in the room. So I lay back down on the bed and immediately dozed off. Then suddenly the movement of my top blanket being removed off my bed awakened me. I don't mean simply removed; the blanket was removed with strong effort. It was literally 'yanked' off, actually catching my leg in the process! Because I was suddenly awakened from a deep sleep, I was semi-aware of my surroundings. In the darkness as I used my hands to attempt to locate the cover, I reached to the floor. Taking hold of it, I brought it back to my bed and covered myself. I didn't think of a ghost. What I did think was that I had a severe dream and nothing more. I never gave any thought that a ghost was in the room with me; it really didn't cross my mind. Because I was so sleepy and tired from driving earlier in the day, I simply reached down, grabbed the blanket, and placed it haphazardly over me.

Closing my eyes for what must have been less then a minute, I heard a voice speak in the Navajo language. I am not conversant in Navajo, so I couldn't make out what was being said, but I can recognize the language. I immediately thought Larry was calling out to me from outside the front door, so I answered, 'Yeah, what is it?' But I didn't get a response. Thinking it must be something important, I got up out of bed and walked over to the door and opened it. Expecting to see Larry, instead no one was standing there. I stepped outside and looked around the small apartment and didn't see anyone. The lights were off in the house, and not even a neighborhood dog was barking. I knew I was imagining things.

When I walked back into the apartment, I didn't need to turn on a light in order to notice that my bed was a mess! The covers had all been removed from the bed, sheets and all, and were now placed in a large pile against the opposite wall! That did it; I grabbed my pants and shirt, and even decided to leave my shoes! I seriously wanted out of there and fast! I quickly walked over to the main house. I reached the back door, opened it and scrambled inside, choosing to spend the night on the living room couch.

In the morning, I was awakened by the sound of Larry turning on the kitchen faucet to make coffee. Larry was surprised to see me on the couch and asked me what caused me to decide to sleep in the house. I told him what I had experienced and he looked at me in a manner that gave me the impression he was well aware of what was going on. He said, 'I'm sorry Hector but I should have told you about my nephew's death. I didn't want you to get the 'willies' but he committed suicide a few months ago in his room—the apartment where you were sleeping in. He died of an overdose. I'm sorry Hector, but you know we don't talk about these things, especially since it's only been a few months.'

I was left speechless. But because I didn't want to cause any ill feelings between my friend and I, after dressing I chose to walk over to the rear apartment and pick up my shoes and shaving kit. But I was very, very hesitant to enter that room again. Before opening the door, I offered a prayer of respect to the young man's spirit and asked him to please not be offended by my entering his personal room. Locating my shoes then picking them up, I walked to the small bathroom and reached for my shaving kit. It was not there. I looked everywhere in that room. Not having a clue as to where it was, I walked out the door and almost tripping on it, my shaving kit had been placed right on the second stair, outside the front door! I had no words to describe the fear that gripped me at that instant. Especially knowing I needed to re-enter the room alone, I had intentionally left the front door wide open. I wanted to be prepared to make a quick dash for safety outside if I needed.

On the long drive to Los Angeles, Larry and I spoke about all types of things that were going on in our lives. We spoke a lot regarding our families, jewelry-making and such. But one topic we mutually knew would best be left unspoken was the topic of my ghost experience back in Tempe. That's all I can say about it. I hope whatever has taken residence in Larry's brother's backyard apartment is at rest and eventually finds peace. I know I'll never go back there again."

EVA MARIE BOWER'S (AFRICAN-AMERICAN) STORY

Eva and I met by shear coincidence within the parish mission office on the Laguna Pueblo. I was visiting the priest regarding another matter. After I concluded my meeting with the priest, and following a brief talk with Eva, I decided her story would add to my book. So, we met a few months later at her

257

home that doubles as a bed and breakfast.

In 1996, Eva Marie and her husband, T.C. Bower, opened the doors for business of their home and began the Apache Canyon Ranch Bed and Breakfast. The longtime residents of Albuquerque moved to Apache Canyon Ranch adjacent to the Laguna Pueblo lands in 1993 and decided to share their friendly retreat with the rest of the world.

--Antonio

"I've lived in New Mexico for thirty-eight years beginning June, 1971. In the mid-sixties, my husband, T.C. Bower, was stationed at Cannon Air Force Base located in eastern New Mexico. I was visiting from the state of Georgia and I immediately fell in love with New Mexico. Martin Luther King had just been assassinated four months prior to my visit and I was determined to move out of Georgia and make New Mexico my new home. I have to say that New Mexicans were very welcoming to my husband, our three children and me. From the beginning, we were made to feel right at home.

I also want to mention this side note; my grandfather, who was a 'great deal of a man' during his time, was born to a Cherokee slave woman and a Dutch man. They had nine children. My husband, children and I lived in Albuquerque from 1971 to 1993. In July of 1993, we made the move to Laguna. In June of 1996, we began the business of our bed and breakfast. Our last child left for West Point in 1982. Another of my sons is currently a physician living in Houston, Texas.

Historically the surrounding land upon which the current location of our house was built was once a part of the 70,000-acre land grant belonging to the King of Spain. It was in many years past, given to the Herrera family. The king took the land from the Native population, then 'granted' it back to them—less land than he took! For instance, the nearby Acoma Pueblo people were granted roughly one million acres, although the king took over two million acres of their land. The same thing took place with the surrounding Indian Nations in the area, including the Laguna and Canyoncito Navajos. The Herrera family arrived in the area from Spain. The Herrera's were originally named Smit, but before leaving Spain they were required to change their name to Herrera and to also adopt Catholicism. The descendants of the Herrera family gave me a copy of their family tree, which outlines what I just informed you of. Anton Smit, who was renamed Antonio de Herrera, was granted the land we presently live upon by the king. Throughout the years since, the Herrera family sold back to the Indians a great portion of this land area.

To the east of us, just a few years ago, a pueblo village site was uncovered. Directly where my house is located was the traditional wintering site of the Apache people. When we were digging the foundation for the house, which later became the bed and breakfast, we uncovered a whole mound of broken pottery shards. At the time Ben, a Navajo gentleman, our handyman, came to me very disturbed. He exclaimed, 'Skin-walkers were on the property last night!' He took me to where he had planted two fruit trees on the property, but overnight the base of the trees had been burned black with fire! He described that this was the work of a 'skin-walker.' A skin-waker is the half-human, half-spirit being of a medicine man or woman who travels at night causing ill and destruction. The worker believed that the burnt trees were a symbolic message directed to me, conveying the thought that because I built my house in the area, I was 'opening up' the land, welcoming the white man to enter! I responded to the man's words by stating, 'You tell the skin-walker that Eva has a big gun, and she'll put a big hole in the skin-walker's belly!' Since then, I never had another problem with skin-walkers on the property.

After opening the bed and breakfast, we always had guests comment on how much they enjoyed staying with us. Comments such as, 'I feel so good here,' or 'This is such a spiritual place,' were not uncommon to receive. Once we had a Presbyterian minister from North Carolina who stayed with us for five days. After the third day she mentioned to me, 'I'm seeing many different people on your property. People dressed in old fashion clothes and also wearing buckskins.' I asked her to not tell me any more. 'I'm scared; I don't want to hear any more about them. I'll die if I see them!' I said. She answered, 'Oh, Eva, don't worry. They seem very happy and I'm sure they're aware that you're not the most bravest person. They're not going to scare you.' She then continued, 'There is also another person I keep seeing in your house. She's a small black woman who sits in the living room who smiles at me. She seems to be such a sweet person.' I asked her to describe the woman to me. As she described the woman's features my jaw dropped! She had described my own mother to a 'T!' My mother had died several years before.

One other thing she mentioned, which I thought was pretty surprising, was during her walks on the trail behind our house, she encountered snakes that were stretched across the dirt trail. She mentioned that the snakes were so unusually placid that she'd simply stepped over them. Not being aroused in the least, they would remain still as she'd continue on her walk. My sister Mary visited me in 2006 from Georgia. She mentioned one morning, 'Eva, I'm seeing spirits in the house. I saw spirits in my room last night.' Not wanting to hear anymore of this because I'm such a chicken, I asked her to keep quiet and not mention the spirits to me ever again! I can't tell you anymore about what other spirits she saw because she never mentioned them to

"This is a picture of my mother standing to my right. She had described my own mother to a 't!"

me again, but she did see many more.

We have an abundance of coyotes on the property that offer up howls most nights. They don't bother me at all. They are very 'respectful' to our property. They carry on with their yapping all through the night, and sometimes when they become a bother, I'll walk outside and yell at them, 'Shut up coyote, coyote!' That's all it takes to keep them quiet. My son took a photo one winter of one of these coyotes that was brave enough to jump over our wall and was sniffing around in the yard. I must confess that I don't want to encourage visits from spirits.

I'm uncomfortable with even the thought of being visited by a ghost. I've grown even more uncomfortable with this idea since my own younger brother, James, who was a Viet Nam veteran, died. He's buried in Georgia, but lived with us in New Mexico for several years. He also had a job as an Albuquerque bus driver. During the war he was a truck driver, transferring supplies to the front line. My brother was in and out of VA hospitals for sometime due to an illness that halted blood from circulating to his limbs. Because of this illness, his right leg had to eventually be amputated. After my brother's funeral, which took place in Georgia, my younger sister Sheryl reported to me that his spirit visited her just two weeks after. She stated he was dressed very nicely and wore a red shirt when he appeared to her in her bedroom. My brother walked to her bedside then sat down on the mattress. His hair was combed nicely and he mentioned to her that he wanted to thank me for all I've done for him. Sheryl spoke to him saying, 'You have your leg back!' He responded, 'Yes, you have no idea how wonderful everything is here. I'm doing very well and mother is also here with me!'

One particular night after going to bed, I fell into a light sleep. I was awakened by the presence of someone in my bedroom. I opened my eyes and saw the spirit of my brother James in my bedroom, just as my sister reported. James appeared to me dressed in the same manner as he had appeared to my sister—red shirt and all. I immediately got out of bed and shot out of the room! Being a Catholic, I had always meditated on the mysteries of the holy rosary. I now regard what I experienced with my brother's spirit as personal growth, a development of my own spirituality. Now let me tell you, if a spirit would appear to me, I wouldn't be fearful for my life, but I would certainly be somewhat scared.

I know of a situation that took place with the Navajo people in the area. A young woman age 31 who had died was taken outside her home. At the moment of her death, they made sure that her body was well outside of the house. The Navajos believe that if a person dies within a house, the spirit of the person will linger after death and haunt the home. That's why they take the dying person outdoors, to release the person's spirit to the elements. When people ask me what's it like living out here in the vast open land, I respond, 'If the Indians like you, they don't bother you. If they don't like you, they don't bother you.' That about says it all, don't you think?"

JEMEZ SPRINGS PUEBLO

The Pueblo of Jemez located 27 miles northwest of Bernalillo is the only remaining Towa- speaking pueblo. Beautifully surrounded by colorful red sandstone mesas, the pueblo is situated within an awe inspiring natural setting of wonder. In the 1830's, survivors of nearby Pecos (Cicúye) Pueblo, a once-mighty trading center which now lies in ruins, joined Jemez. Many Pecos Pueblo warriors at first resisted the invading Spanish forces under conquistador Diego de Vargas twelve years after the Great Pueblo Revolt in 1680, but later allied with the conquerors.

Due to the popularity of all things Indian, which increased in the 70's and 80's, the potters of Jemez refined the quality of their clay art form, searching for a distinctive style of their own. Today, Jemez pottery stands alone and is recognized for its matte-on-gloss designs, stylized feathers and geometric designs. As of the date of this book's printing, the Pueblo of Jemez has generally closed its village to all non-Indians. The pueblo chose this policy due to not having adequate tourism facilities and for issues that arose regarding the privacy of its inhabitants. However, the pueblo village is open to the public only on feast days, but the pueblo chooses to not openly publicize these days. So ask around if you wish to attend.

Jemez Pueblo 1850

MARCUS D. PACHECO'S (JEMEZ) STORY

While visiting the Taos Pueblo, I made a pre-arranged date (my third) for my interview with Marcus. You need to know that Marcus is an interesting guy in that he's always on the go and very difficult to pin down. I was fortunate to eventually rope him in and sit him down for what would become another unique personal story. His particular story takes place both here in the United States and Europe.

Breaking a sincere personal contract between two men has in the past, but sadly lacking in the present, been accepted as a serious breach of personal integrity and not to be treated lightly. As you'll soon come to read, this not only pertains to the living, but also upheld as well by those who have passed. Marcus' story reminds us to hold true when giving our 'word,' and in doing so, we will be judged by our peers, both living and dead.

— Antonio

"My family has lived on the pueblo land for generations and I was born and raised in the Jemez Pueblo. In my family, I was the only one of my siblings to enlist in the armed forces. I chose the army. My father, being a carefree kind of guy, married and remarried three times and I was his oldest boy of his first marriage. Today I live in Taos with my wife's people and our two daughters. The story I'm going to tell you took place at Jemez Pueblo—my pueblo. I was around nineteen years old at the time of my experience. That spring after having decided to join the army, I would be headed out of New Mexico to Texas for training before being deployed to Germany. A few years later, after returning home from Germany, I met my future wife and I married. Because we didn't get along very well with my father's present wife, we chose to move off the Jemez Reservation and onto my wife's reservation in Taos. This is where we have lived since.

My story begins during my military deployment. It all began with a loan of money. Just a couple of months before leaving for Texas, I needed to ask a few friends for financial help. I needed to borrow some money in order to repair my car. As it turned out, my car gave out on me as I was headed back home one evening from the New Mexican town of Los Lunas. First the oil light came on the dash, then the car began to smoke and finally it refused to move. Apparently, a rock or something sharp had somehow punctured the oil pan underneath the engine and all the motor oil had leaked out leaving me with an engine empty of oil! If you know anything about a car's engine, oil is a car's lifeblood. Well, due to driving it without any oil, I managed to burn out the engine. The only way to repair it would be to remove the damaged engine and install a rebuilt one. But this of course would cost money. Money I didn't have. I began to ask around for financial help, but all I kept getting from my friends were excuses. Eventually, I did receive money from my father and from an older friend of the family named Andy. Andy lent me $1,500 with the understanding that I would repay him his money within two months. I agreed with this, and eventually managed to spend the money, only not on the car, but foolishly on other things. So, now I was left without a car and without Andy's money!

As the payment date was approaching within two months came closer, I knowingly kept avoiding Andy whenever possible. I even moved off the pueblo and moved in with my sister's family in Albuquerque. I was holding out for the couple of months that would bring my paperwork from the army, ordering me to ship out to Texas. I thought to myself if only I could avoid Andy for just a few more months—just so I could make my getaway. I know this was not the right thing to do, and if the pueblo governors would hear about this, I know they would intervene for sure and not in my favor. My negative behavior also didn't give my father a very good standing among our pueblo, but I was young, not thinking straight and frankly stupid.

As it turned out, my father was quite angry with me and informed me that Andy had saved the money he had loaned to me for several years. He was going to use it as a down payment to purchase a newer house. My response to my father was to tell Andy that I would make good on the deal once I returned from Germany in two or three years. But without my father relaying my message, or having a hint of illness, the following week Andy died from a stroke. So my message to Andy never made it to his ears.

It was not long after, that as I was doing my army base service in the city of Augsburg, Germany, I began to have what became a series of strange dreams. I would dream of being back home in Jemez, and then I'd be awakened from my sleep by the sensation of someone being in the room with me. I would wake and hear my name being 'yelled out' at me! There was nothing subtle about it; I heard a male voice yell out, 'Marcus, Marcus!' Being Indian, I knew that there was something going on that went beyond having a series of simple nightmares; no, there was much more to this. The voice was familiar, but not distinct enough for me to recognize who it might be. Then it was just a few days later when the thought hit me like a ton of bricks. The familiar voice, the voice that was calling to me in those dreams I was having – it's Andy's voice!

Dwelling on my new found discovery didn't help me. I became very nervous to the point of being straight-out obsessed with trying to make sense of the dreams. There was no way to deny the fact that Andy wanted me to make things right. I knew I had to do all in my power to appease him. Because today he was choosing to contact me in my dreams, how far would his spirit go to make his intentions known? Would the next step be for Andy to actually appear to me? I definitely didn't want that to take place. It didn't take long for me to decide that I had to make everything right with him. The wrong that I had committed by breaking our agreement was now becoming too real for me to ignore. Andy's spirit had taken the monumental action to follow me all the way to Germany!

As soon as I had the first opportunity, I contacted my father by phone and informed him of my dreams, and especially Andy's strong, emotional voice that would awaken me from my sleep. My father stated to me, 'You know our people don't hurt each other or break agreements between us like you did to Andy. Andy was a good man; he trusted you and you must do what's right. I didn't raise you like that. I'll need to contact someone here at the pueblo to pray for Andy's soul, but you'll have to repay him by helping out his family when you get back to the U.S. You be sure to tell him you'll keep your promise this time to make it all right when he calls out your name again!'

I promised my father that I would honor his words and do as he instructed me to. That same night I again had a dream and was awakened by Andy's voice calling my name. As soon as I sat up in my bed I spoke in a low voice, 'I promise I'll repay you. Andy please don't keep waking me up. You know I'll repay you somehow when I return. I promise.' Immediately after having spoken those words, I felt a relief come over me. Strangely, I felt a peace that took all the fear and anxiety I had focused on totally away. And following that night I didn't hear Andy's voice for several months until two nights before I was to get on the plane that would take me back to the states.

I again had the now familiar dream of Andy and was awakened by his voice. Only this time I actually saw standing, in the area at the foot of my bed, the dark outline of Andy's body! I remember saying, 'I'm so sorry. Please, please don't visit me anymore. I'll return you your money. Don't visit me anymore, please!' Within a second or two after saying my last word, his image, or his spirit, disappeared in a flash! As you might imagine, I didn't get much sleep for the remainder of that night.

Arriving in the states a few days later and heading right to the pueblo, I made it a point to immediately walk directly up to my father's house. After hugs and the initial conversation, I mentioned to my father all my encounters with Andy's spirit.

My father was not too surprised by what I spoke. He said, 'As long as you keep your promise to him and offer prayers to his spirit, I'm sure things will begin to get better for you.' I assured my father that I was sincere and showed him the cash I had saved and was carrying in my wallet — the cash which I was going to present to Andy's family. My father said, 'Andy was a good friend of mine and I've been offering him prayers while you were away. Give the money to Andy's daughter; his daughter is all that now remains of his family.' That same day after visiting with my friends and relatives, I slipped away while everyone was watching a baseball game on television and found myself at the pueblo's cemetery. Standing by Andy's grave, I spoke to his spirit sincerely offering my personal prayers over his grave. I had also thought ahead and brought along a small glass jar with a screw top lid. I reached into my pocket and retrieved the jar that contained one of the army caps I wore while in Germany. Using a stick as a shovel, I dug a hole and buried it at the foot of Andy's grave as a sincere gesture or offering. Not knowing what else to do, I stood in attention and saluted him.

Driving the short distance to my father's home, by coincidence I happened to meet up with Andy's daughter who was walking along the road with her young daughter. Not mentioning anything about my visit to her father's grave, or the events that led up to it, I presented her with the money that I had owed her father. She seemed annoyed at first, then after explaining to her my intentions, very surprised. We spoke a short while and after sharing a hug between us, I drove to my father's house and told him what I had done. He patted me on the back and said, 'Son that should take care of any more visits from Andy. I know everything is all now in the past. Andy was a good friend of mine and I know he's now satisfied.'

My father was correct. I have not gotten another visit from Andy's spirit and I don't believe I ever will again. It's been many years that have passed; my father has died and today I sit before you with a diagnosis of cancer. My cancer is a stage three cancer, but I'm not at all afraid of the future. My only concern is for my family. I know that I might not have many days to go, but I leave it for God to know where and when. But you know I do get reassurance from my experience with Andy's spirit. I know we don't stop existing when our bodies die; we just go on our personal road to who-knows-where. This was proven to me years ago when I was visited by Andy's spirit across the sea in Germany."

SAN FELIPE (KATISHTYA) PUEBLO

'Katishtya' today known as the Pueblo of San Felipe, is located 25 miles north of Albuquerque and 30 miles south of Santa Fe. In 1591, the pueblo was named San Felipe by conquistador Castaño de Sosa after the Catholic Jesuit martyr and saint who voluntarily gave his life in Japan. In 1590, the Portuguese Gaspar Castaño de Sosa led an expedition of 170 people from Mexico into the territory known today as New Mexico. The conquistador met his end while aboard a ship in the South China Sea during a slave insurrection. The pueblo has a great number  of artists, who work with pottery, embroidery and silver. Today, the people of this pueblo speak the Keresan language and have over 3,000 enrolled tribal members. The pueblo's Feast Day of San Felipe is celebrated on May 1st each year with hundreds who gather for the Green Corn Dance on the pueblo's central plaza.

IGNACIO F. GARCIA'S (SAN FELIPE) STORY

Here's a story told to me by a person who was fortunate enough to be counseled and directed by an elder in his family. The story is interesting in the fact that it encompasses the family's history of two generations that encountered similar spiritual forces. Animals have their place in Native culture; snakes as well can be counted in this honored position. Throughout the Americas, Native people have included rattlesnakes in their images. These depictions have been included in both the very personal arts, as well as the stone walls of pre-Colombian pyramids and immense earthen structures of North America. Read now a most interesting story of what is surely an example of communication between humans and our animal relations.

—Antonio

"My story is not about a ghost but about another strange thing. I know this story is different from what you might be accustomed to, but I think your readers will find it interesting.

My story took place several years ago on a day when I decided to take a hike directly behind our pueblo's land to the west. I took my younger brother with me and we walked for a few miles into the desert looking for the old roots of junipers that were nicely curved and weather worn. I used these roots in my artwork. I'd collect them, then in my workshop I'd fashion the frames for dreamcatchers. I'd soak the roots in water and after a few days, bend them into a circle, and then weave a cord of artificial sinew within the middle, shaping a dreamcatcher's web. I'd attach several beads and feathers to the dream catcher and sell them to two Indian art shops; one in Albuquerque and another in Santa Fe.

Even though I have a regular job working on a hay farm in Española, I depend on my dreamcatchers that offer me a little extra income. Returning to my story, as my brother and I were walking over the desert, I decided to walk within a dry arroyo. My brother said he didn't like doing this and chose to follow me by walking along the arroyo's upper edge. This would position him looking down upon me. As we walked, I noticed that the arroyo was getting a bit thick with chaparral bushes. After walking a short way within this growth of shrubs, I felt something hit the side of my boot. When I looked down at what it was, right there at my feet was a rattlesnake about two feet in length! Not a very long snake, but a rattler nonetheless. It struck my boot but thankfully missed my lower leg. The wet spot on my boot that was left from the snake's saliva marked the spot of the strike. Although I wanted to run away, I stood as still as I could watching the snake as it began to move slowly away from me and disappear into the undergrowth. Strangely, I've seen several rattlesnakes in my time, but never one like this one. It had an unusual pink color – something close to a red/purple pink. After it moved a safe distance away, I got out of there very quickly. I retraced my steps and eventually found a nicely sloping embankment where I could grab a hold of a few roots that I could use as handles to crawl out of the arroyo. I called out for my brother and after telling him what happened to me he said that we should take this as a sign and head back home. And that's just what we did.

Arriving at our house we found my grandmother seated on the front porch. As my brother went into the house to get something to eat, I stayed outside and described to grandmother about my rattlesnake encounter. Her eyes were wide open and she listened very carefully to all that I had to say. She was especially concerned about the details of the snake's color. She told me that when she was a young girl, she too had seen a snake just like the one I had seen in the pueblo. Her father happened to be in their backyard with her when he spotted the snake.

He told her not to make a move. The snake coiled, but not in a striking mode. It didn't even rattle. After a few minutes, her father spoke directly to the snake asking it to move on its way and not hurt the family. Grandmother said that after doing this, the snake made a few circular movements on the dirt and then slithered away.

Following my own experience that day with the snake then hearing of my grandmother's own encounter years before, grandmother and I concluded that our joint experiences were that they strangely never made a sound. Not a rattle or hissing — absolutely nothing. The other obviously unique thing was that the snakes were both of the same purple/pink color. But one major difference between our experiences was that during my grandmother's encounter, the snake had left a message in the soft dirt. The snake had left very clear impressions in the shape of three rings. No one knew what to make of these rings, but not wanting to take any chances with the spiritual, her father walked into the house and returned with a hand full of cornmeal and a hawk feather. He blessed the area where the three rings were and offered a prayer to the Creator. We pueblo people don't give out information or reasons as to what the symbols the snake left might mean. It's not in our culture to do so. However, not long after this encounter, it became clear to us that what took place that day, and what was to come to pass in the near future, was foretold by the snake.

As the years passed, no one in my grandmother's family spoke of the snake encounter. Everyone was definitely aware of it, but did not speak openly of it. I'm only sharing this with you because I had a dream about meeting you just a few nights ago. I knew you would soon be coming. I'm not going to say more than I already did. There is more, but I don't

want you to repeat this here in this story. I'll tell you the remainder of my dream when we're done.

As pueblo people we know that there are things attached to animals, their spirits and that they can communicate with humans if we allow ourselves to listen and observe. Most of us think we are too important to listen, but when we do listen to our fellow relations, we can receive information and learn very important lessons. Even if it's a small creature like a snake, they too have much to say. I know this story has nothing to do with ghosts, but it is a spiritual one."

SANTA ANA(TAMAYAME) PUEBLO

The original location of Santa Ana Pueblo is unknown. Most of the pueblo's inhabitants were displaced by either voluntarily leaving or were killed during the Great Pueblo Revolt of 1680. Following the re-conquest of the New Mexico territory by the Spanish in 1692-1694, the pueblo originally known as Tamaya, or the Old Santa Ana Pueblo was founded in an area about eight miles northwest of Bernalillo.

The present people of Santa Ana Pueblo tend to maintain two locations of residence; one area is a farming community along the Rio Grande while the other remains a traditional home located on the north bank of the Jemez River.

Today most of the pueblo's population, about 668 people, gather together at the Old Pueblo for their traditional ceremonies, social gatherings and festivals. This pueblo is rich in its ancient arts of pottery, woven articles and beaded jewelry.

SANTA ANA STAR CASINO

I chose to include this story due to having been approached by several casino workers regarding their own encounters with spirits on the property. Granted, most of these individuals wished to not be included or be identified in this book given their spiritual or tribal beliefs. However, for reasons known to them, the following persons in this story absolutely wanted their stories to be told. Having traveled to many Indian-owned casinos in and outside of New Mexico, I've discovered that for some strange reason, each one without exception has a history of ghosts. Might this be due to the extreme desires of economic hope they offer given the slim possibility for a chance of wealth? Could the fact that so many individuals have lost so much in the game of chance they offer? Or, as in this story, does the fact that a burial gravesite exist within walking distance from the main entrance have anything to do with all these accounts?

I'll leave this possibility open for discussion. But if you're ever in the vicinity of this particular casino, enter, relax, and enjoy yourself. You just might return home with much more than a pleasant memory. You never know 'what' might be standing, waiting for your return home, wanting to collect much more than a winning number!

— Antonio

KATIE MARQUEZ'S (SANTA ANA) STORY

"I'm a tribal member of the Santa Ana Pueblo and I've worked at the tribe's casino for over nine years. I know that there are some fellow

pueblo people who would not want me to talk about the spiritual going-ons at the casino, but even though this is the feeling of the tribe, I know that employees talk openly to themselves about the ghosts. I've heard them and I also know that the tribal chairmen are aware of what people have seen and spoken of. If my story helps others to recognize that what is taking place is not in the imagination, that there really are spirits in the building, well then maybe we can have a medicine man or woman bless the grounds once again and put these restless souls at peace.

Speaking for myself, I'm scared of the spirits. I'm not going to lie; I'm really scared having to come into the building alone at night. I don't want to experience anything else like the experiences that I had in the past. So, after people read my story, I hope enough pressure is put on the tribal council to do something about it. The spirits need to know that they are honored and they need to have prayers offered to them. I hope a ceremony is offered to them; the spirits need one and so do we.

It was just a few months after being hired, six years ago, when I had my first experience with a spirit in the casino. Just before my experience, I was personally told by a fellow pueblo woman worker named Estelle about her own experiences with a spirit that she'd seen in the parking lot one early morning. Estelle told me that it took place when she was walking from her car to the sidewalk. She spotted a little girl about eight or nine years of age. The girl was quite a distance from where this woman was standing. However, the strange thing about this girl was that she was running and jumping about the ground like a small deer. The little girl was making movements that a normal child could not ever do. That's what initially caught the woman's attention: the unusually strange, non-human movements the girl was making.

Immediately, the woman told me she knew this was of a spiritual nature. She quickly turned around, got in her car and drove around the casino to another entrance. As soon as she parked her car, Estelle sat inside and visually checked all around to see if there were plenty of people walking about. As soon as she felt enough at ease, she left her car and dashed in through the casino doors! She didn't dare mention to anyone about what she had seen, especially to co- workers. Estelle told me she was concerned people would think she might be losing her mind. 'It's difficult to explain to people about such things as seeing a ghost. Some might say they believe; but most people don't. It wasn't until my second experience that I decided to open up to others,' she said.

She told me that it was about a year later when she was taking her work break in one of the bathrooms. Thinking she was alone in the bathroom, she was looking into one of the bathroom mirrors applying her lipstick. Suddenly she noticed the faint reflected image of a strange woman standing in front of the wall behind her. Surprised to see her, the woman turned around to face the woman, but she disappeared! Immediately she dropped her lipstick, grabbed her purse and ran out the door! Estelle described the woman as being about the age of thirty-five, about five feet or so with waist, length hair and definitely of Native descent! This time, because of how upset she felt, Estelle chose to speak to a fellow worker, a Mexican woman, about the spirit. She felt confident to speak to her because for the four years they had known each other, they both had grown friendly and trusting towards each other. Soon after her second experience, Estelle left her job and didn't return to work for a full month!

Before returning to work, she requested a change of position; a position where she might have plenty of interaction with the public. Estelle did not want to work alone any longer. The casino's human resources department chose to accommodate her request by giving her the job of pushing a coffee and soda cart throughout the casino floor offering drinks to the guests. Estelle felt very satisfied and safe with this new position and stayed with the job for a few more years until she left the casino in 1991.

That same year I was inside the casino's Events Center room. I, together with two other women staff, were in charge of setting up the tables, chairs and decorations for events. The Events Center is a very large indoor area that hosts concerts and conferences throughout the year and is equipped with a state-of-the-art lighting and sound system. At the time of my ghost experience, Elsa and Carolyn and I were in this large room setting up tables and chairs. I was the first to enter the room, and after turning on the lights, walked to the area where the chairs were stored. The other two women walked over to the opposite side of the room and began to remove the folding tables from storage. The only persons in the room were the three of us; absolutely no one else was in the room. Carolyn mentioned to Elsa and me that she needed a bathroom break. Elsa also decided to accompany her, so they both left me alone in the room for a few minutes. There were approximately forty tables to dress and decorate. I walked to each table placing folded tablecloths in the middle of each. After doing this, I'd begin where I started and unfold them. I was very focused on the job that I was doing when suddenly I had the strangest feeling that I was being watched. I turned to look at the doors and they were closed. Then I looked up to the area of the stage and except for the microphone and podium, it was empty. I could see that I was totally alone in the room.

I was unable to shake off this feeling; it was unshakable. I knew someone was staring at me. I just knew it! I decided to stand quietly in place and listen for footsteps or perhaps a voice. All I heard was the slight humming sound of the air conditioner. But just as I was about to return to the job I was doing, I heard the sound of what appeared to be the dropping of dirt, or gravel on the floor. The sound was not abrupt or very loud, so I was not startled just a bit unnerved. I looked in the direction of the stage and noticed nothing unusual. Then suddenly I heard the sound that I can only imagine was of a cardboard box being kicked very hard coming from what could only be the lighting room located up high and directly above me. The lighting room is located opposite the stage at the eastern end of the room. It's a small room that resembles a loft. In this room a person can operate the special lighting effects that are needed for stage productions. Because of its position, the interior is very visible to anyone standing at the floor level below. I turned and looked up to face the lighting room and spotted the image of a person—a male, standing and staring directly at me! I stood in place wondering who this person could be. I waved at him with my left hand and I could see that he noticed me because immediately after I waved at him, he moved from where he was standing just a few feet to his right. Again, I waved at him then said, 'Hey, what are you doing? Spying on me?' He stood in place gazing at me and suddenly just disappeared! A shock of fear came over me. I almost peed myself! I threw the table cloths I was holding next to the table where I was standing and quickly got out of there fast!

I ran into the nearest bathroom looking for Elsa, gasping for air and calling out her name, but I was alone. I felt too afraid to stay in the empty bathroom any longer than a few seconds, so I ran out of there and down the hall to the buffet dining room. People were busy dropping their money in slot machines as I ran past them. Comforted by the noise and activity all around me, I stopped in place and soon I spotted Carolyn and ran up to her. I hugged her with all my might, but didn't waste any time by telling her about what I had just seen. Because of the serious look on my face, Carolyn stood quiet and then I opened up. She listened to my every word. Then she spoke, 'I know you're telling me the truth because you're now the third person who I know that has seen a ghost in this casino.'

She hugged me and attempted to calm me down. She said, 'Katie, don't worry, he won't hurt you. He's probably lonely and is looking for a girlfriend!' Her silly joke made me smile, but I still had tears in my eyes as I gave into a little laugh.

I very hesitantly returned to the room with her and expecting to see Elsa, we entered the empty Events Center room. I didn't want to even accidentally peek at the lighting room. Clutching her arm, I asked Carolyn to take a look around the room for me. She said that there was absolutely no one living or dead that she could see in the room—it was empty. Just when we were wondering where Elsa had gone, walking through the door was Elsa. She looked oddly. I asked her if she was alright, and she asked us not to laugh at her, but she was scared. She stated to us, 'As I was extending the folded legs from one of the tables, I felt as if an unseen hand had touched my left arm. I turned around and noticed there was no one next to me, but I kept feeling the pressure of an invisible hand still holding tight to my upper arm! I got so scared that I started to swat at my arm. When the 'thing' would not let go, I decided to run out of the room and into the safety of the slot machine room! I didn't notice when the invisible hand let go of me, but it finally did. I walked around for a few minutes until I felt ready to come back and locate the both of you.'

I told Elsa about my own experience and we both decided to call it quits for the day. Elsa and I reported the experience to our supervisor and we were surprised to hear that our experience with a spirit in the casino was not an isolated one. We were asked to finish up the day assisting in another department, but were strongly advised not to discuss our 'encounters' with any other employees. Carolyn and three other employees were left to finish up our job. I've spoken to my family about the spirit I saw at the casino as well as Elsa's experience. My mother told me that the spirits are members of our people who are keeping a watch over us. I shouldn't be afraid of them, just respectful.

My older sister Linda mentioned to me that there are graves on the casino grounds and in fact the graves are located just a short distance from the western edge of the casino's main doors; next to the main highway just behind the large wall with the sign that reads, 'Hyatt Regency Tamaya Resort.' The graves are directly behind that wall surrounded by a small wooden fence. I've also seen the photographs of large round circles of light that are called 'spirit orbs.' Lots of people have captured these lights just by accident during weddings and other events. They'll appear flying about the room and even next to people. Just ask around. You'll see I'm telling you the truth.

The last thing I want to say is that people need to respect these graves and not climb over the fence and wander about. The ones who are buried in that area are ancestors; people like you and me. They lived and had families like everyone. It's best to show your respect by being silent when passing the area on foot, or when driving by in your car. Offer a prayer, but never, ever disrespect their resting. We pueblo people know

that even though the remains of our ancestors are underground, the spirits of our brothers and sisters are always involved in our daily routines. So, please respect the area and keep away. I'm not concerned about what people may think about ghosts. I know I've had my own experiences and I'm personally scared of them. I have confidence that our medicine people know about these graves, and that they gave the right offerings and prayers to our ancestors. I know that we, as pueblo people, need our ancestor's guidance and protection to help us all do good. But sometimes even though they might not mean to scare me, I do get scared. And like I said before, perhaps the spirits need to be given more offerings."

Located at the back of the stone wall is the cemetery

CORONADO STATE PARK AND RV PARK

Located north of Albuquerque in Bernalillo, is Coronado State Monument where Francisco Vásquez de Coronado and 300 soldiers and 800 Indian allies from New Spain entered the valley while looking for the fabled Seven Cities of Gold. Instead of the valuable metal, the Spaniards found villages inhabited by prosperous and very knowledgeable Native people. Coronado's party camped near the Tiwa Pueblo of Kuaua, one of the many villages encountered by the explorers.

The visitor center at Coronado State Park was designed by noted architect John Gaw Meem and contains examples of prehistoric and historic Indian and Spanish colonial artifacts. These items remain on permanent exhibition.

JERLINDA HOLLENBECK'S (ANGLO) STORY

Sitting across the dining room table from Jerlinda and her husband Adam, it was clear that their joint paranormal experience fifteen years prior proved to be a significant change regarding their view toward death. Interestingly, in their living room next to the fireplace was a small area that had been set aside for a small altar. Inquiring about it, Jerlinda stated it was placed there to honor their family members who have passed. 'There's a picture of my mother and father. Jerlinda has two pictures of our son, Adrian, and one of my great-grandfather who fought and died in the First World War,' added Adam. This story that follows is a sincere retelling of an unexpected encounter with a spirit on state park land. It

would be well to note that spirits can at times choose to appear to the living for the purpose of assisting us to reconnect with our forgotten past. This purpose might be to direct our lives towards personal betterment. The following story of spiritual intention absolutely gave the Hollenbeck family just such a direction.

— Antonio

"My story took place in the summer of 1995. My husband Adam, who goes by the nickname 'Coach,' and our three poodles and I were on a road trip, traveling in our RV from the Los Angeles suburb of Pico Rivera, California to Denver. Along the way we decided to stop and spend a few days sightseeing in Albuquerque. Coach had read in a travel magazine about some of the unique sites and restaurants that Albuquerque had to offer, so we arranged to spend a few days at the city. I made a reservation prior to leaving California for a few nights at the Coronado State Park RV Campsite, walking distance from the Santa Ana Star Casino. We arrived at the park on a Sunday evening at close to 5 pm. Registering and locating our site, we settled in for the night. After I made a light dinner, Coach and I decided to take our three dogs for a walk on the trails that the park service had constructed. The sun was about to disappear into the horizon, but there was still a little sunlight left as we began our walk. About ten minutes into the walk one of our dogs, a female named Pop-Tart, must have been feeling pretty brave because she ran, passing in front of us and barking loudly. From where we stood, we could see that as she was barking, she was also becoming more and more agitated. Due to being many yards behind, we were unable to see what was causing her to react so aggressively. Soon we could see the other two dogs had caught up to her and even though Coach and I whistled as loud as we could, they all disregarded our commands and continued to bark uncontrollably. I was concerned that all this barking and noise would bother our fellow park residents.

As Coach and I came upon the dogs, I was the first to spot a person who was standing just a few yards away to the north of the trail. I said, 'Coach, do you see that woman over there where those cactus are? What do you think she's up to?' Strangely, the dogs stopped their barking and cowered back behind my husband and me, seeking what appeared to be safety. Noticing that the woman was wearing a dark cloth, or a blanket, which she had wrapped around her body and strangely, draped the top end over her head, I stood silent. Pop-Tart was growling, but stayed close to our side. At the time we didn't think anything that would cause us to imagine the woman might not be of 'the living.' We simply looked in her direction and automatically waved a friendly greeting of hello. She ignored our gesture and instead slowly turned to her right, then faded away! A feeling of dread came over me. Right in front of the two of us the woman disappeared! The dogs were silent. I felt my knees begin to buckle from under me. I called out to my husband, 'Coach, quick take my arm. I think I'm going to faint!' Coach said, 'Gerri, are you all right? Are you alright?' I answered, 'Yes, yes. I saw her disappear!' He said, 'That was a ghost Gerri. That was a GHOST!'

We stood in place, not wanting to take another step. Then I spoke, 'Honey let's go back. I need to sit down. Take me back to the trailer!' Coach whistled for the dogs to follow us as we headed back to our trailer. We were both shaking. Entering the trailer, I noticed that Coach was very nervous and when I asked him if he was alright, he looked at me with eyes filled with a fear that I had never, ever seen in my husband before. He responded, 'No, Gerri I don't think I am.' Coach then told me his personal story; one that I had never heard before.

'The first time I ever saw a ghost was when I was just an eight-year-old kid, living with my father and his second wife, Catherine. Gerri, I know I never told you about this, but Gerri, I've carried this experience with me all my life and it's made an impact on me to this day! That ghost we just witnessed on the trail reminded me of something that took place when I was a boy, when my mother died of a heart attack.'

Coach continued, 'I was in my bedroom when I saw the spirit of my mother. Gerri, my mother came to me in my bedroom! I knew it was my mother. Even though I was only eight-years-old, I was old enough to have known and to recognize my mother before she died. When she appeared to me in my bedroom, she was standing in front of my opened door. I remember the color of the bedroom walls; they were painted a light blue. She was wearing a white dress with the printed design of small red cherries or strawberries. She stood long enough for me to make out even the detail of her dress. At the time I was playing with my army men on the floor and for some reason, I turned to look toward the door and that is when I saw her. I remember being so surprised to see her, and I guess I was in shock because I was unable to speak at first. Then I got the strength to call out for her. As I made the move to reach out my arms to her, she smiled at me and said, 'No, not now, not now, son.' Then she slowly disappeared, just like that woman's spirit we saw on the trail. She disappeared into nothing! Gerri, right at this moment

I'm not alright; in fact, I'm pretty upset!'

I moved over and sat next to my husband and hugged him. He placed his head on my shoulder and began to weep. I didn't know what to do. I knew it must have taken a lot of personal strength to disclose such a powerful experience. I had never seen him reacting in such an emotional way. Eventually we got to bed and in the morning we spoke a little more about the apparition and my husband's thoughts. I was totally unaware that the death of his mother had left him with such lingering memories, and I never knew about her spirit appearing to him. I asked my husband, 'Coach, tell me, honestly, did your mother really appear to you or do you think your emotional state caused you to imagine it all?' Coach answered, 'Gerri, you know I'd tell you the truth. I actually saw my mother in my bedroom that night. She spoke a few words, 'No, not now, not now, son.' That was it, and then she disappeared. Since that moment, I never doubted that my mother would care and protect me. All through my life I carried that childhood experience with me, never repeating what I had seen, or the words she spoke. I never have shared this with anyone until now.'

I was overcome with questions and obvious concern for my husband's mental state, but I could see that he was now relieved to have finally made his feelings clear, and disclosing them to me proved to help his mental state quite a lot. I also knew from the look on his face that the freedom he now was feeling was so healthy. His mother's spirit had appeared to him, and being such a young boy, both that and her death had obviously made a lasting impression on him.

That morning we decided to take a drive into town and to explore the sites that Albuquerque had to offer. We returned to the trailer park at around dinnertime. As we were driving into the park, we had to drive off the road and onto the dirt shoulder because of a rescue fire truck was coming our way. Flashing its lights we knew something was not right. When we arrived at our trailer space, we asked a man who was standing by his trailer on the graveled area, what had gone on. He told us that a woman had had a heart attack and was being taken to the hospital. Now, I'm not sure if the spirit woman's apparition the night before on the trail had symbolized anything that was to come, as this poor woman's heart attack, but I'd have to say that it would be interesting to speculate. I noticed that Coach became quiet, and then turned to me to say, 'Gerri, my mother is taking care of me. She's still with me. This could not be a coincidence.' I felt the blood drain from my face. I took hold of his hand and said, 'Oh, Coach, I was thinking the same thing!'

Well, that's my story; a story that has caused me to believe that there is much more to this life than what we think we know. Yes, I do believe in the afterlife."

PECOS NATIONAL HISTORIC PARK

At midpoint in a passage through the southern Sangre de Cristo Mountains, the ruins of a Pecos Pueblo and Spanish Mission share a small ridge. Long before Spaniards arrived, this village commanded the trade path between Pueblo farmers of the Rio Grande and tribes who hunted the buffalo plains. Its 2,000 residents could marshal 500 fighting men. Its frontier location brought both war and trade. At trade fairs, Plains tribes, mostly nomadic Apaches, brought slaves, buffalo hides, crops, textiles, turquoise, flint and shells to trade for pottery with the river pueblos. Pecos Indians were middlemen, traders and consumers of the goods and cultures of the very different people on either side of the

mountains. They became economically powerful and practiced in the arts and customs of two worlds.

ROXANNA A. WILLIAMS' (ANGLO) STORY

It's strange how situations develop. In the case of this story, I found myself in an art gallery one day in Santa Fe, admiring a painting when an older woman came up to me and we struck up a friendly conversation. One topic led into another and she inquired as to my line of work. After hearing of the topic I write about, she offered her own story and before long we arranged for a time and date for her interview.

Roxanna's experience that is revealed in her story describes both sadness and a spiritual revelation following the death of her husband. The spirit presented itself to her in broad daylight, and as you'll read in her account, she was not alone. She stated, "Many local people have mentioned seeing strange things in that mountain; state forest workers and just normal folks taking a hike within the canyons and flat areas. One thing I'll never do again is go on my own. I learned that lesson."

After reading her account you'll discover that some who have witnessed ghosts are more than willing to relate the experience, while others choose to take the experience to their graves, remaining silent and absolutely tight-lipped forever.

— Antonio

"I presently live in the village of Pecos, a short driving distance from the Pecos Monument. I've lived in the area for most of my life. Today my seventy-nine year old mother lives at my home with me and my two dogs, Lucy and Ricky. My husband died eleven years ago from a long battle with cancer and because of my loneliness, just a few days after his funeral I chose to acquire my two dogs. I needed some companions to help me through the grieving process, and these two dogs who were just puppies, litter-mates at the time, have definitely provided me with the companionship I needed at that difficult time in my life.

After my husband's funeral when I'd take long walks up above nearby Rowe Mesa, I'd take the puppies with me to provide them with exercise. The mesa is located just south of the monument, at the southern side of Interstate 25. Not far at all from the monument in fact, you can easily view it from the visitor center. On these hikes, I'd take advantage of freeing my mind, having the time to think about my life, and the possibility where I might be headed. It wasn't unusual for me, as I'd be hiking, lost in my thoughts, to notice the puppies yelping, barking at a squirrel, or something that would startle them. Soon I'd snap out from my personal meditation and be brought back to reality. This is how I spent my first few weeks alone with my dogs. I'm informing you of this pattern because one early afternoon, all this was about to change.

One day as I was taking my usual hike up on the mesa, my dogs began to bark at something that appeared to be within an area of shrubs and trees. The area was only a few feet from where we were and as I carefully approached the trees, an unusual thing took place. I noticed a foggy mist that began to slowly rise from the area. It was no larger than a few feet across, about five by six feet in total size. This misty fog seemed to come through the shrubs and it became more solid within just a matter of seconds. As the dogs continued barking loudly with their little voices, I was in awe viewing what was taking place right in front of me. The mist rising from the ground suddenly stopped in mid-air and then slowly floated back to the ground. It came up and out from the shrubs, then floated in the air for a few seconds, and then it landed on the ground. All this took place in I'd say, eight to ten seconds total. And in broad daylight I might add. This might sound strange, but I was not in the least scared. I imagine that due to my state of mind, I was somehow emotionally numb and accepting of anything.

So, I stood in place as this mist landed on the ground, simply observing and not doing much else. Immediately after it touched the ground, the mist became visibly very thick in its composition, and I began to see the outline of a man's body! The person was about my height, thin, had very short hair, almost bald and totally naked. I became convinced that I was witnessing a spirit manifesting itself to me. Strangely, I became aware that the dogs were silent. I looked in their direction and saw that they were both lying on their sides in the shadow of one of the trees. This spirit person was about the age of between nine and thirteen. And the one item that he did have on his body was a necklace; a shell type necklace that pueblo people sometimes wear today. As my eyes continued to focus on this little boy, it became clear to me that he was of Native American descent. The spirit was not very clearly defined, his features and the outline of his body were in a somewhat wavy composition, but there was no doubt in my mind that this was a true person. His image lasted for about ten or more seconds, then as the wind became strong enough to move the trees branches, the image slowly faded away.

Reality then reared up in my mind, and my body began to shake. Nervously, I began rubbing my arms. I was scared, but not to the point of being uncontrollably afraid. I soon gathered my thoughts and began to accept what I had seen was a spirit that had appeared to me for a reason; although what that reason could be I was unable to understand. I chose to sit on the ground and somehow try to think through all the 'whys' and possibilities. I kept coming up with empty answers. But the little boy's image could not be erased from my thoughts. In a few minutes, I called to my dogs and we hiked back to the car, and then drove home.

Arriving to my home, I mentioned to my mother my experience with the spirit. She got quiet, and then asked me to promise her that I would not go hiking into the woods alone again for a long time. I agreed with her and responded that I didn't feel comfortable doing this either. And as of that date, I've not gone up to the mesa since.

A little over a month after that experience, I accompanied a friend of mine named Martin to the Pecos Monument. Martin was an established artist, an oil painter, and he had an appointment with the monument's on-site supervisor. Martin wanted to set up his easel and paints in one of the areas of the monument, for the purpose of painting a large canvas, and needed permission from the park service. I was left to busy myself within the museum portion of the visitors' center. A collection of pottery and other artifacts were displayed and I had no problem occupying my time looking over all the displays. I remember gazing at one of the museum's daily-life dioramas of a pueblo community, when I heard a familiar voice call out my name. I turned around and saw Beverly, a girlfriend who moved away from Pecos a few years ago, and was now living in the northern town of Chama. 'Roxie, is that you?' she said. We hugged and she told me all about her home and husband. She also mentioned that she was in town visiting her mother and brother. She happened to be at the monument because of an old pot her brother had recently purchased from a friend. The pot was wrapped in a bath towel and placed in a cardboard box she was holding. Beverly's brother Hector was at home with the flu, and he asked her if she could do him a favor and visit the museum then ask any monument personnel what type of pot it was, it's age, etc.

I asked Beverly if I could take a look at it. 'Sure,' she said. The pot looked old; it could have even been an ancient pot. I'm not very knowledgeable about pots, but to me it looked authentically old. Beverly and I talked about several things that were going on in our lives, but during our conversation, Beverly asked me, 'Roxie, you don't seem right, what's up?' I mentioned to her how difficult it's been for me to get along with life after my husband's death. Not wishing to hide my hesitance, I then mentioned to her my experience with the spirit. A sincere facial gesture overtook her face, 'Are you serious? I need to know everything about what you saw, Roxie,' she said.

After describing what I experienced, she placed the cardboard box down and said, 'Roxie, my brother had the same experience with a young man's spirit up there on that mesa. Hector and his friend Diego were hunting elk when a young boy's spirit appeared to him. Right there in the open, an Indian boy's spirit wearing the necklace you described appeared to him. Diego was several yards away at the time, so he was unable to verify the story, but Hector swears he saw this spirit come right up to him.' 'Do you think Hector would talk to me about the spirit?' I asked. Beverly answered, 'He doesn't speak to anyone about it. He mentioned it to me years ago, and has never spoken about it since. I don't think he would, but you never know. Just ask him.'

After Beverly was done with her appointment, we drove to my home and had dinner. The following day I decided to drive to Beverly's mother's house and speak with her brother. She did not have a phone, so I was unable to call in advance. When I arrived at their house, Beverly's mother answered the door and welcomed me inside. I was told that Beverly was in Santa Fe. When I asked for Hector, his mother stated that he was in bed with the flu. I walked to his bedroom door and when I asked him if he would not mind discussing his experience with me, adding that I had my own encounter with the spirit, he flatly stated, 'No, I don't want to talk about it. Don't ever bring it up again—okay!'

I was taken aback by his stern response. I said, 'Sure. Hope you feel better.'

I left the house with mixed emotions. Knowing that I would never be able to share my experience with Hector, I drove away thinking how terrible his encounter must have been. Mine was quite pleasant, not at all horrible, a little bit startling, yes, but nothing to make me react in the negative way Hector did.

I'll never know what the spirit's intent was, to give me a message, a sign perhaps? I'll never know. I just know that I was not the only person to have seen the spirit, and that there must be others who have seen it besides Hector and myself. Perhaps someone reading my story will come forward and give their account to you. Then again maybe not."

TOWN OF GRANTS

Grants began as a railroad camp in the 1880's, when three Canadian brothers were awarded a contract to build a section of the new Atlantic and Pacific Railroad through the region. The Grant brothers' camp was first called Grants Camp, then Grants Station, and finally Grants. The new city enveloped the existing colonial New Mexican settlement of

Los Alamitos and grew along the tracks of the Atlantic and Pacific Railroad. The region is primarily high desert country dominated by sandstones and lava flows.

Most memorable in the town's history occurred when Paddy Martinez, a Navajo shepherd, discovered uranium ore near Haystack Mesa, sparking a mining boom that lasted until the 1980's. The collapse of mining pulled the town into a depression, but the town has enjoyed a resurgence based on interest in tourism and the scenic beauty of the region. Recent interest in nuclear power has revived the possibility of more uranium mining in the area, and energy companies still own viable mining properties and claims in the area.

STEVEN O. GOODY'S (ANGLO) STORY

There are times during my research when I encounter examples of how hesitant and even stubborn people can be when the evidence for spirits stands literally in front of them. Is it denial or fear that causes such a disregard for facts presented? Steven's story offers much evidence for the existence of ghosts, and in this case, witchcraft. Both Steven and his partner, Patrick, a physician, encountered something unfamiliar to a western, college educated, and thinking mind set. But when has the spiritual world ever cared about education or social standing? If spirits want to communicate, they will. The choice is theirs and all we can do is sit back and admit to ourselves the truth. Or simply remain in a world of denial. My readers already know the position I take on this topic.

— Antonio

"My partner Patrick and I moved to Grants on May 10th, 1988. Originally I'm from Gallup. My parents owned and managed a small hotel in Gallup. After I graduated with a degree in English literature from USC, the University of Southern California, my partner, Patrick, who also completed his education in California, moved to Grants with me. Patrick is a physician, and at the time of my story, he was practicing medicine on the Navajo Reservation, in the Crownpoint area.

Our strange ghost experience with unexplained phenomenon began at the time when Patrick was treating an elderly eighty-five year old Navajo man named Tom-John. His younger sister's family, who stated that the man was suffering from an illness that was brought about by, of all things, a witch, brought this man into the clinic. Perhaps I should state at this point in my story that on the reservation, there are numerous common illnesses that are attributed by the locals as being a direct cause of witchcraft. Your readers also need to understand that culturally, on the reservation, many Navajos view most illness in this manner. Also, practitioners of western medicine who conduct their practice on the reservation are required to complete an in-service training program. These training sessions are actually provided to all medical staff by the Navajo Tribe in order to educate non-Indians in regards to the Navajo culture's views. This service is a cultural sensitivity training that medical staff undergo prior to beginning their employment on the reservation, and it's very informative.

Patrick informed me that when Tom-John was brought into the clinic for medical evaluation, the poor man's eyelids were very much swollen to the extent of being shut, and his legs were equally swollen with edema—a medical term to describe one of the body's reactions to illness by retaining water. The man's family stated to Patrick that Tom-

John had been suffering with these symptoms for a week, and further that they believed that the cause of his illness was due to a witch; a woman in the Crownpoint area who was known locally to the Navajos as 'Mexican Crow.'

Mexican Crow was given this name due to the fact that as a young woman, she learned to do witchcraft from a Mexican woman. Mexican Crow, who was Navajo but fluent in the Spanish language, lived in Sonora, Mexico for many years. The name 'crow' was attached to her due to her practice of having crow feathers on her person whenever out in public. Crow feathers are definitely a taboo for Navajos, since the bird and its feathers are symbolic of dark forces. Apparently, Tom-John's oldest grandson, Shelby, did something to cross the witch that Mexican Crow did not appreciate. She decided to revenge his family by 'witching' the patriarch, Tom-John.

By the time that Tom-John's family had brought him to the clinic, he had already been given a 'Sing,' or a Navajo healing ceremony attended

Traditional Navajo Hogan.

by two medicine men—all without success. The Sing was conducted within a traditional Navajo and log 'hogan' house.

When Patrick asked Tom-John's family to help undress him for the routine physical exam, he was amazed to see how Tom-John's skin was covered in a yellow hue. So he examined his eyes for jaundice, which would be an indication of liver problems. His eyes were clear and after examining his abdomen, nothing to indicate a liver problem was evident. Patrick ordered the usual blood tests and x-rays that were appropriate for discovering a diagnosis. But most unusual about Tom-John's exam was when Patrick lifted Tom-John's left arm, a dark crow feather fell out from his armpit! It was not a long feather but more of a black, short plume.

Immediately, the two family members who were in the room gasped, as one family member said, 'See, there's another one. We've been finding these feathers in his bed! It's the witch; she still wants to hurt him. We don't know what to do.'

Patrick reached down to pick up the feather and examining it said, 'Well, I'll have to put this aside and I'll look it over later.' Not wanting to alarm the family any further, Patrick placed the feather onto the nearby table, covered it with a paper towel and finished Tom-John's examination. After the exam, the family assisted Tom-John out of the clinic and Patrick let them know he would give them the results of the patient's tests within a day. Now comes the part of the story that involves me.

That evening when Patrick returned home, he informed me of his first documented 'witched' patient; then he showed me the feather. Personally having grown up in the area, knowing a little bit of the Navajos and their traditions, I felt a bit nervous sitting in our home and listening to Patrick's story. Viewing the actual feather on the table before me, I got a bit unnerved and asked Patrick what he was going to do with the feather.

'I'm not going to do anything with it. The family doesn't want it, and I'm sure the clinic doesn't want an object with an attachment of witchcraft on the property. So I don't know. I guess I'll just leave it on my desk as an artifact.'

I didn't want to think anymore about the feather, so I walked over to Patrick's home office and placed it on his desk, on a small dish where he kept a few red colored beads, a pencil and two pens. We didn't mention the feather any further and went about our usual routine.

Strangely, later that night while we were asleep in bed, I was awakened by a noise. The noise sounded like an object that hit the wall which carried some weight, but not so heavy that it would make a loud bang; more of a loud thud! I opened my eyes suddenly and in the darkness of the bedroom, I spotted a quick flash of light! The light darted through the room. It appeared as though a person holding a flashlight was quickly moving about the bedroom! I sat up in bed and sensing this, immediately Patrick also woke up. 'Patrick, there is something in the room with us,' I said. He said, "What do you mean? Where?' 'In here, right in this room!' I answered.

Suddenly, we both heard a noise coming down the hall from Patrick's office. It sounded like his file cabinets were being moved about. We both jumped out of bed, switching on the lights in the bedroom and quickly, with nothing more on than smiles, we made our way down the hall to his office making sure to turn on all the lights in the process.

Reaching his office, Patrick turned on the wall light switch and we noticed that strangely, nothing was out of place. Realizing our imaginations were working overtime, or so we thought, we decided to return to the bedroom. Right before Patrick reached for the light switch, we both noticed the faint sound of a voice. It was a murmuring sound, which we both could not understand, but without mistake, we clearly did hear it. As we stood in place, trying our best to hear what was being said, suddenly we were shaken to our core. All of the items that were on top of Patrick's desk came crashing off! It was as if an invisible, angry person had taken his or her arm and with one motion and pushed everything aside! Boy, talk about being scared! We both jumped back! Then an unnerving silence overcame the room. As we stood in place attempting to make sense of things, we cautiously walked over to where everything lay scattered on the floor. Patrick spoke and said, 'Well, Steve, this is one for the books. I don't have an explanation, do you?' I responded, 'Patrick, do you notice something strange? What's missing? Look on the floor. See all your things, everything that was on your desk is on the floor, right? Everything but the feather—it's gone!'

At that moment, I could tell by the look on Patrick's face that fear was taking over. This university-educated physician was actually scared. 'Let's get back to bed. I've had enough of this crap for the night,' he said. We returned to bed, but decided to leave the lights on if, for nothing else, for our own peace of mind. Nothing else of an unusual nature took place that night, but we sure did find it difficult to fall back to sleep. But after talking it through, eventually we did.

In the morning, Patrick drove off to work and I was left to clean up his office.

As I was busy picking up all that lay on the floor and returning it on to the desk, I again was reminded that the feather was nowhere to be found. But later in the day, I walked into the office to use the stapler and I just happened to glance at a picture of Patrick's father and mother that was hanging on the wall. It was a picture of them that was taken while on a cruise to Alaska. What caught my eye was that placed on top of the picture, between the frame and the wall, was the feather! How it could have gotten there was a mystery. I definitely didn't want to touch it, so I left it alone and I decided to give Patrick a call at his clinic. Strangely, after reaching him, but before I ever got a chance to get a single word across, he interrupted my call by saying, 'Oh Steve, I've got to tell you that I just got a call from Tom-John's family informing me that Tom-John died during the night!' Not wanting to upset Patrick, I decided to keep my story about finding the feather on Patrick's parent's picture to myself. After finishing the phone call, I walked to our kitchen, then returned to Patrick's office and with a pair of kitchen tongs in hand. I grasped the feather, walked to the garage, then locating a small can of cigarette lighter fluid, I doused the feather with the liquid, walked out to the backyard and set it on fire! I didn't want to take any chances that something evil might be attached to the feather, so in my mind I chose to burn it back to hell! Perhaps it might be a little too late, but at least I could rest assured that I had destroyed it!

When Patrick returned home that evening, I mentioned to him about finding the feather and what I had done with it. Although he stated what we had witnessed the night before was very unusual, I found his words difficult to accept. Due to his education and training, I knew that Patrick's educational background didn't allow him to believe that witchcraft might have played a role in what had happened. 'I know you think it was a ghost, Steve, I know you do,' he said. 'But there is a rational explanation for it. There has to be.'

Well, a sad ending to this story is that just a couple of weeks later, we received a phone call that Patrick's seventy-three year old father was found dead of a heart attack. The man was as healthy as they come, so his death caught us both off guard. To this day, Patrick refuses to believe that the witch and feather had anything to do with his father's death. But given my personal knowledge of Navajo beliefs, I don't believe that such an experience as what we had was a coincidence. It's all just too strange and unusually weird. What I can say is that as of this day, Patrick's understanding of the Navajo culture has been much enhanced by our experience. There is so much to learn and understand, and the spiritual aspect of this is also very important. Perhaps the most important of all is that such things as ghosts are real."

SANDIA "NA-FIAT" PUEBLO

The pueblo is located in central New Mexico, adjacent to Albuquerque and covers a total of 22,877 acres on the east side of the Rio Grande Valley. Interestingly, the people of Sandia are members of the pre-Columbian Tiwa language group who once dominated the Albuquerque area. They state that their lineage can be traced to the Aztec civilization of old Mexico. The Sandia people have cultivated the land and raised their families in the area since 1300 AD. Of most importance is the Sandia Mountain, which dominates the panorama of Albuquerque to the east. This mountain range provides the source of the Sandia people's

spirituality as well as offering valuable natural resources, which have been of significant historical importance to their survival. Historically, Sandia was at one time the largest pueblo in the area, with over 3,000 people. Today they currently have approximately 500 enrolled members.

DOMINIC SANTIAGO'S (SANDIA) STORY

Ever hear of a funeral worker who is American Indian? They're not very common, but they do exist. And why shouldn't they? Today Native people can be found doing various types of work, from attorneys, administrators, astronauts, physicians and yes, even writers of ghost books! Sadly, the fearful but ignorant stigma associated with the funeral industry still remains. But as Dominic stated during the interview, "It's changing. I tend to get strange looks from people and have interesting conversations when the subject of 'what type of work do you do?' arises at parties. First, they are taken aback by my profession, then the usual follow-up question is asked, 'But you're Indian, doesn't that go against your culture?'

Presented here is the first recorded story that I am aware of which gives a personal ghost account from a mortician, but not your average mortician—an American Indian mortician.

— Antonio

"I've lived at the pueblo for most of my life. I joined the army right after graduating high school. Eight years ago I completed my degree in funeral science in the state of Kansas, took a short break, then passed my board exam as a licensed Funeral Assistant. Following that, I worked for two years at a mortuary in Kansas City and after returning to the pueblo and spending three years at home, I moved away once again. Today, I live in Albuquerque with my cousin Ruth. I decided not to return to the pueblo because of personal reasons.

As I said, I'm a licensed Funeral Assistant. I served my apprenticeship for over a year before deciding on it as a career. So, today I am working my way up the corporate ladder to the position of Funeral Director. I plan to have a job at one of the major funeral offices in Albuquerque.

As it stands, my primary job is to take care of the deceased, assisting with the embalming, cremation and restorative work. I also get involved with arrangements and finalizing actual funerals, do some grief counseling and generally help the families through their bereavement process. It all might sound a bit odd to most people when I explain my job, especially to Indians, and especially when non-Indians figure out I'm Native. But soon they come to realize that it's a job just like any other — well, maybe not like any other, but it pays the rent.

Having been raised from childhood within the pueblo's traditions, which included knowing that poking fun of the dead was a very serious offense, I honestly can say that I always take my work seriously, and always offer a prayer of reverence to each and every body that comes my way. I give them the respect they deserve and do my best to make their spirit content. I believe that in this way, I offer them a small blessing of peace.

Well, I guess I'll now get right to my story. At the time when I was working in Kansas, my office was located on the second floor of a well-known funeral home. The actual mortuary work was done at the first level and basement of the building. It was an older building but very suitable for the business end of the job I was involved with. The whole building had recently been remodeled and I was especially impressed by my work area's up-to-date equipment and the elevator that the owners had installed during the remodeling which made it a breeze to transfer bodies from the street level to the basement and back.

I was working on a woman's body one morning; her death caused by a combination of old age and lung cancer. This woman's body was particularly difficult given the large amount of restorative work needed. The family, against our better judgment, had requested an open viewing. They insisted on having an open casket, and after I strongly advised against such an endeavor, they were still insistent. So, I was in the process of doing my best to comply with their needs. Given the severe degree of disfigurement, however, I knew I would at some point need the assistance of a superior's experience.

The poor woman's face was completely devoid of fatty tissue, so her skin was blotchy and discolored. Restoring this was not going to be a problem, but her lack of subcutaneous tissue was another matter altogether. Luckily for me, I had a great director whose work had impressed me.

Both he and I had worked on this woman's body for almost two hours, until we reached the result we were aiming for. I was left to dress the body after the embalming, restoration and make-up was completed. After this was done, I placed her in her casket. The last step was for our resident beautician to do her hair.

I had finished putting on her dress, and was in the process of slipping on her stockings and shoes. Suddenly to my left, I noticed a figure; the figure of a woman standing close to me, observing my work. Holding one of the woman's lifeless legs in my left hand and her shoe in my right, I turned to face the person who was standing to my left. As I turned, I found myself staring directly into the eyes of this young woman's face! Startled, I dropped the leg and shoe I was holding and admittedly, I let out a scream! Never taking my eyes off this ghost, I saw that she was not only related to the dead woman lying in the casket, but it was she, only a much younger version! The woman's form, or ghost, was giving off a type of amber light, which soon soothed my fear with a wonderful smile of kindness. I was a mixed bag of emotions at that point. Her spirit lingered for only a few seconds, but enough time to convey such a message of approval, a message that I'll never forget.

In my people's language, I repeated a prayer in her honor and gave her my personal blessing. I didn't know what to think, but fear was no longer an issue for me. In fact, I absolutely had no fear at all. I completed my job, dressing the woman's body for the beautician and never mentioned my experience to anyone. I have nothing more to add to this story, only just to say that I hope someone takes from my experience something of value."

PLACITAS

Placitas, located in Sandoval County, lies northeast of Albuquerque and south of Santa Fe. Begun as the original settlement in 1765, San Jose de Las Huertas, its inception was in an area located in the lower Las Huertas Canyon and inhabited by twenty-one original settlers. Not exactly a city nor a town, although it has something of a village center, Placitas remains but a series of small communities of homes that have found themselves nestled in the northern foothills of the Sandia Mountain Range. Paved and dirt roads are common in the area as are a few spring-fed creeks that offer life to box elder, willows and native evergreens.

RUDY LEBECK'S (ANGLO) STORY

Another person that I interviewed in this book named Nanette Pancita, an Apache woman artist from Dulce, referred me to contact Rudy. As you'll read, you will see I was fortunate to follow through with this recommendation. Rudy and I sat outside his Placitas home on comfortable chairs overlooking the Sandia Mountain Range to the distant south. The visual panorama was stunning and awe inspiring. On a small garden table placed between us was Rudy's personal collection of found objects such as rusted bullet casings, small animal bones, a dried foot-long snake-skin and various colored, vintage medicine bottles. As I observed this collection I located a small area where I placed my tape recorder. Rudy's story will lend credence to the fact that if a burial site were ever disturbed, it would be best to make amends to the spirits for the benefit of ceasing any negative 'attachments.' However, if reverence and a respectful attitude are paid to the deceased, there just might be a token of affection that is returned to the living for offering such a positive gesture. Now read Rudy's story to find what his outcome came to be.

— Antonio

"I'm a recent arrival to the Placitas area. Originally, I was born and raised in Buffalo, New York, and at the age of twenty-two, my girlfriend and I married and moved to Tucson, Arizona. I got a job at a local radio station and three years later my wife and I found us with a few dollars in the bank. So we decided to move away from the extreme heat of Arizona and relocate to a milder temperature. We scouted the Southwest and decided on the mountain community of Placitas. Five months after having made our move, I landed another job with a Santa Fe radio station. The 40-minute drive north one way, every day, to and from my house wasn't so bad at first, considering the pleasant views, but eventually it started to become a drag. So I began looking for a new job closer to home. At the time my wife, Maria, was a nurse at Presbyterian Hospital in Rio Rancho, a suburb of Albuquerque. She thoroughly enjoyed her job. After giving my notice of departure from the Santa Fe radio station, I was out of work for close to ten months. I've always been an outdoors kind of guy, hiking, and camping in the wilderness whenever possible. Maria, on the other hand, was perfectly happy staying at home and watching television. It was during this period of lack of work that I chose to occupy my days of unemployment by taking our dog, Hobo, with me hiking the backcountry hills of Placitas.

One early morning Hobo and I headed out to the distant northeastern hills and came upon three small cairns, or mounds of rocks. These rock piles were not a natural formation, but instead human hands had definitely been at work constructing them. I had seen two examples of such small structures much closer to Placitas, but never formations out here in such isolation. The mounds were circular, about six to seven feet in width, and I'd say close to three or four feet high. I knew they had to be older than ten or more years because of their appearance. My dog and I walked around the mounds but I didn't think much more about them. I soon decided to continue on our hike and we headed in a more northeastern direction.

We had left the mounds not more than I'd say, twenty minutes, when Hobo started to sniff at something located in a sloping area of earth. I approached and without thinking twice, recognized what I interpreted as being the unearthed bones of an animal together with a dark grey colored clay pot! Although filled in with reddish colored earth, after removing this hardened mud, the pot's unmistakable form was very much recognizable. I somehow got the feeling that we had come across a very old Indian site, perhaps even a burial site. I know that it had to be ancient due to the pot not having any familiar pueblo designs. It was simply a dark colored clay pot. When I also attempted to move some of the dirt away from the bones, a large portion of dirt gave way, and the bones broke in two! No doubt, these bones were not of a recently buried animal or person. These bones were in my estimation of an ancient period.

I decided to place handfuls of dirt back on top of the small bones and the pot, in order to cover as much of them as I possibly could. My dog went off and didn't seem to give much concern to what I was doing. Within about an hour I finished and after tamping down the fresh earth with my feet, I gathered a few rocks and made a ring around the grave. After doing this, I decided to place a large rock in the middle of this ring as a symbol of respect to whomever these artifacts might have belonged to. Obviously, many years ago, someone took the time and effort to initially bury them. I just thought I'd continue to make the effort helping to preserve the intentions of the family or tribe. Having accomplished this task, I decided to head back home.

About a week passed when I strangely had a dream about the pot

and bones. It was a summer evening and the rain was coming down hard. That night I found it difficult to sleep. I kept thinking over and over in my mind about the bones I had come across the week before. Maria felt my body turning uncomfortably in bed next to hers so she urged me to get out of bed and go into the living room to watch some television. Usually watching a few minutes of television with the volume turned off is enough to lull me into a semi-conscious state, thereby clearing my mind and causing me to drift into sleep.

I thought I'd follow Maria's suggestion, so I got out of bed and walked down the hall to the living room. After switching on the remote control, I sat in my large leather chair and began to change the channels until I found a nature channel broadcasting a program about deep-water crabs. Just what I needed, I thought, to bore me to death and take my mind off of things. As I sat in the chair, with each minute that passed, my eyes grew more and more tired. Eventually I fell asleep! I don't know how long I was asleep, but I was suddenly taken over by the thought of needing to open my eyes. I recall slowly opening my eyes and spotting a young man about the age of fifteen or so, standing in the living room about ten feet from my chair. I kept my head cradled in the bend of my elbow, and my eyes focused on the figure standing before me. I wasn't scared or fearful at all — just interested! The figure didn't speak, or even move. I could only make out its outline. Eventually it nodded its head forward towards me in a gesture I took as meaning 'thank you.' This thought came to me because of all the mental energy I had spent earlier in the night going over and over in my head, regarding the bones and items that were left in that remote area of land. And now before me the message I took from this apparition's gesture was clearly one of gratitude. I never felt the need to speak or to rise up from the chair. Possibly this was due to being so exhausted and sleepy. The total experience at that moment was one of complete peace and calm. We both, the spirit and I, there for the moment, time ceased to exist, and words were not necessary. We were communicating through thoughts and that was all that was needed. Once this thought of thankfulness was conveyed to me, the figure opened its right fist, which was closed, and let drop to the floor something, which I took to be a small round ball. When the ball hit the floor, it made no sound. Immediately after, the figure slowly began to fade into the dark background of the room. I sat up in the chair and again, without feeling any level of fear, I stared into the darkened room with only the glowing light of the television lighting up the walls and floor. My eyes caught the site of the round item lying on the floor, and I rose out of the chair and walked over to pick it up— it was a rock.

I held the grey colored, walnut-size rock in my hand. It was unusually light in weight, and left me with more questions than answers. I switched off the television and walked to the bedroom. As soon as I got under the covers I fell into a deep sleep. The next morning after waking I decided

to make a return hike to the grave. All I can say at this point is that I was 'driven' to return to the grave.

Arriving at the grave, I didn't spot anything that was immediately out of place. All the stones were still arranged in the circle as I had left them. The large stone I had also placed within the middle of the circle was still upright and nothing at all was odd or disturbed. However, on closer inspection, I noticed that a small round stone, similar to the one the spirit visitor had presented me with the night before, was now resting on top of the largest of the stones! Without hesitating, I reached into my pocket, felt for the stone and brought it out of my pants pocket. Standing next to the grave and holding the small stone in my right hand, a feeling came over me, an unexplainable urge to place the stone I was holding right next to the similar stone that was sitting on top of the larger stone. I was 'compelled' to follow through with this urge. After rubbing the large stone with my two hands, I felt I was now ready to place the two smaller, round stones together on top of the larger one.

Not as I might have expected, nothing unusual took place. I said a personal prayer to the spirit of the buried person, and made my return hike back to my home. I was only about, I'd say, fifty feet or so away from the grave when I heard the cawing sounds of a raven. I turned to spot a very large, black raven circling above and watched as it quickly descended to the ground, hopped towards the grave and leaped up upon the large stone. Landing on the stone, I watched from a distance as it picked up one of the round stones in its beak and without hesitation took flight! Up and into the west it flew. At the time, not understanding what all this meant, I was confident to simply hope it was a positive sign from the 'other side' that following through by returning the stone I was presented was welcomed and appreciated.

About two years later, I was speaking to a woman photography artist friend of mine from the Jicarilla Apache Tribe who is from the Dulce area of New Mexico. Her name is Nanette Pancita. After hearing my story she said, 'I don't know how to advise you, Rudy. You were visited by a spirit and you followed through with your instincts. You did what any respectful Apache person might have done being in a similar situation. Your actions were correct and respectful. The fact that you also witnessed the raven come down and retrieve the gift that was given to you, shows it was accepted and taken to the west, which is the area we Apache people believe is the spiritual gate to the next world. You were given an experience few people, even us Indians, can ever claim to have had.'

So, this was my first and only experience to date that I've ever had with a spirit. I don't speak much at all about it. In telling you my story in hope that others can relate on some level, and if they ever come across a grave, artifacts, no matter how old, they should be respectful and leave them alone. Grave robbing goes on so often, all over the state. Indian pottery, old stone beads and artifacts turn up in antique stores all the time. I know that these objects can bring in lots of money. But is money our only focus that we've been reduced to valuing in our society? For our personal dignity as a people, I hope not."

THREE RIVERS PETROGLYPH NATIONAL RECREATION SITE
LAUREN GUTIERREZ'S (MORONGO) STORY

Sometimes when we least expect to encounter a ghost, they might make their presence known in the daylight, symbolically in the form of an animal or even in a hotel room. Such was the case of Lauren and her husband Luis' experience. The spiritual world can be a consciously unfamiliar one for us. But that doesn't preclude us from connecting with it. Evidence to support this remains etched within Native Indian culture and as is evident in the following story, literally etched in stone.

There are moments when we might encounter something so unusually weird that we are at a loss as to which way to turn. A recurring theme I've discovered among these familiar experiences is to focus on the positive and allow it to lead towards protection from the negative. Trust me, this works. As in the following story, Lauren discovered this to work well for her and her husband.

On a personal note, this area is the place from where my very own Apache great-grandmother named 'Little Stars' or 'Little Crosses' described as being the originating homelands of her and my very own ancestors.

— Antonio

"Originally, I'm from Los Angeles and I've been living in Albuquerque for two years. In 1991, my husband Luis and I, who are both originally from the Morongo Reservation in California, were vacationing in New Mexico when we decided to take pictures and hike around the southeastern area of the state. The Morongo Reservation is seated at the foot of the San Gorgonio and San Jacinto Mountains overlooking the Banning Pass. Luis' reservation extends more than 35,000 acres and was at one time one of nine small reservations set aside by President Grant by executive order in 1865. The Morongo Reservation also has one of the oldest and most successful Indian gaming facilities in California. We hadn't made the permanent move to New Mexico, so this trip was to tour the state and take in as much of the sites as our time permitted. We had just visited Carlsbad Caverns, which was spectacular. It was then we decided to take a drive up north from Las Cruces on Highway 70.

Our destination was Albuquerque and we decided to make the drive north and stop at Three Rivers for a few hours. The time of our trip was in the month of July. Knowing that the weather was going to be quite hot, I brought along plenty of bottled water and sunscreen. Arriving at the park, we loaded our backpacks with plenty of supplies for the hike and took off! The area was a wonderful place to view rock art up close. Luis took photos of most every bird, lizard and natural abstract design imaginable. We both were very impressed by all the ancient art that was literally at our feet, surrounding us everywhere we looked!

I decided to walk over to a small ridge and investigate the area for more art. As I reached the ridge I was drawn to another ridge located a distance from where I was standing. I informed Luis to take his time photographing. Luis' lifelong goal was to be known as one of the world's best photographers. The year before our Southwest trip he spent six months studying this art form in London, England, living and learning at a renowned photography school. The Morongo Reservation provided him with a few extra dollars for this endeavor.

But I was at the moment going to make the hike over to the distant ridge. Having to scramble and maneuver over the sharp volcanic formations with both hands and feet was a bit more than I was prepared for, but eventually I did reach the ridge. Admittedly, I was unaware for the unusual surprise I was to soon encounter. Immediately as I looked around, I realized that I had stumbled upon unusual depictions of weird looking symbols, representing faces with wide screaming mouths and bodies having what looked to me to be 'claw-like' arms and legs. In all the times that I've come across ancient art on rocks walls, I'd never encountered such bizarre looking symbols. If I'd brought my own camera, I would have taken a few pictures of these. But I had counted

on Luis with his own camera to be the photographer, and unfortunately he was quite some distance away.

I was captivated by these unusual depictions of who-knows-what, as I carefully walked among them. The area is known to have an abundance of rattlesnakes, so admittedly I was carefully making my way through the rocks and brush. But wouldn't you know it — I soon heard the 'buzzing' sound of what could only be a rattlesnake! I froze in place and turned my head in the direction of the sound.

Sure enough, just a few feet up ahead I spotted the snake, coiled and ready to defend itself. Taking a few steps back, I missed a step and that's when I took my fall! With a thud, I fell right on my right thigh and rolled over on my back! A little bloodied, I straightened up, and then sat down. The snake was a non-threatening distance away. My hat had also taken a fall off my head and landed in between two large rocks. I looked over to where Luis was and I could see the top of his head and his yellow shirt, but he was at least a half-mile from where I was. I decided to not make a scene and just do the best I could to make the return hike.

As I was seated on top of the sharp rocks, my eyes caught the sight of one large rock with a large collection of glyphs. Among these glyphs was an unusual one that stood out from the others. All the glyphs depicted several large heads, but among these heads was one that was in the process of what appeared to be letting out a loud scream. This glyph in particular among the others was most unusual because of the strange movement I noticed taking place on its surface. At first I didn't know what to make of it, but as I leaned in closer for a better look, I noticed that there were hundreds of bees actually crawling along the outline of the glyph! The bees were not randomly crawling all over the glyph and rock, no; they were actually following the outline of the artwork! It was so strange to witness how one bee was trailing the others like an insect 'conga line.' They were crawling, following the glyph's outline, making it appear as if it were moving. I was so emotionally struck by this activity that I decided to get the heck out of there and fast!

I located my hat and made the strenuous return hike to the car. I was not in the most positive of attitude when Luis looked at me and asked,

'What happened to you?' I just remember almost yelling to him to help me into the front seat and then to give me a wet towel to wipe the now dried blood off my legs. However, one thing I do clearly recall saying was telling Luis that I had had enough of this place, and to get his things together because, 'We're getting out of here and heading back onto the highway!'

We arrived later that evening at Albuquerque, had dinner and then checked into a hotel for the night. Throughout the night I was visibly uncomfortable and Luis kept inquiring about my well- being. All I was able to respond was that I felt a strangeness; a heaviness that wouldn't go away. It was as if a heavy, hot fur coat had been placed over my body and even after I had taken a cold shower, it had no effect. I took a few aspirins and went to bed thinking this might blow over and I'd feel better in the morning. During the night, I awoke and walked over to the large window on the tenth floor overlooking the city below. Gazing out the window into the darkness of the night, I suddenly noticed a white bird that was flying in the distance. My eyes were locked on this bird as it flew about the sky and then was surprised as it suddenly came fluttering over to where I was standing at the window. As soon as it came close enough for me to make out its form, I became aware of what type of bird this was. It was an owl! I froze in place! As I stood at the window, the owl changed its direction and came flying directly right up to the window where I was! Fully aware of the negative implications that this symbol conveyed, when this owl came up to me I jumped back into the room and immediately woke Luis up from his sleep. We discussed the events of the day, in addition to the owl. We thought it best to phone Luis' mother the following morning. She informed us that we needed to get home to the Morongo Reservation as soon as possible. But before doing that, she instructed me to visit a local Catholic church and have the priest recite a blessing over me.

Oddly, I didn't feel in the least embarrassed to follow her instructions and after breakfast Luis and I found a church and priest. We met the priest after introducing ourselves to him at the church rectory office. We were escorted into his office and there he heard our story. Without hesitation he blessed both of us, making the sign of the cross on our foreheads and at the nape of our necks. I wept a bit and thanked him. He said, 'There are many avenues which the negative force makes its presence known, but always remember that with all its power, there is One that is greater still.' A few years have past since that day. Luis and I have moved from Los Angeles and now live in Albuquerque. Our lives are filled with peace and we absolutely would not change a thing. The move to New Mexico was the best thing we ever could have hoped for. And Luis is living his dream of being a professional photographer. An art gallery in the village of Corrales currently is doing well selling his work and I'm attending the University of New Mexico with a hope of graduating in three years.

Although the experience we encountered at Three Rivers Petroglyph National Recreation Site was a tormenting one, I did learn from it and came through the experience with a much more positive view of what is sacred, and the role I personally must play in making positive decisions in my life. That's what I took from the experience."

JICARILLA APACHE

The Jicarilla people currently live in the northern portion of New Mexico and speak a southern Athabaskan language. They were one of the six southern bands that migrated south from Canada between 1300 and 1500 A.D. The term Jicarilla comes from Mexican Spanish meaning "little basket." The Jicarilla Reservation has a land area of 1,364 square miles and a population of roughly 3,403. The capital, Dulce, with most of the tribal offices, comprises over 95 percent of the reservation's population. The tribe owns the Apache Nugget Casino located on the reservation and the Best Western Jicarilla Inn and Casino, both located in Dulce.

TOWN OF DULCE

Located in the northern area of New Mexico in Rio Arriba County, I toured the little village and spoke to various persons in town regarding possible paranormal experiences. I was surprised to have encountered at least five people who instead offered me reports of weird legends that they say have persisted in the area for centuries. These stories are about the strange and secretive caverns and the world of celestial beings that

inhabit these underground caverns. Apparently, from these accounts the alien beings and their caverns are centered in the mountains of Dulce. These individuals further informed me that UFO aliens are using these bases to carry out missions involving humans and the earth's weather system. I found this information to be intriguing, but not totally surprising. After all, New Mexico does have an undeniable reputation for firsthand UFO sightings and recalling the southern town of Roswell, even crashes. Perhaps in a future book, I'll cover the UFO phenomenon, but for now I remain satisfied with my present endeavor.

NANETTE PANCITA'S (JICARILLA) STORY

Nanette and I met for her interview at the Jicarilla Inn and Casino located on the reservation. After our initial greetings, we entered the casino and located a quiet spot at a table within the restaurant. What I had imagined would be a simple story turned out to be a real eye-opener for me. Given my research history, I am well aware not to assume before each interview that each story on average is not of a 'typical' nature. But was I in for a surprise. Reading Nanette's story will prove this to be true.

At the end of our interview, Nanette offered some information regarding a personal friend. "A guy I know named Rudy Lebeck, who lives just north of Albuquerque in the mountain village of Placitas, also had a similar story of encountering a ghost. You might want to talk with him. I'll give you his phone number if you'd like. I bet he'll be more than happy to discuss his experiences with you," said Nanette. I interviewed Rudy and his personal story is included in his book as well.

— Antonio

"I was born and have lived on the Jicarilla Reservation on and off all of my forty- eight years of life. I am an artist, and early in my life chose this field to both develop my creative sense and as it turned out, it became my livelihood. In other words, I've made my living creating and producing photographs that I've personally taken in and around the Southwestern region of the U.S. In addition to this, I'm also a bead-worker. My proudest accomplishment, as far as my photography is concerned, was a show which featured my prints in the country of Norway. How that show was developed and put together by my gallery representative is a long and interesting story in itself, but as it turned out was for me a great accomplishment. Today I travel around the U.S. attending numerous art and trade shows; events that I need to attend for the purpose of marketing both my photography and beadwork. These events have afforded me the opportunity to cross paths with other Native artists, which are considered very prominent individuals in their chosen field of expression.

One thing that will impact my career, hopefully in a positive manner, is that I currently am very close to, and plan to marry, an oil painter from the Central American country of Belize. Rodrigo is a descendant of the Mayan people of Belize. When my move takes place, I'll soon be headed south for who knows how long. Oh, I'll still continue my photography, and I'm hoping this change of location will open up new doors of opportunity for me. At least that's our plan.

Rodrigo expressed to me that he finds our Apache people to be friendly, but also somewhat 'very American' in our dress and attitudes. Of course, this opinion is coming from a person whose immediate family still lives in the jungle highlands, speak nothing but their native tongue, and practice primarily their ancient form of spirituality. Rodrigo's culture is fascinating to me. Each moment with him affords me the opportunity to learn about his culture and to hear his spoken language. Obviously, I don't know a word of the Mayan language, but every now and then he'll speak a word or sentence and I become totally amazed by its beauty. Because I also have a very strong pride in my own Apache people's distinct customs and language, I know he and I will get along fine. We might have a few disagreements, but after all we're artists!

I know you want to know about the spiritual things that I personally had happen to me, so before anything else, I'll first say that as a Jicarilla Apache woman, to speak of such things does not come very easily. This is especially true when other Jicarillas are in hearing range. Within our tribe there is a lot of superstitions and fear surrounding the mentioning of ghosts and spirits, even to speak of simple things as 'butterflies' in regards to art. I believe this is due to a strong cultural belief in our traditional ways of respecting all forms of life's energy, including those who have passed over to the spirit form. Personally, I'm glad we still carry this respect within our tribe. I know many other Native tribes do as well. It is an important view and is a healthy one.

That being stated up front, I'll tell you my experience with spirits took place in the late spring of 1998. Prior to the winter of that year, in the early fall I had planned on taking a horseback ride deep within our reservation's forested mountains. Preparing to take many photographs of our beautiful, natural surroundings, I was going to gather as much photographic images as possible for a Native women's show that my agent was organizing for me in Chicago. I made sure to pack enough food, water and digital

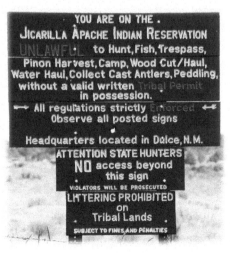

memory cards to last at least a week or more. Taking a trip like this was not unusual for me. I've taken such a trip as this before, so I knew how to prepare. I even packed my pistol just in case I ran into any problems with crazy animals of the 'human two- legged' kind.

It was one early Saturday morning when a friend of mine loaded my horse named Star Child and packing gear into his horse trailer. He hitched the trailer to his pick-up truck and he drove us to a trailhead not far from my house. After unloading and getting my gear in order we said our goodbyes, and just a few minutes later I got fully saddled up and began my ride into the mountains. The morning was uneventful, except for the small herd of elk that I spotted on a hill beyond the one I was on. The trail was a good one, marked clearly and free of any debris so Star Child and I had no problem navigating it. I'd been on this trail a few years past, so I knew from memory the valleys and uphill climbs we'd be traversing. I figured that we'd arrive at camp by four that afternoon if not earlier.

I'd been on the trail for about five hours when suddenly from my left I spotted the movement of a dark figure between the trees. I calmly turned my head all the while keeping my eyes closely focused on the area. I spotted no further unusual movements. A few minutes later, closer to a half hour, once more I saw to my left the same dark figure moving within the tree trunks. The difference between the first one and this one was that before noticing the dark figure, I distinctly heard the sound of a woman's voice speaking in our Apache tongue. The voice said, 'Use the feather. Use the feather.' Star Child came to a stop without having me pull on his reins. I noticed his ears perked up high, and if anyone reading this knows anything about horses, when a horse perks his ears up in this manner, it means watch out, something is not right! Immediately I felt something like a little bolt of electricity that shot up my left leg, starting at the foot. This was followed by the uncomfortable sense that something unusual and what I interpreted to be of a 'spiritual' nature was about. Due to my innate sense of caution, it was clear to me that I had to be alert to any change in the environment, especially to the possibility of an attack on a spiritual level. Native people know that forest spirits do exist, so it's best to be ready and on the alert.

I took my right hand and gently patted Star Child on the base of his neck in order to comfort him. Visually scanning the forest before me, I responded to the voice within the trees in Apache, 'If you are a good spirit, I honor you and ask for your protection. If not, I ask that you leave me alone and go away!' Just as soon as I finished speaking these words, I heard what now was the distinct voice of a woman once more state in our Apache tongue, 'The feather. The feather.' All I could think of was that the eagle feather I had placed on my hat had something to do with this, so I removed it from my hat brim, hopped off my horse and attached it to Star Child's leather rein, just below his left eye. Eagle feathers are very important to Native people and are considered to be holy. This particular feather was given to me by my aunt, so its meaning as a family gift is doubly important to me.

Even though the remainder of my journey into the mountains went without any further spiritual occurrences, I was well aware that something was about. In the forthcoming nights, as soon as the dimming day would give into the night, I always offered my personal prayers to the Creator and asked for my relations to protect me. This definitely gave me the confidence and courage to continue on with my work. And because of my deep spiritual belief regarding the power that comes from such knowledge, I had no doubt that with the assistance of my own personal spirits, I was being protected against any negative ones I might encounter. After spending six days in the mountains finishing up with all my photography work, I was glad to finally make the return trip back and return to my home. And regarding the darting spirits I saw within the trees, I felt that I had made a positive connection with the forces that made their presence known to me in the form of a shadow and voice. This to me was positive and on some level, a guiding one. I knew I had been instructed to attach the eagle feather to my horse for a very good reason. Even though I didn't realize at the time why, I instinctively knew there was a very good reason to obey the voice that projected itself to me from between the trees.

Three days after returning to my house, my cousin Annie's husband Paul asked me to help him with the construction of a wheelchair ramp.

His wife, my cousin, Annie, had been diagnosed with diabetes for a few years and a month before, had her right leg amputated below the knee due to complications of the disease. Annie would need the wooden ramp built as soon as possible to ease the burden of being wheeled in and out of their home. I was eager to begin the project, so I mentioned to Paul that I would help purchase the lumber and other supplies the following day and we'd begin the work on the ramp in two days.

I remember going over to Annie's house on a Thursday morning at about eight in the morning. I measured the area of the front yard to be used for the ramp, which actually did not take up too much square front yard footage. Paul and I headed over to purchase the lumber, screws and metal braces. The only thing left to do was to dig the holes for the pouring of the cement, into which we'd anchor the four-by-four posts.

The following morning I arrived at my aunt's home with two shovels; one for me, the other for Paul. I began digging into the soft soil, while Paul dug opposite of where I stood. We needed to dig a hole roughly ten inches in diameter and two feet deep. After completing the first two holes we moved to the next two, then we'd have two left for a total of six holes. Beginning the digging for the third hole, and after going down about a foot, my shovel hit what I thought appeared to be a hard cream-colored broken dish. After another shovel full of dirt, I heard a cracking sound that knocked off a small portion of what I again thought was a ceramic material, or a chunk of white limestone. Carefully I dug around it and soon brought up a shovelful of moist soil and a large portion of whatever this material was. I dropped the clump of soil next to the hole and with my bare hands began to dislodge the compacted dirt from the cream-colored material. Suddenly I stopped, and let out a controlled scream. Paul came over to where I was standing as I held out my hand. I asked him to tell me what I was holding. He didn't hesitate, 'Nanette, those are teeth!' I dropped the handful of soil and teeth onto the ground.

What I had uncovered from my digging was a human jawbone! I felt ill and so very frightened. Paul was speechless. All sort of thoughts raced through my mind. Above all else was the knowledge that there was a human body buried just below the surface of my aunt's house—in her front yard!

I took a cautious look at the dirt and jawbone lying on the ground and again I felt a nauseous feeling well up in my stomach. I called to Paul to quickly bring me the water hose. I rinsed the soil off my hands and asked Paul to drop the jawbone with the teeth I had been holding back into the hole. Rinsing the mud from my hands and scrubbing so hard I thought my hands would bleed, I didn't want even one spot of soil to be left on my hands from that hole. A feeling of such abhorrence came over me, knowing I had just touched a dead body. I wanted to physically wash away any and all minute molecules that I possibly could from my hands. Throughout all this Paul stood back and began to make the sign of the cross over his chest, then recited out loud the Lord's Prayer in Apache. Then we both sat down and discussed the situation. Because of now having the knowledge of a skeleton on the property, my Aunt Annie and Paul would need to get the assistance of one of our medicine people to come and take care of this in the Apache manner. We mentioned to my aunt what we had uncovered and as I expected, without hesitation she chose to move into her sister's home several miles away that very day. Without getting into the details of what transpired the weeks following this discovery, all I'll say is that the tribal police were called. They did their investigation. Then a blessing ceremony was performed. It was revealed that the bones were centuries old and most importantly, not involved in a murder or crime. My aunt and Paul moved their home to a new location on the reservation and that's all I can say. This was a very important revelation to me. Something that I'd not want to experience again—ever!

I do believe that the woman's voice I heard just a week before during my trip into the woods had something to do with my experience at my aunt's house. After all, the voice urged me to carry the eagle feather. I believe the voice was urging me to be careful, and to guard myself from the unknown forces that could have caused me harm. I'm grateful for that. So since that day I carry a small eagle feather's fluff with me always. It's our people's way to take such precautions and I do believe this is the right thing to do."

CITY OF GALLUP

Gallup was founded in 1891 as a railhead for the Atlantic and Pacific Railroad. The city was named after David Gallup, a paymaster for the Atlantic and Pacific Railroad. It is the most populous city between Albuquerque, New Mexico and Flagstaff, Arizona. Gallup is sometimes called the 'Indian Capital of the World,' for its location in the heart of Native American lands and the presence of Navajo, Zuni, Hopi and other Native Nations. One-third of the city's population has Native American roots. Route 66 runs through Gallup, and the town's name is mentioned in the lyrics to the song, Route 66. In 2003, the U.S. and New Mexico Departments of Transportation renamed U.S. Highway 666, the city's other major highway, to Route 491 since the number '666' is associated with Satan and devil worship. Thus, it was offensive to some people. Local Navajos, some who are superstitious, felt the name change would lift the route from being 'cursed'.

Gallup is a forerunner of racial diversity and civil rights issues. The city long opposed racial discrimination of its black residents; the majority of them lived in the city's west side in the 1940's before the U.S. Civil Rights movement took place. During World War II, the city fought successfully to prevent 800 Japanese-American residents from being placed in wartime internment. A sizable Palestinian community of about 600 persons can be found; they first arrived from Palestine in the 1970's and are found in the Southwestern arts and jewelry industries.

Gallup has more millionaires per capita than any other town in the United States. There is controversy surrounding this, as it is widely believed that most of the so-called Indian jewelry shops and Southwestern arts and jewelry industries are exploiting the local Native American people. Most companies that deal with jewelry from Native Americans often buy the jewelry for as little as 10% of the worth, but turn around and then sell the items for hundreds of dollars with the artist receiving much less for his/her work.

HISTORY OF THE EL RANCHO HOTEL

'Charm of Yesterday, Convenience of Tomorrow.' Thus, is the historic El Rancho Hotel's slogan. It's also known as the 'Home of the Movie Stars.' Of note is the impressive guest list of Hollywood's notable stars from years gone-by that have lodged at the hotel. This list includes the likes of Ronald Reagan, Allan Ladd, Jane Wyman, Betty Hutton, Jackie Cooper, Katharine Hepburn, Kirk Douglas, Paulette Goddard, William Bendix, Humphrey Bogart and Jack Benny. Today, autographed photos of these and other stars adorn the fabulous two-story open lobby, along with mounted trophy animal heads and Navajo rugs. Historically, the hotel, built by the brother of the movie magnate, D.W.

Griffith, opened its doors on December 17, 1937. The Gallup area was well-known to Hollywood filmmakers at the time due to all the westerns that were being filmed in the area. Conveniently located directly on historic Highway 66, the hotel is presently owned by and operated by Armand Ortega.

Decorated throughout in the Spanish/Indian tradition, it's quite a showcase for the eyes. Needless to say, for the visitor it remains to be quite an interesting and uncommon destination!

MARK CANNING'S (ANGLO) STORY

I interviewed Mark while he was standing across from me with the hotel's registration counter between us. The hotel's lobby was silent, having a lull in check-ins during the late evening hour of midnight. The lights were low, the atmosphere was peaceful, and the only break in this state of calm was the occasional ringing phone or nearby passing train. Mark is an easygoing type of person, very welcoming and no hint of agitation. Mark's responses to my questions were free flowing and he wasn't in the least scared or hesitant to inform me of his personal experiences with the paranormal at the hotel. At the end of our interview he even accompanied me to the parking lot and to my car stating, "Maybe the next time you return to Gallup, if you have the time, we can take a hike up to those mesas over there. There are a lot of interesting and historical things. I'm sure you'll be impressed by what you see." I just might take Mike up on that invitation. But for now, I'll busy myself with documenting his ghost experiences. As you'll soon read, there is much to record and much Mark has seen throughout his fifteen years of employment at the historic El Rancho Hotel.

— Antonio

"Originally I'm from Montgomery, New York which is near West

Point. As of today, I've been working at the hotel for about fifteen years. About eighteen years ago, I decided that I wanted to make a change in my life, so I moved to the Gallup area. One thing led to another and I got a job at the hotel. I worked various jobs at the hotel beginning as a desk clerk. Today I'm the night auditor. When I began my employment, at first there was no mention of a ghost or ghosts inhabiting the hotel, but that would soon change when I had my own unusual experience.

I live upstairs in an area of the hotel that is reserved for an employee's living quarters such as myself. I had an apartment that is located in a connecting building, a building that originally housed chauffeurs, maids and other employees. My apartment number was 228, that's over fourteen years ago.

Having recently painted and fixed a few things in it, at the time I had only been living in the apartment for a few months. I had taken the time and care to make sure that everything in the apartment was in place and functioning properly.

My first night in the apartment proved to be a very disturbing one for me. I was abruptly awakened one night by the very loud sounds of items being moved in the room where I was sleeping. It seemed that these sounds were coming from everywhere, so I couldn't pinpoint exactly what was going on, or what was being moved. But the noises were loud enough to wake me from a deep sleep. Suddenly, the dishes, pots and pans that I had carefully placed in the kitchen began to be rattled. I got up and had a look around the apartment and saw nothing. I really got 'creeped out!' I returned to my bed and once more the noises started up. I also heard what I identified as the recognizable sound of a four-footed animal walking above my ceiling! The footsteps were very heavy and obvious. It was as if someone wanted to really make themselves known to me by first, causing me to wake up, then 'they' would rush to the kitchen and begin to rattle the pots and pans.

This only took place the first night of my stay. Then nothing happened for approximately a span of about six months. Because I'd not had another such experience like the one on my first night, I thought it was now all over, but this was not to be the case.

As I said, about six months later during one night, as I was sound asleep, the loud noises in my apartment once again started up! I jumped out of bed several times, and looked all over the apartment and, as before, discovered nothing out of place. The following morning the bar manager of the hotel named Manuel, who also had his own apartment several doors down the hall from mine, remarked to me that he had had some strange 'going-ons' the night before; the same evening as me. He stated that similar to my experience, he was awakened in the middle of the night because of loud noises around his bed. Then the noises moved quickly to the kitchen; he rose out of bed to investigate and found nothing out of place. We decided to check for the possibility that mice were in the apartments. So we looked for the tell-tale signs of mouse droppings and any evidence of rodent damage, and discovered nothing to indicate such. I was somewhat glad that we didn't find mice; I was not looking forward to encountering any mice and having to eradicate them. I remember back to a time when I lived in New York, and I accidentally discovered that my house had mice. One morning as I was going about the usual breakfast routine, I placed two slices of bread in my toaster and within a few minutes discovered that along with the bread, I had toasted a mouse that had entered the toaster the night before!

My wife, who is Navajo, has had her own experiences in the apartment. She tells me she has had numerous occasions when she has heard a male voice speaking to her in the room. This male voice surfaces every now and then. Even to this day, not much time transpires when the voice will make its presence known. She tells me that it is definitely a masculine voice. Interestingly, there was a time when she could make out a few sentences. The voice stated to her, 'Relax, I'm not going to bother you. I just want to rest a bit.' I tend to believe that this spirit might be a relative of mine. I believe this because of my furniture. All the furniture in the apartment I brought to Gallup from New York. I think that the spirit in the apartment is somehow 'attached' to the furniture. I got to admit that the furniture is very 'spooky' looking. Even though it's in good shape, it's dated from the late 1940's. We don't get a feeling of being harmed by the male spirit; I think he just wants us to know he's still watching over his furniture. People get attached to such material things, so this is just one of numerous possibilities that I can think of.

Other strange reports take place on the hotel's third floor level. It is not unusual for our house- keeping staff to state that they have been touched on their backs by an invisible hand. I recall one night, about five years ago, as I was seated at the front desk, a female guest who was staying in room number 305 came up to me and reported something strange had just taken place. Above the bed is a framed poster by a Navajo artist named R.C. Gorman. Prior to this woman's experience, the artist had died just two weeks before. Well, this guest came up to me and stated that the glass-framed print had come away from the wall and had floated, suspended by unseen hands, through the air and then made its way to where she was! Instinctually, she began to swing at it, and making a direct hit, broke the glass! Today the print has been re-framed, with new glass and re-hung on the same wall.

Manuel, the bartender, informed me some years ago, one of the desk clerks reported to him of witnessing the ghost of a woman floating down the stairs in our lobby. The woman's most notable feature is her long white hair. As the ghost made her way down the stairs, reaching the halfway point, she stopped, turned her head in his direction apparently making sure he had a good look at her face. Once this was accomplished, she broke out in a loud crazy sort of laughter! The bartender wasted no time in leaving the hotel for good! He quit and never returned. The man still lives in Gallup, but refuses to enter the hotel. He won't even look at the hotel when he drives by in his car. I have heard similar stories about this apparition, and the stories all mention the ghost's long, white hair. Guests also mention that they see the spirit woman seated in our dining room. When they attempt to approach her, or even stare just a little too long, she will disappear!

I personally am at this counter every night and I must admit that I've heard unusual noises in the lobby, and I've even seen what appear to be shadows of people walking about. But I think this might be due to all the glass and mirrors decorating the lobby. At least, I want to convince myself that this is the case.

The freaky thing that not only I've seen, but also lots of others have been witness to, is the apparition of a ghostly light that moves up and down the railroad tracks. The train tracks that run directly through town are located directly across the street from the hotel and the train passes several times day and night. Oddly, this ghostly light is seen moving along the tracks as if on a smooth traveling bicycle, but never do you hear a sound—it's completely silent. It jumps, speeds up, stops and then floats up in the air without any visible means of suspension. It's a very freaky thing to see! People in town speak of the lights belonging to the spirits of those folks who have died on the tracks. I read of several incidents involving individuals who have been killed by the passing train. In fact, just recently there was an article in our newspaper reporting another such death. I've personally seen these lights quite a few times, and always

in the early mornings. I've looked at my watch and have noticed that the lights appear between three and four in the morning—always within this hour.

As the front desk night auditor for the hotel, from time to time I've had guests come up to me asking, 'Is this hotel haunted?' I try not to engage them in such a conversation only because I can't tell if they sincerely are interested in the history, or if this were not the case, might decide to seek lodging elsewhere. I try to give indirect responses to such questions, but I personally don't have a problem with ghosts. I was raised in an area of New York where the writer Washington Irving wrote his story, 'The Headless Horseman.' The whole area where I grew up is spooky looking, especially during the fall and winter months when the trees are bare and the moon shines. So, having grown up in old farmhouses with huge foreboding barns, I don't have a problem with ghosts.

Aside from these reports, the only other strange incidents that have taken place during my time at the front desk are when local Navajos have come into the lobby seeking refuge from 'skin-walkers.' Navajos believe that skin-walkers are supernatural beings, part human and part animal— usually coyote. They believe that skin-walkers can do harm, cause illness, and even kill. This is a very common belief among the Navajos. Well, I've had several incidents when I'd be working the front desk late at night, the front doors would open, and in would walk a Navajo, visibly upset and seeking protection from what he stated was a skin-walker following him. After a few minutes of conversation, the man would reluctantly leave the hotel.

'Navajo skin-walkers, or 'Yeenaaldlooshii,' literally translated means 'with it, he goes on all fours' in the Navajo language. A Yeenaaldlooshii is one of several varieties of Navajo witch, specifically an 'ánt'!!hnii or practitioner of the Witchery Way, as opposed to a user of curse-objects ('adag"sh) or a practitioner of Frenzy Way ('azh!tee). Technically, the term refers to an 'ánt'!!hnii who is using his (rarely her) powers to travel in animal form. In some versions, men or women who have attained the highest level of priesthood then commit the act of killing an immediate member of their family, and then have thus gained the evil powers that are associated with skin-walkers.'

One incident worth mentioning that my friend Mike and I experienced about five years ago, took place one Easter night outside of the hotel. Mike and I were both employed at the hotel and on our day off decided to go for a hike. For the sake of the story I need to mention that Mike is part Apache. We decided to enter an area of the surrounding cliffs, which historically, the local Navajos are hesitant to enter due to their idea that it's filled with spirits, and is also a known area where evil medicine is practiced. We chose to hike the White Cliffs area just because it is so attractively beautiful. We weren't at all thinking of ghosts.

Mike and I hiked up to a mesa, which is called Jesus Rock due to its highest formation appearing like the crown of thorns. The night was windy and as we hiked the area we discovered evidence of the ancient Anasazi people and a few kivas, or ceremonial subterranean sites. Today, they are all now in ruins, but none-the-less, still remain as evidence of human inhabitation in the area going back several thousand years.

Reaching the top of the mesa, we encountered an area that was totally flat and surrounded by very large boulders. Mike wanted to make our camp there in the middle of this spot, but something told me to move on. So, we agreed to walk away and eventually settled in another area where we pitched our tent for the night. During the night, Mike kept stating to me that he was hearing footsteps walking about the outside of the tent. I didn't hear anything and mentioned to Mike that what he was hearing were squirrels.

Later that night, I had an unusual dream. I dreamt I was beating on a drum. Interestingly, the rhythm I was beating on the drum, without having a personal knowledge of Navajo music, was a very proper and correct one. Suddenly, I woke up and noticed that at the same exact time I awoke, Mike also woke and stood up from his sleep! Without speaking a word, we jointly heard the sound of distinct, human voices chanting. The chanting appeared to be echoing from the top of the nearby mountain. Just then Mike began to once more hear the sound of footsteps walking about the outside of the tent. We spent the remainder of the night in conversation until our lack of sleep got the better of us.

Because I've never been severely bothered by ghosts, I'd like to think that if one were to appear to me, I'd take it in stride and perhaps react with a calm attitude, but I'm not so sure. I'm a pretty spiritual person. I pray a lot and have actually lived in a community of Hare Krishna worshipers. I feel I'm protected from such negative forces. I studied the ancient texts and found it to be a very positive experience. But when it comes to ghosts, well, who can say?"

SAM P. ANSON'S (ANGLO) STORY

A mutual friend of ours who lives in Albuquerque referred me to speak with Sam. I had never met Sam, but after just a few minutes of conversation, found him to be very interesting. I also discovered that although he is Caucasian, he is fluent in the Navajo language. His story is a remarkable one in the sense that, unlike most, his ghost experience took place during the day. I can't write much more about Sam, because he is hesitant to allow others to possibly identify him. "You can't begin to imagine how the local Navajos would avoid me, once they discover that I actually had an encounter with a ghost! That would be very bad for business," he said.

In my experience, I've only had a few such stories when a ghost has made actual contact with the living in broad daylight. It's not a common occurrence, but why should it not happen during the day? After my interview with Sam was over, I drove over to the site where he had his encounter and actually spoke to a couple other individuals in the immediate area who were very well aware of the spiritual haunting. They stated to me, "I'm not surprised by what goes on here. Several people are killed on those train tracks every year. Drunks lay on the tracks and the train runs them over. I'm not surprised by any of it at all." And another shared, "Ghosts here in Gallup. Sure, I've heard some of the stories—some are true, some are not, but I know the spooks hang around town."

— Antonio

"I've lived in Gallup for all my life 55 years and I attended the public schools from grammar to high school. Because of this, I'm familiar with the town and outlying country very well. One weekend I decided with some friends to do a little inexperienced rock climbing in the area known as Mentmore Canyon. I say inexperienced because I wasn't using any ropes, just my sneakers and bare hands! It didn't take long for me to take a tumble. I fell about forty feet—landing on both feet! Regrettably, I broke both ankles and had to be carried out of the canyon. It was the worst pain I'd ever experienced in my life! To this day, I still tend to limp a little when I walk.

Being of Anglo heritage, my family and I were not much into discussing apparitions, ghosts and hauntings. We couldn't care less about them. We just didn't believe in these things, and preferred to leave what we regarded as fake but fun stories to the Navajos. I have to say this at the start of my story, in order to give you an idea as to how difficult it was for me to finally have to admit to actually having had my own ghost encounter.

Since my family had a jewelry store in town, both my parents were always busy interacting with Navajo jewelers coming into our store with silver and turquoise bracelets, rings and necklaces to sell. After my parents passed away, I was left with the family business, and today it remains my livelihood. I still live upstairs on Coal Street with the jewelry business located on the first floor at street level.

It's no secret that alcoholism is a problem with a lot of the Navajos in Gallup. It's a problem that affects everyone, even whites, but is most obvious when you personally witness so many Indian drunks passed out along the streets and alleys. It's really sad to see such a waste of humanity. I know the tribe has attempted to tackle the problem of alcoholism among its members, but it must be a very strong addiction, or disease to conquer because you can still see the evidence of its terrible effects all around town. I first became aware of the stories of ghosts and witchcraft in and around Gallup when as a child. I'd gather together with the other children after school and tell stories. The stories most commonly shared were the ones that were told by the Navajo kids regarding 'skin-walkers.' Skin-walkers are witches who have turned themselves into animal forms then go about causing harm to others. They were very much feared by the Navajos then and even to this very day. Aside from the skin-walkers, I was made aware of a few haunted places in town and the in the surrounding hills and mountains. When at home, I'd attempt to explain all these stories I had heard to my parents, but my father in particular refused hear them and forbade me to even mention anything that included the subject of ghosts in his home. I later discovered the reason for his strong aversion when my uncle informed me that when he and my father were children, they experienced a very terrible ghost in their home. My uncle never did go into detail regarding what that experience was like, he just made me promise not to bring the subject up ever again—and I never did.

Well, thirteen years ago this winter, when I was the age of forty-two, I had my own encounter with a ghost. My experience took place on a Saturday morning within an alleyway, just one-half block south of Coal Street. The time was approximately ten in the morning. I was walking south on Second Street from Coal Street and was about to pass the alley that runs through the middle of most of the blocks going north and south. As I began to pass the alley, I happened to hear a man's voice say, 'Hey brother, can you help me?' I looked over to the direction of

the voice and spotted a young Navajo man wearing jeans and a dark shirt. The guy was about thirty yards away from me and was leaning with his back against a building. I stopped my walk and turned and faced the man. Immediately I thought he was going to ask for money, but instead said, 'I've been hurt and I need to see a doctor.'

Because of his need for medical attention, I cautiously decided to walk over to him to investigate. Normally, I would have just kept walking, but that day for me was somehow strangely a different one. As I got to within ten or so yards from him, he lifted his head and I got a real good look at his face as he turned in my direction. Because his features indicated that he was a full-blood Navajo, I was so surprised to see that his face was completely drained from color, and was totally a very, very pale light white or yellow/grey!

He kept saying over and over, 'I need to see a doctor. Take me to a doctor.' After seeing how unnatural this guy's skin looked, I was very hesitant to approach him. I had never seen anyone who looked in this state of shock or poor health. Something within me, my instinct said, this is death pure and simple. This guy is dead!

Because of his pleas for help, I walked up to him and said, 'What the hell happened to you?' He responded by saying, 'I was hit by the train. I need to see a doctor.' I was confused by his answer because if a train had hit him, he would be dead at the tracks, not standing in an alley. I didn't smell any alcohol on him, but as I was about to ask him another question he began to slide to the ground. I caught him and he spoke, raising and pointing his finger, 'Can you take me over to the Catholic Indian Center? They'll help me.'

The Catholic Indian Center was located just across the street, so I told him I would help him to cross the street. I placed my right arm around his waist and immediately felt such a coldness that I can't explain. He felt so cold that I knew this guy's situation was a serious one. He appeared not only sick, but also dead to the touch! We struggled across the street and around to the front of the building. I helped sit him down upon the stairs at the entrance to the center. The whole right side of my body, at the area during our short walk where I had supported his body, was cold as ice! I thought the poor guy was ready to die any minute. I walked up to the door of the center and began to knock loudly and with force. No answer. I couldn't wait so I told him I was going to walk next door and see if I could fine someone.

'I'll be right back,' I said. I left him there seated bathed in the morning sunlight on the stairs and ran over to Coal Street and found a shopkeeper about to open his store for the day standing outside his building. I explained to the shop owner, who I knew, that I needed to get the guy some medical attention. The shopkeeper seemed very calm and advised me not to be so concerned. 'The guy must be drunk. Just another drunk Indian that's all,' he said. I told him that this guy was not drunk but has something more serious. The shopkeeper turned the key to lock the door, took out his cell phone, and we both walked back to the Catholic Indian Center. This was only a short distance of about a half block. When we arrived at the stairs, the guy was nowhere to be seen. I looked all around the building and glanced at the empty parking lot. I just stood there on the stairs, very confused. I thanked the storekeeper and decided not to give the incident more thought. But I remained perplexed and bothered by everything that had transpired.

I decided to walk back to the alley, and was so surprised to see the same man standing against the same wall! This time I had no hesitation to approach him and ask for an explanation. As I stood at the sidewalk facing in his direction, again about thirty yards away, I yelled at him, 'What are you doing there? I thought you wanted to see a doctor! I went through a lot of trouble for you.' As I walked up to him, he turned to face me and said, 'It's too late, but everything is okay now.'

I stopped and as I kept my eyes on this guy, he slowly began to disappear, in broad daylight. He faded away and was gone! I was shaking with fear. All I remember saying out loud was, 'Oh, God. Oh, God. Oh, God!' I walked out of the alley and back to my home in a dazed state. I didn't dare speak of what I had experienced to anyone. I was both scared and numb. The only people I've ever told my story to are Jon, a fellow neighbor of mine who

moved to the state of Delaware a few months ago, and the other is a Navajo woman, Josephine, who has been a friend of the family for many years.

Josephine, who lives in a very traditional manner on the reservation, does not speak of ghosts at all. But after hearing my story she did arrange for a medicine woman to conduct a 'cleaning ceremony' for me. Because of its sanctity, I'm not allowed to describe the ceremony, but it did help me deal with the after-effects of the experience I went through with the ghost.

At this point, I'll never forget what it was like to actually touch a ghost; it was cold and absolutely the strangest thing I think I'll ever go through. You can't imagine how awful it was to unknowingly hold onto a ghost as I did, holding a person that is lacking any body warmth or feeling of life. The only thing that comes close to this is if you were to visit a mortuary and lift up a body out of a coffin. I guarantee it will change your life forever. Today, whenever I drive past the alley, I always try not to look in the direction of where I spotted that man. But even though I try not to do so, curiosity always makes me sneak a quick glance. I haven't seen him again and I hope not to. I hope he is in peace."

THE SANTA FE LABORATORY OF ANTHROPOLOGY HISTORY AND THE MUSEUM OF INDIAN ARTS AND CULTURE

As the 19th century came to a close, the American Southwest was undergoing enormous transition. Tourists from Europe and the East Coast of America flooded the area, drawn by word-of-mouth from early visitors and quick to take advantage of the railroad, which had

just arrived in the west. Notably, the Southwest's major attraction—its vibrant Native American cultures. In response to unsystematic collecting by eastern museums, anthropologist Edgar Lee Hewett founded the Museum of New Mexico in 1909 with a mission to collect and preserve Southwest Native American material culture. Several years later in 1927, John D. Rockefeller founded the renowned Laboratory of Anthropology with a mission to study the Southwest's indigenous cultures. In 1947, the two institutions merged, bringing together the most inclusive and systematically acquired collection of New Mexican and Southwestern anthropological artifacts in the country.

DOTY FUGATE'S (ANGLO) STORY

I sat across the desk from where Doty was sitting when conducting this interview. Doty's office is located at Museum Hill, on the bottom floor of the Laboratory of Anthropology building. We were surrounded by long tables upon which were numerous archeological examples. Contained within cardboard boxes were carefully placed un-cataloged pottery shards and other artifacts. It was not difficult to feel an aura of ancient history that enveloped the large room as the afternoon sunbeams entered the narrow windows.

Speaking for myself, I was impressed by the array of ancient human evidence that lay just a few feet from where I sat. Not only were Native people of the Southwest represented within arm's length of where I was seated, but in adjacent rooms were also artifacts from the Maya and other pre-Columbian high cultures of the Americas.

I found Doty to be quite informative of her experiences both within her chosen field of study and with the focused details of our discussion. "I'm familiar with the area of ghosts and the supernatural," *she stated.* "I've had my own personal experiences, so I'm not a disbeliever. I've also known of a few fellow archeologists who have had their encounters with spirits at dig sites; some good, some not so good."

Doty Fugate has been employed at the laboratory for many years, and has regularly heard of the personal experiences from fellow staff, and additionally has had her own encounters at the building. Not included with this story for personal reasons, Doty informed me of a girl child's spirit who is today making her presence known in the rooms and halls of the building. I hope Doty's story will

offer another evidential twist to whatever
pre-conceived ideas you might have regarding
museum workers and their vocation.

— *Antonio*

"In 1991, I began my employment as a day laborer at the Museum of Indian Arts & Culture Laboratory of Anthropology. My duty at the time was to organize and make sense of the anthropological lab, as it was in desperate need of a thorough makeover. Prior to arriving in Santa Fe, I was employed as Assistant Curator of Collections at Arizona's State Museum. Today my title is Assistant Curator of Archaeological Research Collections.

Jesse L. Nusbaum and Alfred Vincent Kidder. In 1931, Nusbaum took leave from the NPS to develop the Laboratory of Anthropology, part of the Museum of New Mexico, in Santa Fe. He continued to serve as advisor to the Secretary of the Interior and interior bureaus on archeological issues, and his title was modified to reflect this relationship, becoming 'consulting archeologist,' thus, modifying the title to the one still used today, Departmental Consulting Archeologist (DCA). By 1935, Nusbaum had returned to the NPS and held positions at Mesa Verde and the NPS office in Santa Fe, as well as serving as DCA, until the end of his long career in 1957. Following his retirement, he continued his involvement in archeology as an independent consultant until his death at age 88 in 1975.

Let be begin my story by giving you a little history of the lab and building. Founded in 1928, the building's construction was completed in 1930. During that time, there existed a political conflict between the museum and the lab. Understand that the anthropological lab was independent of the museum. The lab was owned and was supported by the Rockefeller family. At the time, both archeologists, Jesse L. Nusbaum (1887-1975) and Alfred Vincent Kidder (1885- 1963) were the administrators of the lab. That picture of the two was taken in 1907. The building, when constructed, was actually built upon the original Santa Fe Trail, meaning it is situated today astride the historic Santa Fe Trail.

From 1915 to 1929, Kidder conducted site excavations at an

abandoned pueblo in Pecos, near Santa Fe, New Mexico. He excavated levels of human occupation at the pueblo going back more than 2,000 years, and gathered a detailed record of cultural artifacts, including a large collection of pottery fragments and human remains. From these items, he was able to establish a continuous record of pottery styles

Alfred Vincent Kidder   from 2,000 years ago to the mid to late 1800's.

Kidder then analyzed trends and changes in pottery styles in association with changes in the Pecos people's culture and established a basic chronology for the Southwest.

With Samuel J. Guernsey, he established the validity of a chronological approach to cultural periods. Kidder asserted that deductions about the development of human culture could be obtained through a systematic examination of stratigraphy and chronology in archaeological sites. This research laid the foundation and has become New Mexico's state repository, housing millions of artifacts. Generally, if it's dug up in the state, it eventually ends up housed here. For example, see those items sitting on that table over there? Well, those items were dug up at an excavation in the year 1974 at the Santa Fe Plaza, Palace of the Governors. As you can see, there is pottery, nails, and porcelain, from Santa Fe's Spanish era. Additionally, twine and cordage fashioned by Native hands that has been collected is dated to be over 2,000 years.

The lab building has both a basement and sub-basement. My office, where we are currently both seated, is the level of the first basement. I first knew something was unusually strange when soon after beginning my employment, my trash can was not being emptied. When I asked the staff why, I was told that the maintenance personnel were afraid to enter my office during the night hours. Without hesitation, I was given the simple explanation, 'The basement and your office are haunted!'

I did not recall ever being told in a direct conversation, or being informed prior to being hired, of any unusual activity regarding ghosts or spirits at the lab. However, this took a turn when one evening myself, together with the museum's security staff, got together after hours at a bar for a few beers. One of the security officers began telling of his own strange experiences that he had felt and witnessed, and added with his story the stories of other fellow security staff. I immediately found these descriptions to be not just very interesting, but from an archaeological field method, invaluable.

The main areas of the building where most of the occurrences of unexplained activity are frequently reported take place within the library, basement, the boiler room, and the small apartment. Once in the year 1991, we had a high-ranking administrator visit the lab and decide to stay at the apartment. The apartment that is located in the basement of the building is not that easy to get to. To reach the apartment you need to walk through the collections room, a small hallway, and through the boiler room. Well, one night during the time of his stay, he reported being awakened from a deep sleep by a very loud argument, or as he described to the security staff, the sound of an all-out, drag-out, violent, physical altercation that was taking place in the apartment! He also let it be known that being concerned for

his safety, he had a loaded gun and would not hesitate to shoot first and ask questions later. The police were called and no evidence of an intruder or of a fight was ever discovered.

The movement of furniture has also been reported taking place on the first floor on the north side of the building; such furniture as chairs and tables moving at various times of the day and night. The building was meant to house a large and growing collection of American Indian arts and crafts such as pottery, baskets, weavings, etc. Since then, the lab incident I was informed of regarding the Anthropology Lab, is about the ghost of a grey-haired, little old lady. One evening, as a wine and cheese event was taking place at the lab, an older woman dressed head-to-toe in black, entered from the outside and walked among the guests. By her movement she apparently knew the lay of the building because she was observed meandering through the guests and eventually made her way to the room where our collections are housed. Quietly, she was pursued close behind by a security staff member. As the staff member followed this strange woman into the secured room, he stated that she abruptly disappeared and was never seen again.

There is a stairway which leads to the basement where many historical artifacts are housed and catalogued. Let's now take a walk over there. It's just a short walk. This is the basement where at one time there were literally stacked cardboard boxes filled with artifacts. These boxes were

stacked on top of each other to the point that they would actually reach the ceiling. In years past, some of the boxes even held human remains that were gathered by way of excavating Indian sites, but that policy has since changed. We no longer do this.

Today, our policy is to house human remains off-site of this building. We used to have a collection of religious mural paintings that pertained to spiritual Native American sites, such as kivas. Again, today these also have been removed and are housed elsewhere. It took a lot of hours and hard work to re-organize this large storage room. But as you can see, today it is well organized and everything is properly catalogued, as it should be.

In years past, that hand-cranked elevator located at one end of the room was used to move heavy objects between the upper and lower floor levels. It's a dinosaur, to be sure. Because of its iron cogs and wheels, it reminds me of something that would have been used in a torture chamber many years ago. Admittedly, when needed, it must have certainly gotten the job done.

I do want to make sure you see something else. The closet you see here is considered by our staff to be the 'center of unpleasantness.' It personally gives me the creeps! I know of individuals who refuse to come down here because of this very closet. I was actually told by maintenance staff that, 'If I go down there, that 'thing' in the closet will get me!' They didn't go into any long description as to their reason regarding the 'thing', but I could tell that they had one.

When you pay a visit to our research library, you'll note that it's located at the top floor just left of the main entrance. Let's now take a walk over there. Security staff has told me of numerous instances when, after locking up the building and turning off the lights, they would witness 'moving' lights, dancing within the building, and in particular within the area of the library! The security service staff for the building used to have a terrible time with our motion sensors. The sensors would go off constantly. They would have to quickly respond to these alarms and, as you might guess, they would discover nothing out of place and nothing to cause the alarms to malfunction. I had three guards confide in me that at different times, usually at the end of the day, they would hear a loud discussion between women taking place at the basement of the building. The sound of these women would travel as if the women were walking about the building making their way up to where the museum guards were located on the first floor. As soon as the voices of the women reached the doorway where the men were standing, the voices would abruptly cease!

One guard named Pete described to me how, after hearing the voices, he quickly walked to the top of the stairs, where he had a clear view of the stairwell leading to the basement. As soon as he glanced down the stairs, he heard the voices move from the stairwell, reverse direction, then disappear into another room! Of course, Pete and the other security staff would investigate the origin of the voices, but again, nothing would be discovered to be out of the ordinary.

Another incident I'll describe pertains to a lab staff member, who happened to be a Native American man from the San Felipe Pueblo. He related to us that as he would begin the drive from his home to the lab, he would 'get spiritual messages' from his dead ancestors that would caution him not to go to work due to the lab being a 'bad place.' He didn't go into detailed description as to how he would receive the messages, but he was steadfast on this.

Speaking of American Indian spirits, another frequent report from our security staff involves the sighting of the ghost of an Indian. He materializes with such a frequency that we now all refer to him as 'the big Indian.' He is always seen in a crouched dancing position. One guard was so startled to see him that he even drew his gun on the spirit! The guard encountered the spirit as the guard was walking down a hallway and turned the corner. Spotting the big Indian, and not knowing this was a spirit, the guard demanded he stop! When the spirit paid him no heed, the guard drew his gun and again demanded he stop in his tracks! The guard stated that the Indian, who was very large in stature, turned to face the guard, gave him a very grumpy look, then preceded to disappear by walking right into the wall!

Another employee who happened to be a 24-hour live-in staff janitor had his own apartment located in one wing of the basement. He reported seeing the ghost of an Indian man who, at different times, would appear to him sitting at the foot of his bed.

One security guard stated that as he was responding to one of the motion alarms that was triggered, making his way through the basement, a 12' x 6' very heavy wood table actually moved on its own, blocking his access to the short hallway that leads to the boiler room! The table physically moved across the floor and came to a stop directly in front of him! The actual table is still stored down in the basement, exactly at the spot where it has stood for many years. Needless to say, he was quite alarmed and quickly made the decision to get the heck out of there. He scrambled his way up to the main floor when he

noticed that the short wooden gate between the main room and the hallway was actually moving back and forth on its own. It appeared as if an invisible hand was pushing it! I have also had others directly report to me witnessing the unexplained movement of this small wooden gate as it swings back and forth on its own. Keep in mind, that throughout all this, the security guard was the only person in the building at the time!

It's well known by staff that for some unknown reason spirits frequent the boiler room. One reported incident states that the door to the boiler room once opened on its own, and as a work man was standing within the door jam, a very cold breeze passed through the now-opened doorway and suddenly closed with a loud, 'slam!' The guy was fortunate to get out of the way in time, or else he would have had quite a bruise, maybe even possibly could have lost a finger or two!

Located directly next to our Anthropology Lab is the Museum of American Indian Art and Culture. I've been told by a few staff members that work at that museum, that it is just as haunted as the lab. You'd have to speak with staff from that museum for their stories. I bet you'd receive some very interesting responses.

As an anthropologist, fellow associates of mine have spoken of instances when at a digging at a site, they've had strange unexplained paranormal occurrences take place. One story in particular involved an archeologist who was asleep one night within a tent he had pitched at the site. He mentioned being suddenly awakened by the sound of crying children. He opened the tent's door to peer outside expecting to see someone, but didn't see a living soul.

Stories like these, experienced by fellow anthropologists, are not as uncommon as you might think. I was once at a conference in the Pecos area located east of Santa Fe, which took place in the 1970's. There were some paleontologists who were also present. They described to me their experience when excavating within a cave. The cave was located next to the Zuni Pueblo in the Malpais area. Their purpose was to excavate Pleistocene megafauna, or pre-historic animal remains. Suddenly, during their work, they began to hear the sound of a woman singing; singing what they described to resemble antiquated Mexican songs.

Again, my own personal experience has given me much to believe that ghosts do exist. I don't doubt for one instance that there is an afterlife and that ghosts or spirits are very much a part of this. I also believe that animals too have spirit, which carry on after they have died. I can recall my own experience I had as a young child, when my dog visited me sometime after its death. As for the lab being haunted, no doubt this place gets very creepy. I don't find myself working here at night and neither would anyone else if they had any good sense!"

The End

༁ NATIVE AMERICAN GRAVES PROTECTION ༂ AND REPATRIATION ACT OF 1990 (NAGPRA)

(PL 101-601; 25 USC 3001-13; 104 Stat. 3042)
This act was approved November 16, 1990, and in summary states:

This act assigns ownership and control of Native American cultural items, human remains, and associated funerary objects to Native Americans. It also establishes requirements for the treatment of Native American human remains and sacred or cultural objects found on Federal land. This act further provides for the protection, inventory, and repatriation of Native American cultural items, human remains, and associated funerary objects. When these items are inadvertently discovered, cease activity, make a reasonable effort to protect the items, and notify the appropriate Indian tribe(s) and/or Native Hawaiian organization(s). As of November 16, 1995, Federal agencies in possession of any such remains or objects are required to issue an inventory of any human remains or funerary objects.

As of November 16, 1993, agencies must have issued a written summary of all funerary objects not associated with human remains, or sacred or cultural objects under their control, along with all available information on geographical or cultural affiliation of such items. In any case where such items can be associated with specific tribes or groups of tribes, the agency is required to provide notice of the item in question to the tribe or tribes. Upon request, each agency is required to return any such item to any lineal descendant or specific tribe with whom such item is associated. There are various additional requirements imposed upon the Secretary.

CALIFORNIA SENATE BILL 447

On January 1, 1988, California Senate Bill 447 went into effect. This legislation amended Section 5097.99 of the Public Resources Code, making it a felony to obtain or possess Native American remains or associated grave goods:

(a) No person shall obtain or possess any Native American artifacts or human remains, which are taken from a Native American grave or cairn on or after January 1, 1984, except as otherwise provided by law or in accordance with an agreement reached pursuant to Section 5097.98.

(b) Any person who knowingly or willfully obtains or possesses any Native American artifacts or human remains which are taken from a Native American grave or cairn after January 1, 1988, except as otherwise provided by law or in accordance with an agreement reached pursuant to subdivision (1) of Section 5097.94 or pursuant to Section 5097.98, is guilty of a felony which is punishable by imprisonment in the state prison.

(c) Any person who removes, without authority of law, any Native American artifacts or human remains from a Native American grave or cairn with an intent to sell or dissect or with malice or wantonness is guilty of a felony which is punishable by imprisonment in the state prison.

CONTEMPORARY NATIVE AMERICANS

In seeking answers to questions about Native Americans, remember there are more than 554 Indian tribes and Alaska Native groups within the United States that speak more than 250 languages. Each Indian Nation has its own culture, history and identity. Since no two tribes are exactly alike, what is good for one tribe may not be good for another. Consequently, there are no simple solutions to the many challenges facing Indian Nations today.

Although only two generations away from the 'old way' of life — hunting, fishing, gathering, sowing, etc. — American Indians today occupy all professional fields. They are doctors, police, firefighters, foresters and surveyors. Today Indian fathers and mothers work to straddle values between two different worlds; their Indian culture and the current social system of the dominant society. They traverse between the dominant society and their culture as citizens and productive members of both.

Today Indians number approximately 1.2 million, with about 900,000 living on or near Indian reservations. Unemployment on Indian reservations averages about 37%. They experience extreme lack of economic opportunities and a lower-than-average quality of life when measured against the dominant society. Still, the American Indian today proudly maintains an independent cultural identity. American Indians occupy a unique status in this country as it relates to society, political association, cultural identity and relation with the federal government.

TRIBAL RESOURCES

The following are contact resources for the Native American reservations and pueblos mentioned in this book. You may call or write for locations, attractions, and further information pertaining to that specific tribe.

What you may not request is information regarding ghosts, hauntings and the paranormal, for the obvious reason that this information is not available to the public.

When visiting any pueblo or reservation keep in mind that each is a sovereign government. Obey their laws and respect the privacy of the residents.

Be aware that ceremonial events, which are preformed and timed to the earth's seasons, can take place at a moment's notice. Above all, when attending such ceremonies, behave as you would in a church. Avoid asking personal questions regarding the meanings of ceremonial garb, songs, etc. Remember, you are on private property so respect cemeteries and homes, and do not ever climb on kivas, etc. Always check at the pueblo/reservation office before taking movies and photographs. If in doubt, ask the office personnel.

All the reservations referenced in Arizona may be contacted by way of their own web sites or through:

The University of Arizona Economic Development Research Program

The Office of Arid Land Studies

1955 East Sixth Street P.O. Box 210184

Tucson, Arizona 85719-5224

Voice: (520) 621-7899 Fax: (520) 621-7834

(602) 364-3700

edrp.arid.arizona.edu/tribes.html

All reservations in Colorado referenced may be contacted by way of their own web sites or through: www.colorado.gov/ltgovernor/initiatives/indianaffairs.html

All reservations in California referenced may be contacted by way of their own web sites or through:

www.ca.gov/About/Government/Local/Tribes.html

All pueblos and reservations in New Mexico referenced may be contacted by way of their own web sites or through:

Pueblo Cultural Center 2401 12th Street, NW

Albuquerque, New Mexico 87104

(505) 843-7270

1-800-766-4405 (outside of New Mexico)

http://www.indianpueblo.org/index.shtml#toc

REFERENCES

ARIZONA
Arizona Department of Tourism
Arizona Department of Commerce
Arizona State Parks
Arizona State Archives
Infinity Horn Publishing, Chinle AZ, 1997 ISBN #0-9656014-0-4

CALIFORNIA
Sutter Creek Visitors Center—"History of Sutter Creek"
Yosemite Association, "The Miwok In Yosemite"
Lassen Loomis Museum Association photo, "Baskets by Selena La Mare and Atsugewi"
California Native American Heritage Commission, "A Professional Guide."
Photo of Donner Doll courtesy of Bob Basura, Supervising State Park Ranger "Sutter's Fort State Park"
"Chief Shavehead of the Hat Creek Nation" — Lassen Loomis Museum Assoc.
Photo of Bridal Vail Fall — U.S. Department of the Interior

COLORADO
Montrose Daily Press
Montrose Visitor's Guide
"History of Sand Creek Massacre," and "Bent's Fort History"—National Park Service, U.S. Dept. of the Interior
"The Updated Colorado Guide" by Bruce Caughey and Dean Winstanley
Buffalo Bill & Grave/ Koshare Indian Historical Information and Museum
U.S. Army Colonel John Chivington and Delegation of Cheyenne, Kiowa and Arapaho
Photos in the public domain

NEW MEXICO

Apache Canyon Ranch Bed and Breakfast

#4 Canyon Drive Laguna, NM 87026 1-800-808-8310 info@ apachecanyon.net

IAIA-Institute of American Indian Arts, Santa Fe, New Mexico

Santa Fe Visitors Guide, 2000

Santa Fe Convention and Visitors Bureau

New Mexico Department of Tourism

Pueblo Cultural Center, Albuquerque, New Mexico

Photos of Zia Pueblo and Chaco Canyon provided by U.S. National Parks Dept.

Southwestern Indian Tribes, Tom and Mark Bahti, KC Publications, 1999

History of the Laboratory of Anthropology and the Museum of Indian Arts & Culture provided by David E. McNeece, Rights & Reproductions Manager Museum of Indian Arts & Culture/Laboratory of Anthropology Department of Cultural Affairs, State of New Mexico. Web site: www.miaclab.org

Photo of Alfred Kidder, University of Texas Austin

Teller, J. "The Navajo Skin-walker, Witchcraft, & Related Spiritual Phenomena: Spiritual Clues: Orientation to the Evolution of the Circle"

History of Gallup: "Find a County" National Association of Counties

Photo of Acoma Pueblo taken by an unknown individual.

"Plaques to be Guide to City's Past" Gallup Independent. "US Gazetteer files: 2000 and 1990".

Drawing of ancient Pecos Pueblo by Lawrence Ormsby

OTHER POPULAR BOOKS BY ANTONIO R. GARCEZ:
Arizona Ghost Stories ISBN 0-9740988-0-9
Ghost Stories of California's Gold Rush Country and
Yosemite National Park ISBN 0-9634029-8-6
Colorado Ghost Stories ISBN 0-9740988-1-7
Gay and Lesbian Ghost Stories ISBN 0-97809898985-3-9
Ghost Stories of the Medical Profession 0-97809898985-4-6
New Mexico Ghost Stories Vol. I ISBN 0-97809898985-2-2
New Mexico Ghost Stories Vol. II ISBN 0-97809898985-1-5

(Note: All the author's "Adobe Angels" series of books listed below are
OUT OF PRINT)
Adobe Angels - Arizona Ghost Stories Published 1998 ISBN
0-9634029-5-1
Adobe Angels - Ghost Stories of O'Keeffe Country Published 1998
ISBN 0-9634029-6-X
Adobe Angels - The Ghosts of Las Cruces and Southern New Mexico
Published 1996 ISBN 0-9634029-4-3
Adobe Angels - The Ghosts of Santa Fe and Taos Revised 1995 ISBN
0-9634029-3-5
Adobe Angels - The Ghosts of Albuquerque Published 1992 ISBN
0-9634029-2-7

Made in USA - Kendallville, IN
19459_9780974098845
09.23.2022 1313